MARK TWAIN'S
AUTOBIOGRAPHY

MARK TWAIN DICTATING HIS AUTOBIOGRAPHY AT
DUBLIN, NEW HAMPSHIRE, IN THE SUMMER OF 1906

MARK TWAIN

[*New York, Tuesday, January 23, 1906*

About a meeting at Carnegie Hall, in the interest of Booker Washington's Tuskegee Institute.—An unpleasant political incident which happened to Mr. Twichell.

THERE was a great mass meeting at Carnegie Hall last night, in the interest of Booker Washington's Tuskegee Educational Institute in the South, and the interest which New York people feel in that Institute was quite manifest, in the fact that although it was not pleasant weather there were three thousand people inside the Hall and two thousand outside, who were trying to get in when the performances were ready to begin at eight o'clock.[1] Mr. Choate presided, and was received with a grand welcome when he marched in upon the stage. He is fresh from his long stay in England, as our Ambassador, where he won the English people by the gifts of his heart, and won the royalties and the Government by his able diplomatic service, and captured the whole nation with his fine and finished oratory. For thirty-five years Choate has been the

---

[1] They were largely attracted by the announcement that Mark Twain was to be present and would speak.—A. B. P.

handsomest man in America. Last night he seemed to me to be just as handsome as he was thirty-five years ago, when I first knew him. And when I used to see him in England, five or six years ago, I thought him the handsomest man in that country.

It was at a Fourth of July reception in Mr. Choate's house in London that I first met Booker Washington. I have met him a number of times since, and he always impresses me pleasantly. Last night he was a mulatto. I didn't notice it until he turned, while he was speaking, and said something to me. It was a great surprise to me to see that he was a mulatto and had blue eyes. How unobservant a dull person can be! Always, before, he was black, to me, and I had never noticed whether he had eyes at all, or not. He has accomplished a wonderful work in this quarter of a century. When he finished his education at the Hampton Colored School twenty-five years ago he was unknown and hadn't a penny, nor a friend outside his immediate acquaintanceship. But by the persuasions of his carriage and address and the sincerity and honesty that look out of his eyes he has been enabled to gather money by the hatful here in the North, and with it he has built up and firmly established his great school for the colored people of the two sexes in the South. In that school the students are not merely furnished a book education, but are taught thirty-seven useful trades. Booker Washington has scraped together many hundreds of thousands of dollars, in the twenty-five years, and with this money he has taught and sent forth into Southern fields among the colored people six thousand trained colored men and women; and his student roll now numbers fifteen hundred names. The Institute's property is worth a million and a half, and the establishment is in a flourishing condition. A most remarkable man is Booker Washington. And he is a fervent and effective speaker on the platform.

When the affair was over and the people began to climb up on the stage and pass along and shake hands, the usual thing happened. It always happens. I shake hands with people who used to know my mother intimately in Arkansas, in New Jersey, in California, in Jericho—and I have to seem so glad and so happy to meet these persons who knew in this intimate way one who was so near and dear to me. And this is the kind of thing that gradually turns a person into a polite liar and deceiver, for my mother was never in any of those places.

One pretty creature was glad to see me again, and remembered being at my house in Hartford— I don't know when, a great many years ago, it was. Now she was mistaking herself for somebody else. It *couldn't* have happened to her. But I was very cordial, because she *was* very pretty. We might have had a good long chat except for the others that I had to talk with and work up reminiscences that belonged in somebody else's experiences, not theirs or mine.

There was one young fellow, brisk, but not

bright, overpoweringly pleasant and cordial, in his way. He said his mother used to teach school in Elmira, New York, where he was born and bred and where the family continued to reside, and that she would be very glad to know that he had met me and shaken hands, for he said: "She is always talking about you. She holds you in high esteem, although, as she says, she has to confess that of all the boys that ever she had in her school, you were the most troublesome."

"Well," I said, "those were my last school days, and through long practice in being troublesome, I had reached the summit by that time, because I was more than thirty-three years old."

It didn't affect him in the least. I don't think he even heard what I said, he was so eager to tell me all about it, and I said to him once more, so as to spare him, and me, that I was never in a schoolhouse in Elmira, New York, even on a visit, and that his mother must be mistaking *me* for some of the Langdons, the family into which I married. No matter, he didn't hear it—kept on his talk with animation and delight, and has gone to tell his mother, I don't know what. He didn't get any-thing out of me to tell her, for he never heard anything I said.

These episodes used to vex me, years and years ago. But they don't vex me now. I am older. If a person thinks that he has known me at some time or other, all I require of him is that he shall consider it a distinction to have known me; and then, as a rule, I am perfectly willing to remember all about it and add some things that he has forgotten.

Twichell came down from Hartford to be present at that meeting, and we chatted and smoked after we got back home. And reference was made again to that disastrous Boston speech which I made at Whittier's seventieth-birthday dinner; and Joe asked me if I was still minded to submit that speech to that club in Washington, day after to-morrow, where Colonel Harvey and I are to be a couple of the four guests. And I said, "No," I had given that up—which was true. Because I have examined that speech a couple of times since, and have changed my notion about it—changed it entirely. I find it gross, coarse—well, I needn't go on with particulars. I didn't like any part of it, from the beginning to the end. I found it always offensive and detestable. How do I account for this change of view? I don't know. I can't account for it. I am the person concerned. If I could put myself outside of myself and examine it from the point of view of a person not personally concerned in it, then no doubt I could analyze it and explain to my satisfaction the change which has taken place. As it is, I am merely moved by instinct. My instinct said, formerly, that it was an innocent speech, and funny. The same instinct, sitting cold and judicial, as a court of last resort, has reversed that verdict. I expect this latest verdict to remain.

Twichell's congregation—the only congregation he has ever had since he entered the ministry—

celebrated the fortieth anniversary of his accession to that pulpit, a couple of weeks ago. Joe entered the army as chaplain in the very beginning of the Civil War. He was a young chap, and had just been graduated from Yale and the Yale Theological Seminary. He made all the campaigns of the Army of the Potomac. When he was mustered out, that congregation I am speaking of called him, and he has served them ever since, and always to their satisfaction—except once.

I have found among my old MSS. one which I perceive to be about twenty-two years old. It has a heading and looks as if I had meant it to serve as a magazine article. I can clearly see, now, why I didn't print it. It is full of indications that its inspiration was what happened to Twichell about that time, and which produced a situation for him which he will not forget until he is dead, if he even forgets it then. I think I can see, all through this artful article, that I was trying to hint at Twichell, and the episode of that preacher whom I met on the street, and hint at various things that were exasperating me. And now that I read that old article, I perceive that I probably saw that my art was not ingenious enough—that I hadn't covered Twichell up, and hadn't covered up the episode that I was hinting at—that anybody in Hartford could read everything between the lines that I was trying to conceal.

I will insert this venerable article in this place, and then take up that episode in Joe's history and tell about it.

THE CHARACTER OF MAN

CONCERNING Man—he is too large a subject to be treated as a whole; so I will merely discuss a detail or two of him at this time. I desire to contemplate him from this point of view—this premise: that he was not made for any useful purpose, for the reason that he hasn't served any; that he was most likely not even made *intentionally;* and that his working himself up out of the oyster bed to his present position was probably matter of surprise and regret to the Creator. . . . For his history, in all climes, all ages and all circumstances, furnishes oceans and continents of proof that of all the creatures that were made he is the most detestable. Of the entire brood he is the only one—the solitary one—that possesses malice.

That is the basest of all instincts, passions, vices —the most hateful. That one thing puts him below the rats, the grubs, the trichinæ. He is the only creature that inflicts pain for sport, knowing *it* to *be* pain. But if the cat knows she is inflicting pain when she plays with the frightened mouse, then we must make an exception here; we must grant that in one detail man is the moral peer of the cat. *All* creatures kill—there seems to be no exception; but of the whole list, man is the only one that kills for fun; he is the only one that kills in malice, the only one that kills for revenge. Also—in all the list he is the only creature that has a nasty mind.

Shall he be extolled for his noble qualities, for his gentleness, his sweetness, his amiability, his lov-

ingness, his courage, his devotion, his patience, his
fortitude, his prudence, the various charms and
graces of his spirit? The other animals share *all*
these with him, yet are free from the blacknesses and
rottennesses of his character.

   . . . There are certain sweet-smelling sugar-
coated lies current in the world which all politic men
have apparently tacitly conspired together to support and perpetuate. One of these is, that there
is such a thing in the world as independence: independence of thought, independence of opinion,
independence of action. Another is, that the world
loves to *see* independence—admires it, applauds it.
Another is, that there is such a thing in the world
as toleration—in religion, in politics, and such
matters; and with it trains that already mentioned
auxiliary lie that toleration is admired and applauded. Out of these trunk-lies spring many
branch ones: to wit, the lie that not all men are
slaves; the lie that men are glad when other men
succeed; glad when they prosper; glad to see them
reach lofty heights; sorry to see them fall again.
And yet other branch lies: to wit, that there is
heroism in man; that he is not mainly made up of
malice and treachery; that he is sometimes not a
coward; that there is something about him that
ought to be perpetuated—in heaven, or hell, or
somewhere. And these other branch lies, to wit:
that conscience, man's moral medicine chest, is not
only created by the Creator, but is put into man
ready charged with the right and only true and
authentic correctives of conduct—and the duplicate

chest, with the self-same correctives, unchanged, un-
modified, distributed to all nations and all epochs.
And yet one other branch lie: to wit, that I am I,
and you are you; that we are units, individuals, and
have natures of our own, instead of being the tail
end of a tapeworm eternity of ancestors extending
in linked procession back and back and back—to our
source in the monkeys, with this so-called individu-
ality of ours a decayed and rancid mush of inherited instincts and teachings derived, atom by
atom, stench by stench, from the entire line of
that sorry column, and not so much new and original
matter in it as you could balance on a needle point
and examine under a microscope. This makes well-
nigh fantastic the suggestion that there can be such
a thing as a personal, original, and responsible nature in a man, separable from that in him which
is not original, and findable in such quantity as to
enable the observer to say, This is a man, not a procession.

. . . Consider the first-mentioned lie: that there
is such a thing in the world as independence; that
it exists in individuals; that it exists in bodies of
men. Surely if anything *is* proven, by whole oceans
and continents of evidence, it is that the quality of
independence was almost wholly left out of the human race. The scattering exceptions to the rule
only emphasize it, light it up, make it glare. The
whole population of New England meekly took
their turns, for years, in standing up in the railway
trains, without so much as a complaint above their
breath, till at last these uncounted millions were

able to produce exactly one single independent man, who stood to his rights and made the railroad give him a seat. Statistics and the law of probabilities warrant the assumption that it will take New England forty years to breed his fellow. There is a law, with a penalty attached, forbidding trains to occupy the Asylum Street crossing more than five minutes at a time. For years people and carriages used to wait there nightly as much as twenty minutes on a stretch while New England trains monopolized that crossing. I used to hear men use vigorous language about that insolent wrong—but they waited, just the same.

We are discreet sheep; we wait to see how the drove is going, and then go with the drove. We have two opinions: one private, which we are afraid to express; and another one—the one we use—which we force ourselves to wear to please Mrs. Grundy, until habit makes us comfortable in it, and the custom of defending it presently makes us love it, adore it, and forget how pitifully we came by it. Look at it in politics. Look at the candidates whom we loathe, one year, and are afraid to vote against, the next; whom we cover with unimaginable filth, one year, and fall down on the public platform and worship, the next—and keep on doing it until the habitual shutting of our eyes to last year's evidences brings us presently to a sincere and stupid belief in this year's. Look at the tyranny of party—at what is called party allegiance, party loyalty—a snare invented by designing men for selfish purposes—and which turns voters into chattels, slaves, rabbits, and all the while their masters, and they themselves are shouting rubbish about liberty, independence, freedom of opinion, freedom of speech, honestly unconscious of the fantastic contradiction; and forgetting or ignoring that their fathers and the churches shouted the same blasphemies a generation earlier when they were closing their doors against the hunted slave, beating his handful of humane defenders with Bible texts and billies, and pocketing the insults and licking the shoes of his Southern master.

If we would learn what the human race really *is* at bottom, we need only observe it in election times. A Hartford clergyman met me in the street and spoke of a new nominee—denounced the nomination, in strong, earnest words—words that were refreshing for their independence, their manliness.[1] He said, "I ought to be proud, perhaps, for this nominee is a relative of mine; on the contrary, I am humiliated and disgusted, for I know him intimately—familiarly—and I know that he is an unscrupulous scoundrel, and always has been." You should have seen this clergyman preside at a political meeting forty days later, and urge, and plead, and gush—and you should have heard him paint the character of this same nominee. You would have supposed he was describing the Cid, and Greatheart, and Sir Galahad, and Bayard the Spotless all rolled into one. Was he sincere? Yes—by that

---

[1] *Jan. 11, '06.*—I can't remember his name. It began with K, I think. He was one of the American revisers of the New Testament, and was nearly as great a scholar as Hammond Trumbull.

time; and therein lies the pathos of it all, the hopelessness of it all. It shows at what trivial cost of effort a man can teach himself to lie, and learn to believe it, when he perceives, by the general drift, that that is the popular thing to do. Does he believe his lie *yet?* Oh, probably not; he has no further use for it. It was but a passing incident; he spared to it the moment that was its due, then hastened back to the serious business of his life.

And what a paltry poor lie is that one which teaches that independence of action and opinion is prized in men, admired, honored, rewarded. When a man leaves a political party, he is treated as if the party owned him—as if he were its bond slave, as most party men plainly are—and had stolen himself, gone off with what was not his own. And he is traduced, derided, despised, held up to public obloquy and loathing. His character is remorselessly assassinated; no means, however vile, are spared to injure his property and his business.

The preacher who casts a vote for conscience' sake runs the risk of starving. And is rightly served, for he has been teaching a falsity—that men respect and honor independence of thought and action.

Mr. Beecher may be charged with a *crime,* and his whole following will rise as one man, and stand by him to the bitter end; but who so poor to be his friend when he is charged with casting a vote for conscience' sake? Take the editor so charged—take—take anybody.

All the talk about tolerance, in anything or anywhere, is plainly a gentle lie. It does not exist. It is in no man's heart; but it unconsciously, and by moss-grown inherited habit, drivels and slobbers from all men's lips. Intolerance is everything for oneself, and nothing for the other person. The mainspring of man's nature is just that—selfishness.

Let us skip the other lies, for brevity's sake. To consider them would prove nothing, except that man is what he is—loving toward his own, lovable to his own—his family, his friends—and otherwise the buzzing, busy, trivial enemy of his race—who tarries his little day, does his little dirt, commends himself to God, and then goes out into the darkness, to return no more, and send no messages back —selfish even in death.

[New York, Wednesday, January 24, 1906

Tells of the defeat of Mr. Blaine for the Presidency, and how Mr. Clemens's, Mr. Twichell's, and Mr. Goodwin's votes were cast for Cleveland.

IT is plain, I think, that this old article was written about twenty-two years ago, and that it followed by about three or four months the defeat of James G. Blaine for the Presidency and the election of Grover Cleveland, the Democratic candidate —a temporary relief from a Republican-party domination which had lasted a generation. I had been accustomed to vote for Republicans more frequently than for Democrats, but I was never a Republican and never a Democrat. In the community, I was regarded as a Republican, but I had never so re-garded myself. As early as 1865 or '66 I had had this curious experience: that whereas up to that time I had considered myself a Republican, I was converted to a no-party independence by the wisdom of a rabid Republican. This was a man who was afterward a United States Senator, and upon whose character rests no blemish that *I* know of, except that he was the father of the William R. Hearst of to-day, and therefore grandfather of Yellow Journalism—that calamity of calamities.

Hearst was a Missourian; I was a Missourian. He was a long, lean, practical, common-sense, un-educated man of fifty or thereabouts. I was shorter and better informed—at least I thought so. One day, in the Lick House in San Francisco, he said:

"I am a Republican; I expect to remain a Re-publican always. It is my purpose, and I am not a changeable person. But look at the condition of things. The Republican party goes right along, from year to year, scoring triumph after triumph, until it has come to think that the political power of the United States is its property and that it is a sort of insolence for any other party to aspire to any part of that power. Nothing can be worse for a country than this. To lodge all power in one party and keep it there is to insure bad gov-ernment and *the sure and gradual deterioration of the public morals.* The parties ought to be so nearly equal in strength as to make it necessary for the leaders on both sides to choose the very best men they can find. Democratic fathers ought to divide up their sons between the two parties if they can, and do their best in this way to equalize the powers. I have only one son. He is a little boy, but I am already instructing him, persuading him, preparing him, to vote against me when he comes of age, let me be on whichever side I may. He is already a good Democrat, and I want him to remain a good Democrat—until I become a Democrat myself. Then I shall shift him to the other party, if I can."

It seemed to me that this unlettered man was at least a wise one. And I have never voted a straight ticket from that day to this. I have never belonged to any party from that day to this. I have never belonged to any church from that day to this. I have remained absolutely free in those matters. And in this independence I have found a spiritual comfort and a peace of mind quite above price.

When Blaine came to be talked of by the Republican leaders as their probable candidate for the Presidency, the Republicans of Hartford were very sorry, and they thought they foresaw his defeat, in case he should be nominated. But they stood in no great fear of his nomination. The convention met in Chicago and the balloting began. In my house we were playing billiards. Sam Dunham was present; also F. G. Whitmore, Henry C. Robinson, Charles E. Perkins, and Edward M. Bunce. We took turns in the game, and, meanwhile, discussed the political situation. George, the colored butler, was down in the kitchen on guard at the telephone. As fast as a ballot was received at the political headquarters downtown, it was telephoned out to the house, and George reported it to us through the speaking-tube. Nobody present was seriously expecting the nomination of Mr. Blaine. All these men were Republicans, but they had no affection for Blaine. For two years the Hartford *Courant* had been holding Blaine up to scorn and contumely. It had been denouncing him daily. It had been mercilessly criticizing his political conduct and backing up the criticisms with the deadly facts. Up to that time the *Courant* had been a paper which could be depended on to speak its sincere mind about the prominent men of both parties, and its judgments could be depended upon as being well and candidly considered, and sound. It had been my custom to pin my faith to the *Courant* and accept its verdicts at par.

The billiard game and the discussion went on and on, and by and by, about mid-afternoon, George furnished us a paralyzing surprise through the speaking-tube. Mr. Blaine was the nominee! The butts of the billiard cues came down on the floor with a bump, and for a while the players were dumb. They could think of nothing to say. Then Henry Robinson broke the silence. He said, sorrowfully, that it was hard luck to have to vote for that man. I said:

"But we *don't* have to vote for him."

Robinson said, "Do you mean to say that you are not going to vote for him?"

"Yes," I said, "that is what I mean to say. I am not going to vote for him."

The others began to find their voices. They sang the same note. They said that when a party's representatives choose a man, that ends it. If they choose unwisely it is a misfortune, but no loyal member of the party has any right to withhold his vote. He has a plain duty before him and he can't shirk it. He must vote for that nominee.

I said that no party held the privilege of dictating to me how I should vote. That if party loyalty was a form of patriotism, I was no patriot, and that I didn't think I was much of a patriot, anyway, for oftener than otherwise what the general body of Americans regarded as the patriotic course was not in accordance with my views; that if there was any valuable difference between being an American and a monarchist it lay in the theory that the American could decide for himself what is patriotic and what isn't; whereas the king could dictate the monarchist's patriotism for him—a decision which was final and must be accepted by the victim; that in my belief I was the only person in the sixty millions —with Congress and the Administration back of the sixty millions—who was privileged to construct my patriotism for me.

They said, "Suppose the country is entering upon a war—where do you stand then? Do you arrogate to yourself the privilege of going your own way in the matter, in the face of the nation?"

"Yes," I said, "that is my position. If I thought it an unrighteous war I would say so. If I were invited to shoulder a musket in that cause and march under that flag, I should decline. I would not voluntarily march under this country's flag, or any other, when it was my private judgment that the country was in the wrong. If the country *obliged* me to shoulder the musket, I could not help myself, but I would never volunteer. To volunteer would be the act of a traitor to myself, and consequently traitor to my country. If I refused to volunteer, I should be *called* a traitor, I am well aware of that —but that would not make me a traitor. The unanimous vote of the sixty millions could not make me a traitor. I should still be a patriot, and, in my opinion, the only one in the whole country."

There was a good deal of talk, but I made no converts. They were all candid enough to say that they did not want to vote for Mr. Blaine, but they all said they would *do* it, nevertheless. Then Henry Robinson said:

"It is a good while yet before election. There is time for you to come around, and you will come around. The influences about you will be too strong for you. On election day you will vote for Blaine."

I said I should not go to the polls at all.

The *Courant* had an uncomfortable time thence until midnight. General Hawley, the editor-in-chief (and he was also commander-in-chief of the paper), was at his post in Congress, and the telegraphing to and fro between the *Courant* and him went on diligently until midnight. For two years the *Courant* had been making a "tar baby" of Mr.

Blaine, and adding tar every day—and now it was called upon to praise him, hurrah for him, and urge its well-instructed clientele to elevate the "tar baby" to the Chief Magistracy of the nation. It was a difficult position and it took the *Courant* people and General Hawley nine hours to swallow the bitter pill. But at last General Hawley reached a decision and at midnight the pill was swallowed. Within a fortnight the *Courant* had acquired some facility in praising where it had so long censured; within another month the change in its character was become complete—and to this day it has never recovered its virtue entirely, though under Charles Hopkins Clark's editorship it has gotten back 90 per cent of it, by my estimate.

Charles Dudley Warner was the active editor of the time. He could not stomach the new conditions. He found himself unable to turn his pen in the other direction and make it proceed backward, therefore he decided to retire his pen altogether. He withdrew from the editorship, resigned his salary, lived thenceforth upon his income as a part proprietor of the paper and upon the proceeds of magazine work and lecturing, and kept his vote in his pocket on election day.

The conversation with the learned American member of the board of scholars which revised the New Testament did occur as I have outlined it in that old article. He was vehement in his denunciation of Blaine, his relative, and said he should never vote for him. But he was so used to revising New Testaments that it took him only a few days to revise this one. I had hardly finished with *him* when I came across James G. Batterson. Batterson was president of the great Travelers' Insurance Company. He was a fine man, a strong man, and a valuable citizen. He was fully as vehement as that clergyman had been in his denunciations of Blaine—but inside of two weeks he was presiding at a great Republican ratification meeting; and to hear him talk about Blaine and his perfections, a stranger would have supposed that the Republican party had had the good fortune to secure an archangel as its nominee.

Time went on. Election day was close at hand. Late one frosty night, Twichell, the Rev. Francis Goodwin, and I were tramping homeward through the deserted streets in the face of a wintry gale, after a séance of our Monday Evening Club, and after a supper-table debate over the political situation, in which the fact had come out—to the astonishment and indignation of everybody, the ladies included—that three traitors were present. That Goodwin, Twichell, and I were going to keep our votes in our pockets instead of casting them for the archangel. Along in that homeward tramp, somewhere, Goodwin had a happy idea, and brought it out. He said:

"Why are we keeping back these three votes from Blaine? Plainly the answer is, to do what we can to defeat Blaine. Very well, then, these are three votes against Blaine. The common-sense procedure would be to cast six votes against him by turning in our three votes for Cleveland."

Even Twichell and I could see that there was sense in that, and we said:

"That is a very good thing to do and we'll do it."

On election day we went to the polls and consummated our hellish design. At that time the voting was public. Any spectator could see how a man was voting—and straightway this crime was known to the whole community. This double crime—in the eyes of the community. To withhold a vote from Blaine was bad enough, but to add to that iniquity by actually voting for the Democratic candidate was criminal to a degree for which there was no adequate language discoverable in the dictionary.

From that day forth, for a good while to come, Twichell's life was a good deal of a burden to him. To use a common expression, his congregation "soured" on him and he found small pleasure in the exercise of his clerical office—unless, perhaps, he got some healing for his hurts, now and then, through the privilege of burying some of those people of his. It would have been a benevolence to bury the whole of them, I think, and a profit to the community. But if that was Twichell's feeling about it, he was too charitable in his nature and too kindly to expose it. He never said it to me, and I think that if he would have said it to anyone, I should have been the one.

Twichell had most seriously damaged himself with his congregation. He had a young family to support. It was a large family already, and it was growing. It was becoming a heavier and heavier burden every year—but his salary remained always the same. It became less and less competent to keep up with the domestic drain upon it, and if there had ever been any prospect of increasing this salary, that prospect was gone now. It was not much of a salary. It was four thousand dollars. He had not asked for more, and it had not occurred to the congregation to offer it. Therefore his vote for Cleveland was a distinct disaster to him. That exercise of his ostensible great American privilege of being free and independent in his political opinions and actions proved a heavy calamity. But the Rev. Francis Goodwin continued to be respected as before—that is, publicly; privately he was damned. But publicly he had suffered no harm. Perhaps it was because the public approval was not a necessity in his case. His father was worth seven millions, and was old. The Rev. Francis was in the line of promotion and would soon inherit.

As far as I was myself concerned, I did not need to worry. I did not draw my living from Hartford. It was quite sufficient for my needs. Hartford's opinion of me could not affect it, and besides it had long been known among my friends that I had never voted a straight ticket, and was therefore so accustomed to crime that it was unlikely that disapproval of my conduct could reform me—and maybe I wasn't worth the trouble, anyway.

By and by, about a couple of months later, New-

Year's Eve arrived, and with it the annual meeting of Joe's congregation and the annual sale of the pews.

[New York, Thursday, February 1, 1906

Subject of January 24th continued.—Mr. Twichell's unpopular vote.

JOE was not quite present. It was not etiquette for him to be within hearing of the business talks concerning the church's affairs. He remained in the seclusion of the church parlor, ready to be consulted if that should be necessary. The congregation was present in full force; every seat was occupied. The moment the house was called to order, a member sprang to his feet and moved that the connection between Twichell and the church be dissolved. The motion was promptly seconded. Here, and there, and yonder, all over the house, there were calls of, "Question! Question!" But Mr. Hubbard, a middle-aged man, a wise and calm and collected man, business manager and part owner of the *Courant,* rose in his place and proposed to discuss the motion before rushing it to a vote. The substance of his remarks was this (which I must put in my own language, of course, as I was not there) :

"Mr. Twichell was the first pastor you have ever had. You have never wanted another until two months ago. You have had no fault to find with his ministrations as your pastor, but he has suddenly become unfit to continue them because he is unorthodox in his politics, according to your views. Very well, he *was* fit; he has become unfit. He *was* valuable; his value has passed away, apparently—but only apparently. His highest value remains—if I know this congregation. When he assumed this pastorate this region was an outlying district, thinly inhabited, its real estate worth next to nothing. Mr. Twichell's personality was a magnet which immediately began to draw population in this direction. It has continued to draw it from that day to this. As a result, your real estate, almost valueless in the beginning, ranges now at very high prices. Reflect before you vote upon this resolution. The church in West Hartford is waiting upon this vote with deep solicitude. That congregation's real estate stands at a low figure. What they are anxious to have now above everything else under God, is a price-raiser. Dismiss Mr. Twichell to-night, and they will hire him to-morrow. Prices there will go up; prices here will go down. That is all. I move the vote."

Twichell was not dismissed. That was twenty-two years ago. It was Twichell's first pulpit after his consecration to his vocation. He occupies it yet, and has never had another. The fortieth anniversary of his accession to it was celebrated by that congregation and its descendants a couple of weeks ago, and there was great enthusiasm. Twichell has never made any political mistakes since. His persistency in voting right has been an exasperation to me these many years and has been the cause and inspiration of more than one vicious letter from me to him. But the viciousness was all a pretense. I have never found any real fault with him for voting his infernal Republican ticket, for the reason that, situated as he was, with a large family to support, his first duty was not to his political conscience, but to his family conscience. A sacrifice had to be made; a duty had to be performed. His very first duty was to his family, not to his political conscience. He sacrificed his political independence, and saved his family by it. In the circumstances, this was the highest loyalty, and the best. If he had been a Henry Ward Beecher it would not have been his privilege to sacrifice his political conscience, because in case of dismissal a thousand pulpits would have been open to him, and his family's bread secure. In Twichell's case, there would have been some risk—in fact, a good deal of risk. That he, or any other expert, could have raised the prices of real estate in West Hartford is, to my mind, exceedingly doubtful. I think Mr. Hubbard worked his imagination to the straining point when he got up that scare that night. I believe it was safest for Twichell to remain where he was if he could. He saved his family, and that was his first duty, in my opinion.

In this country there are perhaps eighty thousand preachers. Not more than twenty of them are politically independent—the rest cannot be politically independent. They must vote the ticket of their congregations. They do it, and are justified. They themselves are mainly the reason why they have no political independence, for they do not preach political independence from their pulpits. They have their large share in the fact that the people of this nation have no political independence.

[*New York, February 1, 1906*

TO-MORROW will be the thirty-sixth anniversary of our marriage. My wife passed from this life one year and eight months ago, in Florence, Italy, after an unbroken illness of twenty-two months' duration.

I saw her first in the form of an ivory miniature in her brother Charley's stateroom in the steamer *Quaker City* in the Bay of Smyrna, in the summer of 1867, when she was in her twenty-second year. I saw her in the flesh for the first time in New York in the following December. She was slender and beautiful and girlish—and she was both girl and woman. She remained both girl and woman to the last day of her life. Under a grave and gentle exterior burned inextinguishable fires of sympathy, energy, devotion, enthusiasm, and absolutely limitless affection. She was *always* frail in body, and she lived upon her spirit, whose hopefulness and courage were indestructible. Perfect truth, perfect honesty, perfect candor, were qualities of her character which were born with her. Her judgments of people and things were sure and accurate. Her intuitions almost never deceived her. In her judgments of the characters and acts of both friends and strangers there was always room for charity, and this charity never failed. I have compared and contrasted her with hundreds of persons, and my conviction remains that hers was the most perfect character I have ever met. And I may add that she was the most winningly dignified person I have ever known. Her character and disposition were of the sort that not only invite worship, but command it. No servant ever left her service who deserved to remain in it. And as she could choose with a glance of her eye, the servants she selected did in almost all cases deserve to remain, and they *did* remain. She was always cheerful; and she was always able to communicate her cheerfulness to others. During the nine years that we spent in poverty and debt she was always able to reason me out of my despairs and find a bright side to the clouds and make me see it. In all that time I never knew her to utter a word of regret concerning our altered circumstances, nor did I ever know her children to do the like. For she had taught them, and they drew their fortitude from her. The love which she bestowed upon those whom she loved took the form of worship, and in that form it was returned—returned by relatives, friends, and the servants of her household. It was a strange combination which wrought into one individual, so to speak, by marriage—her disposition and character and mine. She poured out her prodigal affections in kisses and caresses, and in a vocabulary of endearments whose profusion was always an astonishment to me. I was born *reserved* as to endearments of speech, and caresses, and hers broke upon me as the summer waves break upon Gibraltar. I was reared in that atmosphere of reserve. As I have already said, I never knew a member of my father's family to kiss another member of it except once, and that at a death-bed. And our village was not a kissing community. The kissing and caressing ended with court-ship—along with the deadly piano-playing of that day.

She had the heart-free laugh of a girl. It came seldom, but when it broke upon the ear it was as inspiring as music. I heard it for the last time when she had been occupying her sick bed for more than a year, and I made a written note of it at the time —a note not to be repeated.

To-morrow will be the thirty-sixth anniversary. We were married in her father's house in Elmira, New York, and went next day, by special train, to Buffalo, along with the whole Langdon family, and with the Beechers and the Twichells, who had sol-emnized the marriage. We were to live in Buffalo, where I was to be one of the editors of the Buf-falo *Express* and a part owner of the paper. I knew nothing about Buffalo, but I had made my household arrangements there through a friend, by letter. I had instructed him to find a boarding-house of as respectable a character as my light sal-ary as editor would command. We were received at about nine o'clock at the station in Buffalo and were put into several sleighs and driven all over America, as it seemed to me—for apparently we turned all the corners in the town and followed all the streets there were—I scolding freely and characterizing that friend of mine in very uncomplimentary ways for securing a boarding-house that apparently had no definite locality. But there was a conspiracy—and my bride knew of it, but I was in ignorance. Her father, Jervis Langdon, had bought and furnished a new house for us in the fashionable street, Delaware Avenue, and had laid in a cook and housemaids and a brisk and electric young coachman, an Irishman, Patrick McAleer—and we were being driven all over that city in order that one sleighful of these people could have time to go to the house and see that the gas was lighted all over it, and a hot supper prepared for the crowd. We arrived at last, and when I entered that fairy place my indignation reached high-water mark, and without any reserve I delivered my opinion to that friend of mine for being so stupid as to put us into a boarding-house whose terms would be far out of my reach. Then Mr. Langdon brought forward a very pretty box and opened it and took from it a deed of the house. So the comedy ended very pleasantly and we sat down to supper.

The company departed about midnight, and left us alone in our new quarters. Then Ellen, the cook, came in to get orders for the morning's marketing—and neither of us knew whether beefsteak was sold by the barrel or by the yard. We exposed our ignorance, and Ellen was full of Irish delight over it. Patrick McAleer, that brisk young Irishman, came in to get his orders for next day—and that was our first glimpse of him.

Thirty-six years have gone by. And this letter from Twichell comes this morning, from Hartford:

HARTFORD, *January* 31.

DEAR MARK:

I am sorry to say that the news about Patrick is very bad. I saw him Monday. He *looked* pretty well and was in cheerful spirits. He told me that he was fast recovering from an operation performed on him last week Wednesday, and would soon be out again. But a nurse who followed me from the room when I left told me that the poor fellow was deceived. The operation had simply disclosed the fact that nothing could be done for him.

Yesterday I asked the surgeon (Johnson, living opposite us) if that were so. He said "Yes," that the trouble was cancer of the liver and that there was no help for it in surgery; the case was quite hopeless; the end was not many weeks off. A pitiful case, indeed!

Poor Patrick! His face brightened when he saw me. He told me, the first thing, that he had just heard from Jean. His wife and son were with him. Whether they suspect the truth I don't know. I doubt if the wife does; but the son looked very sober. Maybe he only has been told.

Yrs. aff.,

JOE.

Jean had kept watch of Patrick's case by correspondence with Patrick's daughter Nancy, and so we already knew that it was hopeless. In fact, the end seems to be nearer than Twichell suspects. Last night I sent Twichell word that I *knew* Patrick had only a day or two to live, and he must not forget to provide a memorial wreath and pin a card to it with my name and Clara's and Jean's signed to it, worded, "In loving remembrance of Patrick McAleer, faithful and valued friend of our family for thirty-six years."

I wanted to say that he had *served* us thirty-six years, but some people would not have understood that. He served us constantly for twenty-one years. Then came that break when we spent nine or ten years in Europe. But if Patrick himself could see his funeral wreath—then I should certainly say, in so many words, that he served us thirty-six years. For last summer, when we were located in the New Hampshire hills, at Dublin, we had Patrick with us. Jean had gone to Hartford the 1st of May and secured his services for the summer. Necessarily, a part of our household was Katy Leary, who has been on our roster for twenty-six years, and one day Jean overheard Katy and Patrick disputing about this length of service. Katy said she had served the family longer than Patrick had. Patrick said it was nothing of the kind; that he had already served the family ten years when Katy came, and that he had now served it thirty-six years.

He was just as brisk there in the New Hampshire hills as he was thirty-six years ago. He was sixty-four years old, but was just as slender and trim and handsome, and just as alert and springy on his feet, as he was in those long-vanished days of his youth. He was the most perfect man in his office that I have ever known, for this reason: that he never neglected any detail, howsoever slight, of his duties, and there was never any occasion to give

him an order about anything. He conducted his
affairs without anybody's help. There was always
plenty of feed for the horses; the horses were always shod when they needed to be shod; the carriages and sleighs were always attended to; he kept
everything in perfect order. It was a great satisfaction to have such a man around. I was not capable of telling anybody what to do about anything.
He was my particular servant, and I didn't need
to tell him anything at all. He was just the same
in the New Hampshire hills. I never gave him
an order while he was there, the whole five months;
and there was never anything lacking that belonged
in his jurisdiction.

When we had been married a year or two Patrick
took a wife, and they lived in a house which we
built and added to the stable. They reared eight
children. They lost one, two or three years ago
—a thriving young man, assistant editor of a Hartford daily paper, I think. The children were all
educated in the public schools and in the high school.
They are all men and women now, of course. . . .

Our first child, Langdon Clemens, was born the
7th of November, 1870, and lived twenty-two
months. Susy was born the 19th of March, 1872,
and passed from life in the Hartford home, the
18th of August, 1896. With her, when the end
came, were Jean, and Katy Leary, and John and
Ellen (the gardener and his wife). Clara and
her mother and I arrived in England from around
the world on the 31st of July, and took a house
in Guildford. A week later, when Susy, Katy, and

Jean should have been arriving from America, we got a letter instead.

Subject of February first continued.—The death of Susy Clemens. Ends with mention of Dr. John Brown.

IT explained that Susy was slightly ill—nothing of consequence. But we were disquieted and began to cable for later news. This was Friday. All day no answer—and the ship to leave Southampton next day, at noon. Clara and her mother began packing, to be ready in case the news should be bad. Finally came a cablegram saying, "Wait for cablegram in the morning." This was not satisfactory—not reassuring. I cabled again, asking that the answer be sent to Southampton, for the day was now closing. I waited in the post-office that night till the doors were closed, toward midnight, in the hope that good news might still come, but there was no message. We sat silent at home till one in the morning, waiting—waiting for we knew not what. Then we took the earliest morning train, and when we reached Southampton the message was there. It said the recovery would be long, but certain. This was a great relief to me, but not to my wife. She was frightened. She and Clara went aboard the steamer at once and sailed for America, to nurse Susy. I remained behind to search for another and larger house in Guildford.

That was the 15th of August, 1896. Three days

later, when my wife and Clara were about halfway
across the ocean, I was standing in our dining-room,
thinking of nothing in particular, when a cablegram
was put into my hand. It said, "Susy was peacefully
released to-day.'

It is one of the mysteries of our nature that a
man, all unprepared, can receive a thunder-stroke
like that and live. There is but one reasonable
explanation of it. The intellect is stunned by the
shock and but gropingly gathers the meaning of
the words. The power to realize their full import
is mercifully wanting. The mind has a dumb sense
of vast loss—that is all. It will take mind and
memory months, and possibly years, to gather together the details and thus learn and know the
whole extent of the loss. A man's house burns
down. The smoking wreckage represents only a
ruined home that was dear through years of use
and pleasant associations. By and by, as the days
and weeks go on, first he misses this, then that,
then the other thing. And when he casts about
for it he finds that it was in that house. Always
it is an *essential*—there was but one of its kind.
It cannot be replaced. It was in that house. It is
irrevocably lost. He did not realize that it was an
essential when he had it; he only discovers it now
when he finds himself balked, hampered, by its
absence. It will be years before the tale of lost
essentials is complete, and not till then can he truly
know the magnitude of his disaster.

The 18th of August brought me the awful tid-
ings. The mother and the sister were out there

in mid-Atlantic, ignorant of what was happening, flying to meet this incredible calamity. All that could be done to protect them from the full force of the shock was done by relatives and good friends. They went down the Bay and met the ship at night, but did not show themselves until morning, and then only to Clara. When she returned to the stateroom she did not speak, and did not need to. Her mother looked at her and said, "Susy is dead."

At half past ten o'clock that night Clara and her mother completed their circuit of the globe, and drew up at Elmira by the same train and in the same car which had borne them and me westward from it one year, one month, and one week before. And again Susy was there—not waving her welcome in the glare of the lights as she had waved her farewell to us thirteen months before, but lying white and fair in her coffin, in the house where she was born.

The last thirteen days of Susy's life were spent in our own house in Hartford, the home of her childhood and always the dearest place in the earth to her. About her she had faithful old friends— her pastor, Mr. Twichell, who had known her from the cradle and who had come a long journey to be with her; her uncle and aunt, Mr. and Mrs. Theodore Crane; Patrick, the coachman; Katy, who had begun to serve us when Susy was a child of eight years; John and Ellen, who had been with us many years. Also Jean was there.

At the hour when my wife and Clara set sail for America, Susy was in no danger. Three hours later there came a sudden change for the worse. Meningitis set in, and it was immediately apparent that she was death-struck. That was Saturday, the 15th of August.

"That evening she took food for the last time." (Jean's letter to me.) The next morning the brain fever was raging. She walked the floor a little in her pain and delirium, then succumbed to weakness and returned to her bed. Previously she had found hanging in a closet a gown which she had seen her mother wear. She thought it was her mother, dead, and she kissed it and cried. About noon she became blind (an effect of the disease) and bewailed it to her uncle.

From Jean's letter I take this sentence, which needs no comment:

"About one in the afternoon Susy spoke for the last time."

It was only one word that she said when she spoke that last time, and it told of her longing. She groped with her hands and found Katy, and caressed her face and said, "Mamma."

How gracious it was that in that forlorn hour of wreck and ruin, with the night of death closing around her, she should have been granted that beautiful illusion—that the latest vision which rested upon the clouded mirror of her mind should have been the vision of her mother, and the latest emotion she should know in life the joy and peace of that dear imagined presence.

About two o'clock she composed herself as if for sleep, and never moved again. She fell into unconsciousness and so remained two days and five hours, until Tuesday evening at seven minutes past seven, when the release came. She was twenty-four years and five months old.

On the 23d her mother and her sisters saw her laid to rest—she that had been our wonder and our worship.

The summer seasons of Susy's childhood were spent at Quarry Farm on the hills east of Elmira, New York; the other seasons of the year at the home in Hartford. Like other children, she was blithe and happy, fond of play; *un*like the average of children, she was at times much given to retiring within herself and trying to search out the hidden meanings of the deep things that make the puzzle and pathos of human existence, and in all the ages have baffled the inquirer and mocked him. As a little child aged seven, she was oppressed and perplexed by the maddening repetition of the stock incidents of our race's fleeting sojourn here, just as the same thing has oppressed and perplexed maturer minds from the beginning of time. A myriad of men are born; they labor and sweat and struggle for bread; they squabble and scold and fight; they scramble for little mean advantages over each other. Age creeps upon them; infirmities follow; shames and humiliations bring down their prides and their vanities. Those they love are taken from them, and the joy of life is turned to aching grief. The burden of pain, care, misery, grows heavier year by year. At length ambition is dead; pride is dead; vanity is dead; longing for

release is in their place. It comes at last—the
only unpoisoned gift earth ever had for them—
and they vanish from a world where they were of
no consequence; where they achieved nothing; where
they were a mistake and a failure and a foolish-
ness; where they have left no sign that they have
existed—a world which will lament them a day and
forget them forever. Then another myriad takes
their place, and copies all they did, and goes along
the same profitless road, and vanishes as they vanished—to make room for another and another and
a million other myriads to follow the same arid
path through the same desert and accomplish what
the first myriad, and all the myriads that came
after it, accomplished—nothing!

"Mamma, what is it all for?" asked Susy, pre-
liminarily stating the above details in her own halt-
ing language, after long brooding over them alone
in the privacy of the nursery.

A year later, she was groping her way alone
through another sunless bog, but this time she
reached a rest for her feet. For a week, her mother
had not been able to go to the nursery, evenings,
at the child's prayer hour. She spoke of it—was
sorry for it, and said she would come to-night, and
hoped she could continue to come every night and
hear Susy pray, as before. Noticing that the child
wished to respond, but was evidently troubled as
to how to word her answer, she asked what the
difficulty was. Susy explained that Miss Foote (the
governess) had been teaching her about the Indians and their religious beliefs, whereby it ap-

peared that they had not only a god, but several. This had set Susy to thinking. As a result of this thinking she had stopped praying. She qualified this statement—that is, she modified it—saying she did not now pray "in the same way" as she had formerly done. Her mother said, "Tell me about it, dear."

"Well, mamma, the Indians believed they knew, but now we know they were wrong. By and by it can turn out that we are wrong. So now I only pray that there may be a God and a heaven—or something better."

I wrote down this pathetic prayer in its precise wording, at the time, in a record which we kept of the children's sayings, and my reverence for it has grown with the years that have passed over my head since then. Its untaught grace and simplicity are a child's, but the wisdom and the pathos of it are of all the ages that have come and gone since the race of man has lived, and longed, and hoped, and feared, and doubted.

To go back a year—Susy aged seven. Several times her mother said to her, "There, there, Susy, you mustn't cry over little things."

This furnished Susy a text for thought. She had been breaking her heart over what had seemed vast disasters—a broken toy; a picnic canceled by thunder and lightning and rain; the mouse that was growing tame and friendly in the nursery caught and killed by the cat—and now came this strange revelation. For some unaccountable reason, these were not vast calamities. Why? How is the size of calamities measured? What is the rule? There must be some way to tell the great ones from the small ones; what is the law of these proportions? She examined the problem earnestly and long. She gave it her best thought, from time to time, for two or three days—but it baffled her—defeated her. And at last she gave up and went to her mother for help.

"Mamma, what is 'little things'?"

It seemed a simple question—at first. And yet before the answer could be put into words, unsuspected and unforeseen difficulties began to appear. They increased; they multiplied; they brought about another defeat. The effort to explain came to a standstill. Then Susy tried to help her mother out—with an instance, an example, an illustration. The mother was getting ready to go downtown, and one of her errands was to buy a long-promised toy watch for Susy.

"If you forgot the watch, mamma, would that be a little thing?"

She was not concerned about the watch, for she knew it would not be forgotten. What she was hoping for was that the answer would unriddle the riddle and bring rest and peace to her perplexed little mind.

The hope was disappointed, of course—for the reason that the size of a misfortune is not determinable by an outsider's measurement of it, but only by the measurements applied to it by the person specially affected by it. The king's lost crown is a vast matter to the king, but of no consequence to the child. The lost toy is a great matter to the child, but in the king's eyes it is not a thing to break the heart about. A verdict was reached, but it was based upon the above model, and Susy was granted leave to measure her disasters thereafter with her own tape-line.

I will throw in a note or two here touching the time when Susy was seventeen. She had written a play modeled upon Greek lines, and she and Clara and Margaret Warner, and other young comrades, had played it to a charmed houseful of friends in our house in Hartford. Charles Dudley Warner and his brother, George, were present. They were near neighbors and warm friends of ours. They were full of praises of the workmanship of the play, and George Warner came over the next morning and had a long talk with Susy. The result of it was this verdict:

"She is the most interesting person I have ever known, of either sex."

Remark of a lady—Mrs. Cheney, I think, author of the biography of her father, Rev. Dr. Bushnell:

"I made this note after one of my talks with Susy: 'She knows all there is of life and its meanings. She could not know it better if she had lived it out to its limit. Her intuitions and ponderings and analyzings seem to have taught her all that my sixty years have taught me.'"

Remark of another lady; she is speaking of Susy's last days:

"In those last days she walked as if on air, and

her walk answered to the buoyancy of her spirits and the passion of intellectual energy and activity that possessed her."

I return now to the point where I made this diversion. From her earliest days, as I have already indicated, Susy was given to examining things and thinking them out by herself. She was not trained to this; it was the make of her mind. In matters involving questions of fair or unfair dealing, she reviewed the details patiently and surely arrived at a right and logical conclusion. In Munich, when she was six years old, she was harassed by a recurrent dream, in which a ferocious bear figured. She came out of the dream each time sorely frightened, and crying. She set herself the task of analyzing this dream. The reasons of it? The purpose of it? The origin of it? No—the moral aspect of it. Her verdict, arrived at after candid and searching investigation, exposed it to the charge of being one-sided and unfair in its construction: for (as she worded it) *she* was "never the one that ate, but always the one that was eaten."

Susy backed her good judgment in matters of morals with conduct to match—even upon occasions when it caused her sacrifice to do it. When she was six and her sister Clara four, the pair were troublesomely quarrelsome. Punishments were tried as a means of breaking up this custom—these failed. Then rewards were tried. A day without a quarrel brought candy. The children were their own witnesses—each for or against her own self. Once Susy took the candy, hesitated, then returned it with a suggestion that she was not fairly entitled to it. Clara kept hers, so, here was a conflict of evidence —one witness *for* a quarrel, and one against it. But the better witness of the two was on the affirmative side, and the quarrel stood proved, and no candy due to either side. There seemed to be no defense for Clara—yet there was, and Susy furnished it; and Clara went free. Susy said, "I don't know whether she felt wrong in *her* heart, but I didn't feel right in *my* heart."

It was a fair and honorable view of the case, and a specially acute analysis of it for a child of six to make. There was no way to convict Clara now, except to put her on the stand again and review her evidence. There was a doubt as to the fairness of this procedure, since her former evidence had been accepted, and not challenged at the time. The doubt was examined, and canvassed—then she was given the benefit of it and acquitted; which was just as well, for in the meantime she had eaten the candy, anyway.

Whenever I think of Susy I think of Marjorie Fleming. There was but one Marjorie Fleming. There can never be another. No doubt I think of Marjorie when I think of Susy mainly because Dr. John Brown, that noble and beautiful soul— rescuer of marvelous Marjorie from oblivion—was Susy's great friend in her babyhood—her worshiper and willing slave.

In 1873, when Susy was fourteen months old, we arrived in Edinburgh from London, fleeing thither for rest and refuge, after experiencing what had

been to us an entirely new kind of life—six weeks
of daily lunches, teas, and dinners away from home.
We carried no letters of introduction; we hid ourselves away in Veitch's family hotel in George
Street and prepared to have a comfortable season
all to ourselves. But by good fortune this did not
happen. Straightway Mrs. Clemens needed a
physician, and I stepped around to 23 Rutland
Street to see if the author of *Rab and His Friends*
was still a practicing physician. He was. He came,
and for six weeks thereafter we were together every
day, either in his house or in our hotel.

[*New York, Monday, February 5, 1906*

*Dr. John Brown continued.—Incidents connected with
Susy Clemens's childhood.—Bad spelling, etc.*

His was a sweet and winning face—as beautiful
a face as I have ever known. Reposeful, gentle,
benignant—the face of a saint at peace with all
the world and placidly beaming upon it the sunshine
of love that filled his heart. Doctor John was beloved by everybody in Scotland; and I think that
on its downward sweep southward it found no frontier. I think so because when, a few years later,
infirmities compelled Doctor John to give up his
practice, and Mr. Douglas, the publisher, and other
friend set themselves the task of raising a fund
of a few thousand dollars, whose income was to be
devoted to the support of himself and his maiden
sister (who was in age), the fund was not only

promptly made up, but so *very* promptly that the books were closed before friends a hundred miles south of the line had had an opportunity to contribute. No public appeal was made. The matter was never mentioned in print. Mr. Douglas and the other friends applied for contributions by private letter only. Many complaints came from London, and everywhere between, from people who had not been allowed an opportunity to contribute. This sort of complaint is so new to the world—so strikingly unusual—that I think it worth while to mention it.

Doctor John was very fond of animals, and particularly of dogs. No one needs to be told this who has read that pathetic and beautiful masterpiece, *Rab and His Friends*. After his death, his son, Jock, published a brief memorial of him which he distributed privately among the friends; and in it occurs a little episode which illustrates the relationship that existed between Doctor John and the other animals. It is furnished by an Edinburgh lady whom Doctor John used to pick up and carry to school or back in his carriage frequently at a time when she was twelve years old. She said that they were chatting together tranquilly one day, when he suddenly broke off in the midst of a sentence and thrust his head out of the carriage window eagerly —then resumed his place with a disappointed look on his face. The girl said: "Who is it? Some one you know?" He said, "No, a dog I don't know."

He had two names for Susy—"Wee wifie" and

"Megalopis." This formidable Greek title was conferred in honor of her big, big dark eyes. Susy and the Doctor had a good deal of romping together. Daily he unbent his dignity and played "bear" with the child. I do not now remember which of them was the bear, but I think it was the child. There was a sofa across a corner of the parlor with a door behind it opening into Susy's quarters, and she used to lie in wait for the Doctor behind the sofa—not lie in wait, but stand in wait; for you could only get just a glimpse of the top of her yellow head when she stood upright. According to the rules of the game, she was invisible, and this glimpse did not count. I think she must have been the bear, for I can remember two or three occasions when she sprang out from behind the sofa and surprised the Doctor into frenzies of fright, which were not in the least modified by the fact that he knew that the "bear" was there and was coming.

It seems incredible that Doctor John should ever have wanted to tell a grotesque and rollicking anecdote. Such a thing seems so out of character with that gentle and tranquil nature that—but no matter. I tried to teach him the anecdote, and he tried his best for two or three days to perfect himself in it—and he never succeeded. It was the most impressive exhibition that ever was. There was no human being, nor dog, of his acquaintance in all Edinburgh that would not have been paralyzed with astonishment to step in there and see Doctor John trying to do that anecdote. It was one which I have told some hundreds of times on the platform, and which I was always very fond of, because it worked the audience so hard. It was a stammering man's account of how he got cured of his infirmity—which was accomplished by introducing a whistle into the midst of every word which he found himself unable to finish on account of the obstruction of the stammering. And so his whole account was an absurd mixture of stammering and whistling—which was irresistible to an audience properly keyed up for laughter. Doctor John learned to do the mechanical details of the anecdote, but he was never able to inform these details with expression. He was preternaturally grave and earnest all through, and so when he fetched up with the climaxing triumphant sentence at the end—but I must quote that sentence, or the reader will not understand. It was this:

"The doctor told me that whenever I wanted to sta— (whistle) sta— (whistle) sta— (whistle) *ammer,* I must whistle; and I did, and it k— (whistle) k— (whistle) k— (whistle) k— ured me *entirely!*"

The Doctor could not master that triumphant note. He always gravely stammered and whistled and whistled and stammered it through, and it came out at the end with the solemnity and the gravity of the judge delivering sentence to a man with the black cap on.

He was the loveliest creature in the world—except his aged sister, who was just like him. We made the round of his professional visits with him in his carriage every day for six weeks. He always brought a basket of grapes, and we brought books.

The scheme which we began with on the first round of visits was the one which was maintained until the end—and was based upon this remark, which he made when he was disembarking from the carriage at his first stopping place, to visit a patient, "Entertain yourselves while I go in here and reduce the population."

As a child, Susy had a passionate temper; and it cost her much remorse and many tears before she learned to govern it, but after that it was a wholesome salt, and her character was the stronger and healthier for its presence. It enabled her to be good with dignity; it preserved her not only from being good for vanity's sake, but from even the appearance of it. In looking back over the long-vanished years it seems but natural and excusable that I should dwell with longing affection and preference upon incidents of her young life which made it beautiful to us, and that I should let its few and small offenses go unsummoned and unreproached.

In the summer of 1880, when Susy was just eight years of age, the family were at Quarry Farm, on top of a high hill, three miles from Elmira, New York, where we always spent our summers, in those days. Hay-cutting time was approaching, and Susy and Clara were counting the hours, for the time was big with a great event for them; they had been promised that they might mount the wagon and ride home from the fields on the summit of the hay mountain. This perilous privilege, so dear to their age and species, had never been granted them before. Their excitement had no bounds. They could talk of nothing but this epoch-making adventure, now. But misfortune overtook Susy on the very morning of the important day. In a sudden outbreak of passion she corrected Clara—with a shovel, or stick, or something of the sort. At any rate, the offense committed was of a gravity clearly beyond the limit allowed in the nursery. In accordance with the rule and custom of the house, Susy went to her mother to confess and to help decide upon the size and character of the punishment due. It was quite understood that as a punishment could have but one rational object and function—to act as a reminder and warn the transgressor against transgressing in the same way again—the children would know about as well as any how to choose a penalty which would be rememberable and effective. Susy and her mother discussed various punishments, but none of them seemed adequate. This fault was an unusually serious one, and required the setting up of a danger signal in the memory that would not blow out nor burn out, but remain a fixture there and furnish its saving warning indefinitely. Among the punishments mentioned was deprivation of the hay-wagon ride. It was noticeable that this one hit Susy hard. Finally, in the summing up, the mother named over the list and asked, "Which one do you think it ought to be, Susy?"

Susy studied, shrank from her duty, and asked, "Which do you think, mamma?"

"Well, Susy, I would rather leave it to you. *You* make the choice, yourself."

It cost Susy a struggle, and much and deep thinking and weighing—but she came out where anyone who knew her could have foretold she would:

"Well, mamma, I'll make it the hay wagon, because, you know, the other things might not make me remember not to do it again, but if I don't get to ride on the hay wagon I can remember it easily."

In this world the real penalty, the sharp one, the lasting one, never falls otherwise than on the wrong person. It was not *I* that corrected Clara, but the remembrance of poor Susy's lost hay ride still brings *me* a pang—after twenty-six years.

Apparently Susy was born with humane feelings for the animals and compassion for their troubles. This enabled her to see a new point in an old story, once, when she was only six years old—a point which had been overlooked by older, and perhaps duller, people for many ages. Her mother told her the moving story of the sale of Joseph by his brethren, the staining of his coat with the blood of the slaughtered kid, and the rest of it. She dwelt upon the inhumanity of the brothers, their cruelty toward their helpless young brother, and the unbrotherly treachery which they practiced upon him; for she hoped to teach the child a lesson in gentle pity and mercifulness which she would remember. Apparently her desire was accomplished, for the tears came into Susy's eyes and she was deeply moved. Then she said, "Poor little kid!"

A child's frank envy of the privileges and distinctions of its elders is often a delicately flattering attention and the reverse of unwelcome, but sometimes the envy is not placed where the beneficiary is expecting it to be placed. Once when Susy was seven, she sat breathlessly absorbed in watching a guest of ours adorn herself for a ball. The lady was charmed by this homage, this mute and gentle admiration, and was happy in it. And when her pretty labors were finished, and she stood at last perfect, unimprovable, clothed like Solomon in his glory, she paused, confident and expectant, to receive from Susy's tongue the tribute that was burning in her eyes. Susy drew an envious little sigh and said, "I wish *I* could have crooked teeth and spectacles!"

Once, when Susy was six months along in her eighth year, she did something one day in the presence of company which subjected her to criticism and reproof. Afterward, when she was alone with her mother, as was her custom she reflected a little while over the matter. Then she set up what I think—and what the shade of Burns would think— was a quite good philosophical defense: "Well, mamma, you know I didn't see myself, and so I couldn't know how it looked."

In homes where the near friends and visitors are mainly literary people—lawyers, judges, professors, and clergymen—the children's ears become early familiarized with wide vocabularies. It is natural for them to pick up any words that fall in their way; it is natural for them to pick up big and little ones indiscriminately; it is natural for them to use

without fear any word that comes to their net, no
matter how formidable it may be as to size. As a
result, their talk is a curious and funny musketry-
clatter of little words, interrupted at intervals by
the heavy-artillery crash of a word of such im-
posing sound and size that it seems to shake the
ground and rattle the windows. Sometimes the child
gets a wrong idea of a word which it has picked
up by chance, and attaches to it a meaning which
impairs its usefulness—but this does not happen
as often as one might expect it would. Indeed, it
happens with an infrequency which may be regarded
as remarkable. As a child, Susy had good fortune
with her large words, and she employed many of
them. She made no more than her fair share of
mistakes. Once when she thought something very
funny was going to happen (but it didn't) she was
racked and torn with laughter, by anticipation. But
apparently she still felt sure of her position, for
she said, "If it had happened, I should have been
transformed [transported] with glee."

And earlier, when she was a little maid of five
years, she informed a visitor that she had been in a
church only once, and that was the time when Clara
was "crucified" (christened).

In Heidelberg, when she was six, she noticed that
the Schloss gardens——

Dear me, how remote things do come together!
I break off that sentence to remark that at a luncheon
uptown yesterday, I reminded the hostess that she
had not made me acquainted with all the guests.
She said yes, she was aware of that—that by re-

quest of one of the ladies she had left me to guess
that lady out for myself; that I had known that
lady for a day, more than a quarter of a century
ago, and that the lady was desirous of finding out
how long it would take me to dig her up out of my
memory. The rest of the company were in the
game and were anxious to see whether I would succeed or fail. It seemed to me, as the time drifted
along, that I was never going to be able to locate
that woman; but at last, when the luncheon was
nearly finished, a discussion broke out as to where
the most comfortable hotel in the world was to
be found. Various hotels on the several sides of the
ocean were mentioned, and at last somebody reminded her that she had not put forward a preference yet, and she was asked to name the hotel that
she thought was, from her point of view, the most
satisfactory and comfortable hotel on the planet,
and she said, promptly, "The 'Slosh,' at Heidelberg."

I said at once, "I am sincerely glad to meet you
again, Mrs. Jones, after this long stretch of years—
but you were Miss Smith in those days. Have I
located you?"

"Yes," she said, "you have."

I *knew* I had. During that day at Heidelberg,
so many ages ago, many charitable people tried
furtively to get that young Miss Smith to adopt
the prevailing pronunciation of Schloss, by *saying*
Schloss softly and casually every time she said
"Slosh," but nobody succeeded in converting her.
And I knew perfectly well that this was that same

old Smith girl, because there could not be two persons on this planet at one and the same time who
could preserve and stick to a mispronunciation like
that for nearly a generation.

As I was saying, when I interrupted myself—
in Heidelberg, when Susy was six, she noticed that
the Schloss gardens were populous with snails creep-
ing all about everywhere. One day she found a
new dish on her table and inquired concerning it,
and learned that it was made of snails. She was
awed and impressed, and said, "Wild ones,
mamma?"

She was thoughtful and considerate of others—
an acquired quality, no doubt. No one seems to be
born with it. One hot day, at home in Hartford,
when she was a little child, her mother borrowed
her fan several times (a Japanese one, value five
cents), refreshed herself with it a moment or two,
then handed it back with a word of thanks. Susy
knew her mother would use the fan all the time
if she could do it without putting a deprivation
upon its owner. She also knew that her mother
could not be persuaded to do that. A relief must
be devised somehow; Susy devised it. She got five
cents out of her money box and carried it to Patrick
and asked him to take it downtown (a mile and
a half) and buy a Japanese fan and bring it home.
He did it—and thus thoughtfully and delicately was
the exigency met and the mother's comfort secured.
It is to the child's credit that she did not save herself
expense by bringing down another and more costly
kind of fan from upstairs, but was content to act

upon the impression that her mother desired the Japanese kind—content to accomplish the desire and stop with that, without troubling about the wisdom or unwisdom of it.

Sometimes while she was still a child, her speech fell into quaint and strikingly expressive forms. Once—aged nine or ten—she came to her mother's room when her sister Jean was a baby and said Jean was crying in the nursery, and asked if she might ring for the nurse. Her mother asked, "Is she crying hard?"—meaning cross, ugly.

"Well, no, mamma. It is a weary, lonesome cry."

It is a pleasure to me to recall various incidents which reveal the delicacies of feeling which were so considerable a part of her budding character. Such a revelation came once in a way which, while creditable to her heart, was defective in another direction. She was in her eleventh year, then. Her mother had been making the Christmas purchases, and she allowed Susy to see the presents which were for Patrick's children. Among these was a handsome sled for Jimmy, on which a stag was painted; also in gilt capitals the word "DEER." Susy was excited and joyous over everything until she came to this sled. Then she became sober and silent—yet the sled was the choicest of all the gifts. Her mother was surprised and also disappointed, and said:

"Why, Susy, doesn't it please you? Isn't it fine?"

Susy hesitated, and it was plain that she did not want to say the thing that was in her mind. However, being urged, she brought it haltingly out:

"Well, mamma, it *is* fine, and of course it *did* cost a good deal—but—but—why should that be mentioned?"

Seeing that she was not understood, she reluctantly pointed to that word "DEER." It was her orthography that was at fault, not her heart. She had inherited both from her mother.

The ability to spell is a natural gift. The person not born with it can never become perfect in it. I was always able to spell correctly. My wife and her sister, Mrs. Crane, were always bad spellers. Once when Clara was a little chap her mother was away from home for a few days, and Clara wrote her a small letter every day. When her mother returned, she praised Clara's letters. Then she said, "But in one of them, Clara, you spelled a word wrong."

Clara said, with quite unconscious brutality, "Why, mamma, how did *you* know?"

More than a quarter of a century has elapsed, and Mrs. Crane is under our roof here in New York for a few days. Her head is white now, but she is as pretty and winning and sweet as she was in those ancient times at her Quarry Farm, where she was an idol and the rest of us were the worshipers. Her gift of imperfect orthography remains unimpaired. She writes a great many letters. This was always a passion of hers. Yesterday she asked me how to spell New Jersey, and I knew by her look, after she got the information, that she was regretting she hadn't asked somebody years ago. The miracles which she and her sister, Mrs.

Clemens, were able to perform without help of dictionary or spelling book are incredible. During the year of my engagement—1869—while I was out on the lecture platform, the daily letter that came for me generally brought me news from the front—by which expression I refer to the internecine war that was always going on in a friendly way between these two orthographists about the spelling of words. One of these words was scissors. They never seemed to consult a dictionary; they always wanted something or somebody that was more reliable. Between them, they had spelled scissors in seven different ways, a feat which I am certain no person now living, educated or uneducated, can match. I have forgotten how I was required to say which of the seven ways was the right one. I couldn't do it. If there had been fourteen ways, none of them would have been right. I remember only one of the instances offered—the other six have passed from my memory. That one was "sicisiors." That way of spelling it looked so reasonable—so plausible, to the discoverer of it, that I was hardly believed when I decided against it. Mrs. Crane keeps by her, to this day, a little book of about thirty pages of note-paper, on which she has written, in a large hand, words which she needs to use in her letters every day—words which the cat could spell without prompting or tuition, and yet are words which Mrs. Crane never allows herself to risk upon paper without looking at that vocabulary of hers, each time, to make certain.

During my engagement year, thirty-seven years

ago, a considerable company of young people amused
themselves in the Langdon homestead one night with
the game of Verbarium, which was brand new at
the time and very popular. A text word was chosen
and each person wrote that word in large letters
across the top of a sheet of paper, then sat with
pencil in hand and ready to begin as soon as game
was called. The player could begin with the first
letter of that text word and build words out of the
text word during two minutes by the watch. But
he must not use a letter that was not *in* the text
word and he must not use any letter in the text
word twice, unless the letter occurred twice in the
text word. I remember the first bout that we had
at that game.   The text word was *California*. When
game was called everybody began to set down words
as fast as he could make his pencil move—"corn,"
"car," "cone," and so on, digging out the shortest
words first because they could be set down more
quickly than the longer ones. When the two minutes were up, the scores were examined, and the prize
went to the person who had achieved the largest
number of words. The good scores ranged along
between thirty and fifty or sixty words. But Mrs.
Crane would not allow her score to be examined.
She was plainly doubtful about getting that prize.
But when persuasion failed to avail we chased her
about the place, captured her, and took her score
away from her by force. She had achieved only one
word, and that was *calf*—which she had spelled
"caff." And she never would have gotten even that

one word honestly—she had to introduce a letter that didn't belong in the text word in order to get it.

[*New York, Tuesday, February 6, 1906*

Playing "The Prince and the Pauper."—Acting charades, etc.

WHEN Susy was twelve and a half years old, I took to the platform again, after a long absence from it, and raked the country for four months in company with George W. Cable. Early in November we gave a reading one night in Chickering Hall, in New York, and when I was walking home in a dull gloom of fog and rain I heard one invisible man say to another invisible man, this, in substance: "General Grant has actually concluded to write his autobiography." That remark gave me joy, at the time, but if I had been struck by lightning in place of it, it would have been better for me and mine. However, that is a long story, and this is not the place for it.

To Susy, as to all Americans, General Grant was the supremest of heroes, and she longed for a sight of him. I took her to see him one day— However, let that go. It belongs elsewhere. I will return to it by and by.

In the midst of our reading campaign, I returned to Hartford from the far West, reaching home one evening just at dinner time. I was expecting to have a happy and restful season by a hickory fire in the library with the family, but was required to go at once to George Warner's house, a hundred and fifty yards away, across the grounds. This was a heavy disappointment, and I tried to beg off, but did not succeed. I couldn't even find out why I must waste this precious evening in a visit to a friend's house when our own house offered so many and superior advantages. There was a mystery somewhere, but I was not able to get to the bottom of it. So we tramped across in the snow, and I found the Warner drawing-room crowded with seated people. There was a vacancy in the front row, for me—in front of a curtain. At once the curtain was drawn, and before me, properly costumed, was the little maid, Margaret Warner, clothed in Tom Canty's rags, and beyond an intercepting railing was Susy Clemens, arrayed in the silks and satins of the prince. Then followed with good action and spirit the rest of that first meeting between the prince and the pauper. It was a charming surprise, and to me a moving one. Other episodes of the tale followed, and I have seldom in my life enjoyed an evening so much as I enjoyed that one. This lovely surprise was my wife's work. She had patched the scenes together from the book and had trained the six or eight young actors in their parts, and had also designed and furnished the costumes.

Afterward, I added a part for myself (Miles Hendon), also a part for Katy and a part for George. I think I have not mentioned George before. He was a colored man—the children's darling and a remarkable person. He had been a member of the family a number of years at that time. He had been born a slave, in Maryland, was set free by the Proclamation when he was just entering young manhood. He was body servant to General Devens all through the war, and then had come North and for eight or ten years had been earning his living by odd jobs. He came out to our house once, an entire stranger, to clean some windows— and remained eighteen years. Mrs. Clemens could always tell enough about a servant by the look of him—more, in fact, than she, or anybody else, could tell about him by his recommendations.

We played "The Prince and the Pauper" a number of times in our house to seated audiences of eighty-four persons, which was the limit of our space, and we got great entertainment out of it. As *we* played the piece it had several superiorities over the play as presented on the public stage in England and America, for we always had both the prince and the pauper on deck, whereas these parts were always doubled on the public stage—an economical but unwise departure from the book, because it necessitated the excision of the strongest and most telling of the episodes. We made a stirring and handsome thing out of the coronation scene. This could not be accomplished otherwise than by having both the prince and the pauper present at the same time. Clara was the little Lady Jane Grey, and she performed the part with electrifying spirit. Twichell's littlest cub, now a grave and reverend clergyman, was a page. He was so small that people on the back seats could not see him without an opera-glass, but he held up Lady Jane's train very well. Jean was only something past three years old, therefore was too young to have a part, but she produced the whole piece every day independently, and played all the parts herself. For a one-actor piece it was not bad. In fact, it was very good—very entertaining. For she was in very deep earnest, and, besides, she used an English which none but herself could handle with effect.

Our children and the neighbors' children played well; easily, comfortably, naturally, and with high spirit. How was it that they were able to do this? It was because they had been in training all the time from their infancy. They grew up in our house, so to speak, playing charades. We never made any preparation. We selected a word, whispered the parts of it to the little actors; then we retired to the hall where all sorts of costumery had been laid out ready for the evening. We dressed the parts in three minutes and each detachment marched into the library and performed its syllable, then retired, leaving the fathers and mothers to guess that syllable if they could. Sometimes they could.

Will Gillette, now world-famous actor and dramatist, learned a part of his trade by acting in our charades. Those little chaps, Susy and Clara, invented charades themselves in their earliest years, and played them for the entertainment of their mother and me. They had one high merit—none but a high-grade intellect could guess them. Obscurity is a great thing in a charade. These babies invented one once which was a masterpiece in this regard. They came in and played the first syllable, which was a conversation in which the word *red* occurred with suggestive frequency. Then they retired—came again, continuing an angry dispute which they had begun outside, and in which several words like *just, fair, unfair, unjust,* and so on, kept occurring; but we noticed that the word *just* was in the majority—so we set that down along with the word *red* and discussed the probabilities while the children went out to recostume themselves. We had thus "red," "just." They soon appeared and began to do a very fashionable morning call, in which the one made many inquiries of the other concerning some lady whose name was persistently suppressed, and who was always referred to as "her," even when the grammar did not permit of that form of the pronoun. The children retired. We took an account of stock and, so far as we could see, we had three syllables, "red," "just," "her." But that was all. The combination did not seem to throw any real glare on the future completed word. The children arrived again, and stooped down and began to chat and quarrel and carry on, and fumble and fuss at the *register!*— (red—just—her). With the exception of myself, this family was never strong on spelling.

In "The Prince and the Pauper" days, and earlier and later—especially later, Susy and her nearest neighbor, Margaret Warner, often devised tragedies and played them in the school-room, with little Jean's help—with closed doors—no admission to anybody. The chief characters were always a couple of queens, with a quarrel in stock—historical when possible, but a quarrel anyway, even if it had to be a work of the imagination. Jean always had one function—only one. She sat at a little table about a foot high and drafted death warrants for these queens to sign. In the course of time they completely wore out Elizabeth and Mary, Queen of Scots—also all of Mrs. Clemens's gowns that they could get hold of—for nothing charmed these monarchs like having four or five feet of gown dragging on the floor behind. Mrs. Clemens and I spied upon them more than once, which was treacherous conduct—but I don't think we very seriously minded that. It was grand to see the queens stride back and forth and reproach each other in three- or four-syllable words dripping with blood; and it was pretty to see how tranquil Jean was through it all. Familiarity with daily death and carnage had hardened her to crime and suffering in all their forms, and they were no longer able to hasten her pulse by a beat. Sometimes when there was a long interval between death warrants she even leaned her head on her table and went to sleep. It was then a curious spectacle of innocent repose and crimson and volcanic tragedy.

[*Wednesday, February 7, 1906*

Susy Clemens's biography of her father.—Mr. Clemens's opinion of critics, etc.

WHEN Susy was thirteen, and was a slender little maid with plaited tails of copper-tinged brown hair down her back, and was perhaps the busiest bee in the household hive, by reason of the manifold studies, health exercises, and recreations she had to attend to, she secretly, and of her own motion, and out of love, added another task to her labors— the writing of a biography of me. She did this work in her bedroom at night, and kept her record hidden. After a little, the mother discovered it and filched it, and let me see it; then told Susy what she had done, and how pleased I was and how proud. I remember that time with a deep pleasure. I had had compliments before, but none that touched me like this; none that could approach it for value in my eyes. It has kept that place always since. I have had no compliment, no praise, no tribute from any source, that was so precious to me as this one was and still is. As I read it *now*, after all these many years, it is still a king's message to me, and brings me the same dear surprise it brought me then—with the pathos added of the thought that the eager and hasty hand that sketched it and scrawled it will not touch mine again—and I feel as the humble and unexpectant must feel when their eyes fall upon the edict that raises them to the ranks of the noble.

Yesterday while I was rummaging in a pile of ancient note-books of mine which I had not seen for years, I came across a reference to that biography. It is quite evident that several times, at breakfast and dinner, in those long-past days, I was posing for the biography. In fact, I clearly remember that I *was* doing that—and I also remember that Susy detected it. I remember saying a very smart thing, with a good deal of an air, at the breakfast table one morning, and that Susy observed to her mother privately, a little later, that papa was doing that for the biography.

I cannot bring myself to change any line or word in Susy's sketch of me, but will introduce passages from it now and then just as they came in—their quaint simplicity out of her honest heart, which was the beautiful heart of a child. What comes from that source has a charm and grace of its own which may transgress all the recognized laws of literature, if it choose, and yet be literature still, and worthy of hospitality.

The spelling is frequently desperate, but it was Susy's, and it shall stand. I love it, and cannot profane it. To me, it is gold. To correct it would alloy it, not refine it. It would spoil it. It would take from it its freedom and flexibility and make it stiff and formal. Even when it is most extravagant I am not shocked. It is Susy's spelling, and she was doing the best she could—and nothing could better it for me.

She learned languages easily; she learned history easily; she learned music easily; she learned all things easily, quickly, and thoroughly—except spelling. She even learned that, after a while. But it would have grieved me but little if she had failed in it—for, although good spelling was my one accomplishment, I was never able to greatly respect it. When I was a schoolboy, sixty years ago, we had two prizes in our school. One was for good spelling, the other for amiability. These things were thin, smooth, silver disks, about the size of a dollar. Upon the one was engraved in flowing Italian script the words "Good Spelling," on the other was engraved the word "Amiability." The holders of these prizes hung them about the neck with a string—and those holders were the envy of the whole school. There wasn't a pupil that wouldn't have given a leg for the privilege of wearing one of them a week, but no pupil ever got a chance except John RoBards and me. John RoBards was eternally and indestructibly amiable. I may even say devilishly amiable; fiendishly amiable; exasperatingly amiable. That was the sort of feeling that we had about that quality of his. So he always wore the amiability medal. I always wore the other medal. That word "always" is a trifle too strong. We lost the medals several times. It was because they became so monotonous. We needed a change—therefore several times we traded medals. It was a satisfaction to John RoBards to *seem* to be a good speller—which he wasn't. And it was a satisfaction to me to seem to be amiable, for a change. But of course these changes could not long endure—for some schoolmate or other would presently notice what had been happening, and that schoolmate would not have been human if he had lost any time in reporting this treason. The teacher took the medals away from us at once, of course—and we always had them back again before Friday night. If we lost the medals Monday morning, John's amiability was at the top of the list Friday afternoon when the teacher came to square up the week's account. The Friday-after-noon session always closed with "spelling down." Being in disgrace, I necessarily started at the foot of my division of spellers, but I always slaughtered both divisions and stood alone with the medal around my neck when the campaign was finished. I *did* miss on a word once, just at the end of one of these conflicts, and so lost the medal. I left the first *r* out of February—but that was to accommodate a sweetheart. My passion was so strong just at that time that I would have left out the whole alphabet if the word had contained it.

As I have said before, I never had any large respect for good spelling. That is my feeling yet. Before the spelling-book came with its arbitrary forms, men unconsciously revealed shades of their characters, and also added enlightening shades of expression to what they wrote by their spelling, and so it is possible that the spelling-book has been a doubtful benevolence to us.

Susy began the biography in 1885, when I was in the fiftieth year of my age, and she in the fourteenth of hers. She begins in this way:

We are a very happy family. We consist of Papa, Mamma, Jean, Clara and me. It is papa I am writing about, and I shall have no trouble in not knowing what to say about him, as he is a *very* striking character.

But wait a minute—I will return to Susy presently. In the matter of slavish imitation, man is the monkey's superior all the time. The average man is destitute of independence of opinion. He is not interested in contriving an opinion of his own, by study and reflection, but is only anxious to find out what his neighbor's opinion is and slavishly adopt it. A generation ago, I found out that the latest review of a book was pretty sure to be just a reflection of the *earliest* review of it. That whatever the first reviewer found to praise or censure in the book would be repeated in the latest reviewer's report, with nothing fresh added.[1] Therefore more than once I took the precaution of sending my book, in manuscript, to Mr. Howells, when he was editor of the *Atlantic Monthly,* so that he could prepare a review of it at leisure. I knew he would say the truth about the book—I also knew that he would find more merit than demerit in it, because I already knew that that was the condition of the book. I allowed no copy of that book to go out to the press until after Mr. Howells's notice of it had appeared. That book was always safe. There wasn't a man behind a pen in all America that had the courage to find anything in the book which Mr. Howells had not found—there wasn't a man behind a pen in America that had spirit enough to say a brave and original thing about the book on his own responsibility.

I believe that the trade of critic, in literature, music, and the drama, is the most degraded of all trades, and that it has no real value—certainly no large value. When Charles Dudley Warner and I were about to bring out *The Gilded Age,* the editor of the *Daily Graphic* persuaded me to let him have

---

[1] Hardly true to-day.—A. B. P.

an advance copy, he giving me his word of honor
that no notice of it should appear in his paper
until after the *Atlantic Monthly* notice should have
appeared. This reptile published a review of the
book within three days afterward. I could not really
complain, because he had only given me his word
of honor as security. I ought to have required of
him something substantial. I believe his notice did
not deal mainly with the merit of the book, or the
lack of it, but with my moral attitude toward the
public. It was charged that I had used my reputation to play a swindle upon the public—that Mr.
Warner had written as much as half of the book,
and that I had used my name to float it and give
it currency—a currency which it could not have
acquired without my name—and that this conduct
of mine was a grave fraud upon the people. The
Graphic was not an authority upon any subject whatever. It had a sort of distinction in that it was the
first and only illustrated daily newspaper that the
world had seen; but it was without character, it
was poorly and cheaply edited, its opinion of a book
or of any other work of art was of no consequence.
Everybody knew this, yet all the critics in America,
one after the other, copied the *Graphic's* criticism,
merely changing the phraseology, and left me under
that charge of dishonest conduct. Even the great
Chicago *Tribune,* the most important journal in the
Middle West, was not able to invent anything fresh,
but adopted the view of the humble *Daily Graphic,*
dishonesty charge and all. However, let it go. It
is the will of God that we must have critics, and

missionaries, and congressmen, and humorists, and we must bear the burden.

What I have been traveling toward all this time is this: The first critic that ever had occasion to describe my personal appearance littered his description with foolish and inexcusable errors whose aggregate furnished the result that I was distinctly and distressingly unhandsome. That description floated around the country in the papers, and was in constant use and wear for a quarter of a century. It seems strange to me that apparently no critic in the country could be found who could look at me and have the courage to take up his pen and destroy that lie. That lie began its course on the Pacific coast, in 1864, and it likened me in personal appearance to Petroleum V. Nasby, who had been out there lecturing. For twenty-five years afterward, no critic could furnish a description of me without fetching in Nasby to help out my portrait. I knew Nasby well, and he was a good fellow, but in my life I have not felt malignantly enough about any more than three persons to charge those persons with resembling Nasby. It hurts me to the heart, these things. To this day, it hurts me to the heart, and it had long been a distress to my family— including Susy—that the critics should go on making this wearisome mistake, year after year, when there was no foundation for it. Even when a critic wanted to be particularly friendly and complimentary to me, he didn't dare to go beyond my clothes. He did not venture beyond that frontier. When he had finished with my clothes he had said all the kind things, the pleasant things, the complimentary things he could risk. Then he dropped back on Nasby.

Yesterday I found this clipping in the pocket of one of those ancient memorandum-books of mine. It is of the date of thirty-nine years ago, and both the paper and the ink are yellow with the bitterness that I felt in that old day when I clipped it out to preserve it and brood over it and grieve about it. I will copy it here, to wit:

A correspondent of the Philadelphia *Press,* writing of one of Schuyler Colfax's receptions, says of our Washington correspondent: "Mark Twain, the delicate humorist, was present; quite a lion, as he deserves to be. Mark is a bachelor, faultless in taste, whose snowy vest is suggestive of endless quarrels with Washington washerwomen; but the heroism of Mark is settled for all time, for such purity and smoothness were never seen before. His lavender gloves might have been stolen from some Turkish harem, so delicate were they in size; but more likely—anything else were more likely than that. In form and feature he bears some resemblance to the immortal Nasby; but whilst Petroleum is brunette to the core, Twain is golden, amber-hued, melting, blonde."

Let us return to Susy's biography now, and get the opinion of one who is unbiased.

Papa's appearance has been described many times, but very incorrectly. He has beautiful gray hair, not any too thick or any too long, but just right; a Roman nose, which greatly improves the beauty of his features; kind blue eyes and a small mustache. He has a wonderfully shaped head and profile. He has a very good figure—in short, he is

an extrodinarily fine looking man. All his features are
perfect, exept that he hasn't extrodinary teeth. His complexion is very fair, and he doesn't ware a beard. He is a
very good man and a very funny one. He *has* got a temper,
but we all of us have in this family. He is the loveliest
man I ever saw or ever hope to see—and oh, so absent-
minded. He does tell perfectly delightful stories. Clara
and I used to sit on each arm of his chair and listen while
he told us stories about the pictures on the wall.

I remember the story-telling days vividly. They
were a difficult and exacting audience—those little
creatures.

[*New York, Thursday, February 8, 1906*

*Susy Clemens's biography continued.—Romancer to the
children.—Incident of the spoon-shaped drive.—The burglar
alarm does its whole duty.*

ALONG one side of the library, in the Hartford
home, the bookshelves joined the mantelpiece—
in fact, there were shelves on both sides of the
mantelpiece. On these shelves, and on the mantelpiece, stood various ornaments. At one end of the
procession was a framed oil-painting of a cat's
head; at the other end was a head of a beautiful
young girl, life size, called Emmeline, an impres-
sionist water-color. Between the one picture and the
other there were twelve or fifteen of the bric-à-brac
things already mentioned, also an oil-painting by
Elihu Vedder, "The Young Medusa." Every now
and then the children required me to construct a

romance—always impromptu—not a moment's preparation permitted—and into that romance I had to get all that bric-à-brac and the three pictures. I had to start always with the cat and finish with Emmeline. I was never allowed the refreshment of a change, end for end. It was not permissible to introduce a bric-à-brac ornament into the story out of its place in the procession. These bric-à-bracs were never allowed a peaceful day, a reposeful day, a restful Sabbath. In their lives there was no Sabbath. In their lives there was no peace. They knew no existence but a monotonous career of violence and bloodshed. In the course of time the bric-à-brac and the pictures showed wear. It was because they had had so many and such violent adventures in their romantic careers.

As romancer to the children I had a hard time, even from the beginning. If they brought me a picture and required me to build a story to it, they would cover the rest of the page with their pudgy hands to keep me from stealing an idea from it. The stories had to be absolutely original and fresh. Sometimes the children furnished me simply a character or two, or a dozen, and required me to start out at once on that slim basis and deliver those characters up to a vigorous and entertaining life of crime. If they heard of a new trade, or an unfamiliar animal, or anything like that, I was pretty sure to have to deal with those things in the next romance. Once Clara required me to build a sudden tale out of a plumber and a "bawgun strictor," and I had to do it. She didn't know what a boa-constrictor was until he developed in the tale—then she was better satisfied with it than ever.

FROM SUSY'S BIOGRAPHY

Papa's favorite game is billiards, and when he is tired and wishes to rest himself he stays up all night and plays billiards, it seems to rest his head. He smokes a great deal almost incessantly. He has the mind of an author exactly, some of the simplest things he can't understand. Our burglar alarm is often out of order, and papa had been obliged to take the mahogany room off from the alarm altogether for a time, because the burglar alarm had been in the habit of ringing even when the mahogany-room window was closed. At length he thought that perhaps the burglar alarm might be in order, and he decided to try and see; accordingly he put it on and then went down and opened the window; consequently the alarm bell rang, it would even if the alarm had been in order. Papa went despairingly upstairs and said to mamma, "Livy the mahogany room won't go on. I have just opened the window to see."

"Why, Youth," mamma replied. "If you've opened the window, why of course the alarm will ring!"

"That's what I've opened it for, why I just went down to see if it would ring!"

Mamma tried to explain to papa that when he wanted to go and see whether the alarm would ring while the window was closed he *mustn't* go and open the window— but in vain, papa couldn't understand, and got very impatient with mamma for trying to make him believe an impossible thing true.

This is a frank biographer, and an honest one; she uses no sandpaper on me. I have, to this day, the same dull head in the matter of conundrums and perplexities which Susy had discovered in those long-gone days. Complexities annoy me; then irritate me; then this progressive feeling presently warms into anger. I cannot get far in the reading of the commonest and simplest contract—with its "parties of the first part," and "parties of the second part," and "parties of the third part,"—my temper is all gone.

In the days which Susy is talking about, a perplexity fell to my lot one day. F. G. Whitmore was my business agent, and he brought me out from town in his buggy. We drove by the porte-cochère and toward the stable. Now this was a *single* road, and was like a spoon whose handle stretched from the gate to a great round flower bed in the neighborhood of the stable. At the approach to the flower bed the road divided and circumnavigated it, making a loop, which I have likened to the bowl of the spoon. I was sitting on the starboard side. As we neared the loop, I sitting as I say, on the starboard side (and that was the side on which the house was), I saw that Whitmore was laying his course to port and was going to start around that spoon bowl on that left-hand side. I said: "Don't do that, Whitmore; take the right-hand side. Then I shall be next to the house when we get to the door."

He said: "That will happen in any case. It doesn't make any difference which way I go around this flower bed."

I explained to him that he was an ass, but he stuck to his proposition, and I said, "Go on and try it, and see."

He went on and tried it, and sure enough he fetched me up at the door on the side that he said I would be. I was not able to believe it then, and I don't believe it yet. I said: "Whitmore, that is merely an accident. You can't do it again." He said he could—and we drove down into the street, fetched around, came back—did it again. I was stupefied, paralyzed, petrified, with these strange results, but they did not convince me. I didn't believe he could do it another time, but he did. He said he could do it all day and fetch up the same way every time—and by that time my temper was gone, and I asked him to go home and apply to the asylum and I would pay the expenses. I didn't want to see him any more for a week. I went upstairs in a rage and started to tell Livy about it, expecting to get her sympathy for me and to breed aversion in her for Whitmore; but she merely burst into peal after peal of laughter as the tale of my adventure went on, for her head was like Susy's. Riddles and complexities had no terrors for it. Her mind and Susy's were analytical. I have tried to make it appear that mine was different. Many and many a time I have told that buggy experiment, hoping against hope that I would some time or other find somebody who would be on my side— but it has never happened. And I am never able to go glibly forward and state the circumstances of that buggy's progress without having to halt and consider, and call up in my mind the spoon handle, the bowl of the spoon, the buggy and the horse, and my position in the buggy—and the minute I have got that far and try to turn it to the left, it goes to ruin. I can't see how it is ever going to fetch me out right when we get to the door. Susy is right in her estimate. I can't understand things.

That burglar alarm which Susy mentions led a gay and careless life, and had no principles. It was generally out of order at one point or another, and there was plenty of opportunity, because all the windows and doors in the house, from the cellar up to the top floor, were connected with it. In its seasons of being out of order it could trouble us for only a very little while. We quickly found out that it was fooling us and that it was buzzing its blood-curdling alarm merely for its own amusement. Then we would shut it off and send to New York for the electrician—there not being one in all Hartford in those days. Then when the repairs were finished we would set the alarm again and re-establish our confidence in it. It never did any real business except upon one single occasion. All the rest of its expensive career was frivolous and without purpose. Just that one time it performed its duty, and its whole duty—gravely, seriously, admirably. It let fly about two o'clock one black and dreary March morning, and I turned out promptly, because I knew that it was not fooling, this time. The bathroom door was on my side of the bed. I stepped in there, turned up the gas, looked at the annunciator, turned off the alarm—so far as the door indicated was concerned—thus stopping the racket. Then I came back to bed.

Mrs. Clemens said, "What was it?"

I said, "It was the cellar door."

She said, "Was it a burglar, do you think?"

"Yes," I said, "of course it was. Do you suppose it was a Sunday-school superintendent?"

She said, "What do you suppose he wants?"

I said: "I suppose he wants jewelry, but he is not acquainted with the house and he thinks it is in the cellar. I don't like to disappoint a burglar whom I am not acquainted with and who has done me no harm, but if he had had common sagacity enough to inquire, I could have told him we kept nothing down there but coal and vegetables. Still, it may be that he *is* acquainted with this place and that what he really wants is coal and vegetables. On the whole, I think it is vegetables he is after."

She said, "Are you going down to see?"

"No," I said; "I could not be of any assistance. Let him select for himself."

Then she said, "But suppose he comes up to the ground floor!"

I said: "That's all right. We shall know it the minute he opens a door on that floor. It will set off the alarm."

Just then the terrific buzzing broke out again. I said: "He has arrived. I *told* you he would. I know all about burglars and their ways. They are systematic people."

I went into the bathroom to see if I was right, and I was. I shut off the dining-room and stopped the buzzing and came back to bed. My wife said:

"What do you suppose he is after now?"

I said: "I think he has got all the vegetables he

wants and is coming up for napkin rings and odds and ends for the wife and the children. They all have families—burglars have—and they are always thoughtful of them; always take a few necessaries of life for themselves, and the rest as tokens of remembrance for the family. In taking them they do not forget us. Those very things represent tokens of his remembrance of us also. We never get them again. The memory of the attention remains embalmed in our hearts."

She said, "Are you going down to see what it is he wants now?"

"No," I said; "I am no more interested than I was before. These are experienced people. *They* know what they want. I should be no help to him. I *think* he is after ceramics and bric-à-brac and such things. If he knows the house he knows that that is all that he can find on the dining-room floor."

She said, "Suppose he comes up here!"

I said: "It is all right. He will give us notice."

She said, "What shall we do then?"

I said, "Climb out of the window."

She said, "Well, what is the use of a burglar alarm for us?"

I said, "You have seen that it has been useful up to the present moment, and I have explained to you how it will be continuously useful after he gets up here."

That was the end of it. He didn't ring any more alarms.

Presently I said: "He is disappointed, I think.

He has gone off with the vegetables and the bric-à-brac and I think he is dissatisfied."

We went to sleep, and at a quarter before eight in the morning I was out, and hurrying, for I was to take the 8:29 train for New York. I found the gas burning brightly—full head—all over the first floor. My new overcoat was gone; my old umbrella was gone; my new patent-leather shoes, which I had never worn, were gone. The large window which opened into the ombra at the rear of the house was standing wide. I passed out through it and tracked the burglar down the hill through the trees; tracked him without difficulty, because he had blazed his progress with imitation-silver napkin rings and my umbrella, and various other things which he had disapproved of; and I went back in triumph and proved to my wife that he *was* a disappointed burglar. I had suspected he would be, from the start, and from his not coming up to our floor to get human beings.

Things happened to me that day in New York. I will tell about them another time.

From Susy's Biography

Papa has a peculiar gait we like, it seems just to sute him, but most people do not; he always walks up and down the room while thinking and between each coarse at meals.

A lady distantly related to us came to visit us once in those days. She came to stay a week, but all our efforts to make her happy failed, and we could not imagine why. We did much guessing, but could not solve the mystery. Later we found out what the trouble was. It was my tramping up and down between the courses. She conceived the idea that I could not stand her society.

That word "Youth," as the reader has perhaps already guessed, was my wife's pet name for me. It was gently satirical, but also affectionate. I had certain mental and material peculiarities and customs proper to a much younger person than I was.

FROM SUSY'S BIOGRAPHY

Papa is very fond of animals particularly of cats, we had a dear little gray kitten once that he named "Lazy" (papa always wears gray to match his hair and eyes) and he would carry him around on his shoulder, it was a mighty pretty sight! the gray cat sound asleep against papa's gray coat and hair. The names that he has given our different cats, are realy remarkably funny, they are namely Stray Kit, Abner, Motley, Fraeulein, Lazy, Bufalo Bill, Soapy Sall, Cleveland, Sour Mash, and Pestilence and Famine.

At one time when the children were small we had a very black mother-cat named Satan, and Satan had a small black offspring named Sin. Pronouns were a difficulty for the children. Little Clara came in one day, her black eyes snapping with indignation, and said: "Papa, Satan ought to be punished. She is out there at the greenhouse and there she stays and stays, and his kitten is downstairs, crying."

FROM SUSY'S BIOGRAPHY

Papa uses very strong language, but I have an idea not nearly so strong as when he first maried mamma. A lady acquaintance of his is rather apt to interupt what one is saying, and papa told mamma that he thought he should say to the lady's husband "I am glad your wife wasn't present when the Deity said Let there be light."

It is as I have said before. This is a frank historian. She doesn't cover up one's deficiencies, but gives them an equal showing with one's handsomer qualities. Of course I made the remark which she has quoted—and even at this distant day I am still as much as half persuaded that if the lady mentioned had been present when the Creator said "Let there be light" she would have interrupted him, and we shouldn't ever have got it.

FROM SUSY'S BIOGRAPHY

Papa said the other day, "I am a mugwump and a mugwump is pure from the marrow out." (Papa knows that I am writing this biography of him, and he said this for it.) He doesn't like to go to church at all, why I never understood, until just now, he told us the other day that he couldn't bear to hear any one talk but himself, but that he could listen to himself talk for hours without getting tired, of course he said this in joke, but I've no dought it was founded on truth.

[New York, Friday, February 9, 1906

The "strong language" episode in the bathroom. Susy's reference to "The Prince and the Pauper."—The mother and the children help edit the books.—Reference to an-cestors.

SUSY's remark about my strong language troubles me, and I must go back to it. All through the first ten years of my married life I kept a constant and discreet watch upon my tongue while in the house, and went outside and to a distance when circumstances were too much for me and I was obliged to seek relief. I prized my wife's respect and approval above all the rest of the human race's respect and approval. I dreaded the day when she should discover that I was but a whited sepulcher partly freighted with suppressed language. I was so careful, during ten years, that I had not a doubt that my suppressions had been successful. There-fore I was quite as happy in my guilt as I could have been if I had been innocent.

But at last an accident exposed me. I went into the bathroom one morning to make my toilet, and carelessly left the door two or three inches ajar. It was the first time that I had ever failed to take the precaution of closing it tightly. I knew the necessity of being particular about this, because shaving was always a trying ordeal for me, and I could seldom carry it through to a finish without verbal helps. Now this time I was unprotected, and did not suspect it. I had no extraordinary trouble with my razor on this occasion, and was able to worry through with mere mutterings and growlings of an improper sort, but with nothing noisy or emphatic about them—no snapping and barking. Then I put on a shirt. My shirts are an invention of my own. They open in the back, and are buttoned there—when there are buttons. This time the button was missing. My temper jumped up several degrees in a moment and my remarks rose accordingly, both in loudness and vigor of expression. But I was not troubled, for the bathroom door was a solid one and I supposed it was firmly closed. I flung up the window and threw the shirt out. It fell upon the shrubbery where the people on their way to church could admire it if they wanted to; there was merely fifty feet of grass between the shirt and the passer-by. Still rumbling and thundering distantly, I put on another shirt. Again the button was absent. I augmented my language to meet the emergency and threw that shirt out of the window. I was too angry—too insane—to examine the third shirt, but put it furiously on. Again the button was absent, and that shirt followed its comrades out of the window. Then I straightened up, gathered my reserves, and let myself go like a cavalry charge. In the midst of that great assault, my eye fell upon that gaping door, and I was paralyzed.

It took me a good while to finish my toilet. I extended the time unnecessarily in trying to make up my mind as to what I would best do in the circumstances. I tried to hope that Mrs. Clemens was asleep, but I knew better. I could not escape by the window. It was narrow and suited only to shirts. At last I made up my mind to boldly loaf through the bedroom with the air of a person who had not been doing anything. I made half the journey successfully. I did not turn my eyes in her direction, because that would not be safe. It is very difficult to look as if you have not been doing anything when the facts are the other way, and my confidence in my performance oozed steadily out of me as I went along. I was aiming for the left-hand door because it was farthest from my wife. It had never been opened from the day that the house was built, but it seemed a blessed refuge for me now. The bed was this one, wherein I am lying now and dictating these histories morning after morning with so much serenity. It was this same old elaborately carved black Venetian bedstead— the most comfortable bedstead that ever was, with space enough in it for a family, and carved angels enough surmounting its twisted columns and its headboard and footboard to bring peace to the sleepers, and pleasant dreams. I had to stop in the middle of the room. I hadn't the strength to go on. I believed that I was under accusing eyes —that even the carved angels were inspecting me with an unfriendly gaze. You know how it is when you are convinced that somebody behind you is looking steadily at you. You *have* to turn your face—you can't help it. I turned mine. The bed was placed as it is now, with the foot where the head ought to be. If it had been placed as it should have been, the high headboard would have sheltered me. But the footboard was no sufficient protection and I could be seen over it. I was exposed. I was wholly without protection. I turned, because

I couldn't help it—and my memory of what I saw is still vivid, after all these years.

Against the white pillows I saw the black head —I saw that young and beautiful face; and I saw the gracious eyes with a something in them which I had never seen there before. They were snapping and flashing with indignation. I felt myself crumbling; I felt myself shrinking away to nothing under that accusing gaze. I stood silent under that desolating fire for as much as a minute, I should say—it seemed a very, very long time. Then my wife's lips parted, and from them issued—*my latest bathroom remark*. The language perfect, but the expression unpractical, apprentice-like, ignorant, inexperienced, comically inadequate, absurdly weak and unsuited to the great language. In my lifetime I had never heard anything so out of tune, so inharmonious, so incongruous, so ill suited to each other as were those mighty words set to that feeble music. I tried to keep from laughing, for I was a guilty person in deep need of charity and mercy. I tried to keep from bursting, and I succeeded—until she gravely said, "There, now you know how it sounds."

Oh, then I exploded! I said, "Oh, Livy, if it sounds like that, God forgive me, I will never do it again."

Then she had to laugh, herself. Both of us broke into convulsions, and went on laughing until we were exhausted.

The children were present at breakfast—Clara, aged six, and Susy, eight—and the mother made a guarded remark about strong language; guarded because she did not wish the children to suspect anything—a guarded remark which censured strong language. Both children broke out in one voice with this comment, "Why, mamma, papa uses it!" I was astonished. I had supposed that that secret was safe in my own breast and that its presence had never been suspected. I asked, "How did you know, you little rascals?"

"Oh," they said, "we often listen over the balusters when you are in the hall explaining things to George."

From Susy's Biography

One of papa's latest books is "The Prince and the Pauper" and it is unquestionably the best book he has ever written, some people want him to keep to his old style, some gentleman wrote him, "I enjoyed Huckleberry Finn immensely and am glad to see that you have returned to your old style." That enoyed me that enoyed me greatly, because it trobles me [Susy was troubled by that word, and uncertain; she wrote a *u* above it in the proper place, but reconsidered the matter and struck it out] to have so few people know papa, I mean realy know him, they think of Mark Twain as a humorist joking at everything; "And with a mop of reddish brown hair which sorely needs the barbars brush a roman nose, short stubby mustache, a sad care-worn face, with maney crow's feet," etc. That is the way people picture papa, I have wanted papa to write a book that would reveal something of his kind sympathetic nature, and "The Prince and the Pauper" partly does it. The book is full of lovely charming ideas, and oh the language! It is *perfect*. I think that one of the most touching scenes in it, is where the pauper is riding on horseback with his nobles in the "recognition procession" and he sees his mother oh and then what followed! How she runs to his side, when she sees him throw up his hand palm outward, and is rudely pushed off by one of the King's officers, and then how the little pauper's consceince troubles him when he remembers the shameful words that were falling from his lips, when she was turned from his side "I know you not woman" and how his grandeurs were stricken valueless, and his pride consumed to ashes. It is a wonderfully beautiful and touching little scene, and papa has described it so wonderfully. I never saw a man with so much variety of feeling as papa has; now the "Prince and the Pauper" is full of touching places, but there is most always a streak of humor in them somewhere. Now in the coronation—in the stirring coronation, just after the little king has got his crown back again papa brings that in about the Seal, where the pauper says he used the Seal "to crack nuts with." Oh it is so funny and nice! Papa very seldom writes a passage without some humor in it somewhere, and I dont think he ever will.

The children always helped their mother to edit my books in manuscript. She would sit on the porch at the farm and read aloud, with her pencil in her hand, and the children would keep an alert and suspicious eye upon her right along, for the belief was well grounded in them that whenever she came across a particularly satisfactory passage she would strike it out. Their suspicions were well founded. The passages which were so satisfactory to them always had an element of strength in them which sorely needed modification or expurgation, and was always sure to get it at their mother's hand.

For my own entertainment, and to enjoy the protests of the children, I often abused my editor's innocent confidence. I often interlarded remarks of a studied and felicitously atrocious character purposely to achieve the children's delight and see the pencil do its fatal work. I often joined my supplications to the children's for mercy, and strung the argument out and pretended to be in earnest. They were deceived, and so was their mother. It was three against one, and most unfair. But it was very delightful, and I could not resist the temptation. Now and then we gained the victory and there was much rejoicing. Then I privately struck the passage out myself. It had served its purpose. It had furnished three of us with good entertainment, and in being removed from the book by me it was only suffering the fate originally intended for it.

FROM THE BIOGRAPHY

Papa was born in Missouri. His mother is Grandma Clemens (Jane Lampton Clemens) of Kentucky. Grandpa Clemens was of the F. F. V's of Virginia.

Without doubt it was I that gave Susy that impression. I cannot imagine why, because I was never in my life much impressed by grandeurs which proceed from the accident of birth. I did not get this indifference from my mother. She was always strongly interested in the ancestry of the house. She traced her own line back to the Lambtons of Durham, England—a family which had been occupying broad lands there since Saxon times. I am not sure, but I think that those Lambtons got along without titles of nobility for eight or nine hundred years, then produced a great man, three-quarters of a century ago, and broke into the peerage. My mother knew all about the Clemenses of Virginia, and loved to aggrandize them to me, but she has long been dead. There has been no one to keep those details fresh in my memory, and they have grown dim.

[*New York, Monday, February 12, 1906*

Susy's biography continued.—Some of the tricks played in "Tom Sawyer."—The broken sugar bowl.—Skating on the Mississippi with Tom Nash, etc.

From Susy's Biography

Clara and I are sure that papa played the trick on Grandma, about the whipping, that is related in "The Adventures of Tom Sawyer": "Hand me that switch." The switch hovered in the air, the peril was desperate—"My, look behind you Aunt!" The old lady whirled around and snatched her skirts out of danger. The lad fled on the instant, scrambling up the high board fence and disappeared over it.

Susy and Clara were quite right about that. Then Susy says:

And we know papa played "Hookey" all the time. And how readily would papa pretend to be dying so as not to have to go to school!

These revelations and exposures are searching, but they are just. If I am as transparent to other people as I was to Susy, I have wasted much effort in this life.

Grandma couldn't make papa go to school, so she let him go into a printing-office to learn the trade. He did so, and gradually picked up enough education to enable him to do about as well as those who were more studious in early life.

It is noticeable that Susy does not get overheated when she is complimenting me, but maintains a proper judicial and biographical calm. It is noticeable, also, and it is to her credit as a biographer, that she distributes compliment and criticism with a fair and even hand.

My mother had a good deal of trouble with me, but I think she enjoyed it. She had none at all with my brother Henry, who was two years younger than I, and I think that the unbroken monotony of his goodness and truthfulness and obedience would have been a burden to her but for the relief and variety which I furnished in the other direction. I was a tonic. I was valuable to her. I never thought of it before, but now I see it. I never knew Henry to do a vicious thing toward me, or toward anyone else—but he frequently did righteous ones that cost me as heavily. It was his duty to report me, when I needed reporting and neglected to do it myself, and he was very faithful in discharging that duty. He is Sid in *Tom Sawyer*.

But Sid was not Henry. Henry was a very much finer and better boy than ever Sid was.

It was Henry who called my mother's attention to the fact that the thread with which she had sewed my collar together to keep me from going in swimming had changed color. My mother would not have discovered it but for that, and she was manifestly piqued when she recognized that that prominent bit of circumstantial evidence had escaped her sharp eye. That detail probably added a detail to my punishment. It is human. We generally visit our shortcomings on somebody else when there is a possible excuse for it—but no matter. I took it out of Henry. There is always compensation for such as are unjustly used. I often took it out of him—sometimes as an advance payment for something which I hadn't yet done. These were occasions when the opportunity was too strong a temptation, and I had to draw on the future. I did not need to copy this idea from my mother, and probably didn't. It is most likely that I invented it for myself. Still, she wrought upon that principle upon occasion.

If the incident of the broken sugar bowl is in *Tom Sawyer*—I don't remember whether it is or not—that is an example of it. Henry never stole sugar. He took it openly from the bowl. His mother knew he wouldn't take sugar when she wasn't looking, but she had her doubts about me. Not exactly doubts, either. She knew very well I *would*. One day when she was not present Henry took sugar from her prized and precious old-English sugar bowl, which was an heirloom in the family —and he managed to break the bowl. It was the first time I had ever had a chance to tell anything on him, and I was inexpressibly glad. I told him I was going to tell on him, but he was not disturbed. When my mother came in and saw the bowl lying on the floor in fragments, she was speechless for a minute. I allowed that silence to work; I judged it would increase the effect. I was waiting for her to ask, "Who did that?"—so that I could fetch out my news. But it was an error of calculation. When she got through with her silence she didn't ask anything about it—she merely gave me a crack on the skull with her thimble that I felt all the way down to my heels. Then I broke out with my injured innocence, expecting to make her very sorry that she had punished the wrong one. I expected her to do something remorseful and pathetic. I told her that I was not the one—it was Henry. But there was no upheaval. She said, without emotion: "It's all right. It isn't any matter. You deserve it for something you've done that I didn't know about; and if you haven't done it, why then you deserve it for something that you are going to do that I shan't hear about."

There was a stairway outside the house, which led up to the rear part of the second story. One day Henry was sent on an errand, and he took a tin bucket along. I knew he would have to ascend those stairs, so I went up and locked the door on the inside, and came down into the garden, which had been newly plowed and was rich in choice, firm clods of black mold. I gathered a generous equipment of these and ambushed him. I waited till he had climbed the stairs and was near the landing and couldn't escape. Then I bombarded him with clods, which he warded off with his tin bucket the best he could, but without much success, for I was a good marksman. The clods smashing against the weather-boarding fetched my mother out to see what was the matter, and I tried to explain that I was amusing Henry. Both of them were after me in a minute, but I knew the way over that high board fence and escaped for that time. After an hour or two, when I ventured back, there was no one around and I thought the incident was closed. But it was not so. Henry was ambushing me. With an unusually competent aim for him, he landed a stone on the side of my head which raised a bump there which felt like the Matterhorn. I carried it to my mother straightway for sympathy, but she was not strongly moved. It seemed to be her idea that incidents like this would eventually reform me if I harvested enough of them. So the matter was only educational. I had had a sterner view of it than that before.

Whenever my conduct was of such exaggerated impropriety that my mother's extemporary punishments were inadequate, she saved the matter up for Sunday and made me go to church Sunday night —which was a penalty sometimes bearable, perhaps, but as a rule it was not, and I avoided it for the sake of my constitution. She would never believe that I had been to church until she had applied her test. She made me tell her what the text was. That was a simple matter—caused me no trouble. I didn't have to go to church to get a text. I selected one for myself. This worked very well until one time when my text and the one furnished by a neighbor, who had been to church, didn't tally. After that my mother took other methods. I don't know what they were now.

In those days men and boys wore rather long cloaks in the wintertime. They were black, and were lined with very bright and showy Scotch plaids. One winter's night when I was starting to church to square a crime of some kind committed during the week, I hid my cloak near the gate and went off and played with the other boys until church was over. Then I returned home. But in the dark I put the cloak on wrong side out, entered the room, threw the cloak aside, and then stood the usual examination. I got along very well until the temperature of the church was mentioned. My mother said, "It must have been impossible to keep warm there on such a night."

I didn't see the art of that remark, and was foolish enough to explain that I wore my cloak all the time that I was in church. She asked if I kept it on from church home, too. I didn't see the bearing of that remark. I said that that was what I had done. She said: "You wore it with that red Scotch plaid outside and glaring? Didn't that attract any attention?"

Of course to continue such a dialogue would have

been tedious and unprofitable, and I let it go and took the consequences.

That was about 1849. Tom Nash was a boy of my own age—the postmaster's son. The Mississippi was frozen across, and he and I went skating one night, probably without permission. I cannot see why we should go skating in the night unless without permission, for there could be no considerable amusement to be gotten out of skating at midnight if nobody was going to object to it. About midnight, when we were more than half a mile out toward the Illinois shore, we heard some ominous rumbling and grinding and crashing going on between us and the home side of the river, and we knew what it meant—the river was breaking up. We started for home, pretty badly scared. We flew along at full speed whenever the moonlight sifting down between the clouds enabled us to tell which was ice and which was water. In the pauses we waited, started again whenever there was a good bridge of ice, paused again when we came to naked water, and waited in distress until a floating vast cake should bridge that place. It took us an hour to make the trip—a trip which we made in a misery of apprehension all the time. But at last we arrived within a very brief distance of the shore. We waited again. There was another place that needed bridging. All about us the ice was plunging and grinding along and piling itself up in mountains on the shore, and the dangers were increasing, not diminishing. We grew very impatient to get to solid ground, so we started too early

and went springing from cake to cake. Tom made
a miscalculation and fell short. He got a bitter
bath, but he was so close to shore that he only
had to swim a stroke or two—then his feet struck
hard bottom and he crawled out. I arrived a little
later, without accident. We had been in a drench-
ing perspiration and Tom's bath was a disaster for
him. He took to his bed, sick, and had a procession
of diseases. The closing one was scarlet fever,
and he came out of it stone deaf. Within a year
or two speech departed, of course. But some years
later he was taught to talk, after a fashion—one
couldn't always make out what it was he was trying to say. Of course he could not modulate his
voice, since he couldn't hear himself talk. When
he supposed he was talking low and confidentially,
you could hear him in Illinois.

Four years ago (1902) I was invited by the
University of Missouri to come out there and receive the honorary degree of LL.D. I took that
opportunity to spend a week in Hannibal—a city
now, a village in my day. It had been fifty-five
years since Tom Nash and I had had that adventure. When I was at the railway station ready
to leave Hannibal, there was a great crowd of citizens there. I saw Tom Nash approaching me across
a vacant space, and I walked toward him, for I recognized him at once. He was old and white-headed,
but the boy of fifteen was still visible in him. He
came up to me, made a trumpet of his hands at
my ear, nodded his head toward the citizens, and

said, confidentially—in a yell like a fog horn—
"Same damned fools, Sam."

FROM SUSY'S BIOGRAPHY

Papa was about twenty years old when he went on the
Mississippi as a pilot. Just before he started on his tripp
Grandma Clemens asked him to promise her on the Bible
not to touch intoxicating liquors or swear, and he said
"Yes, mother, I will," and he kept that promise seven
years when Grandma released him from it.

Under the inspiring influence of that remark,
what a garden of forgotten reforms rises upon my
sight.

[*New York, Tuesday, February 13, 1906*

*Susy's biography continued.—Cadet of Temperance.—
First meeting of Mr. Clemens and Miss Langdon.—Miss
Langdon an invalid.—Doctor Newton.*

I RECALL several of them without much difficulty. In Hannibal, when I was about fifteen, I was
for a short time a Cadet of Temperance, an organization which probably covered the whole United
States during as much as a year—possibly even
longer. It consisted in a pledge to refrain, during
membership, from the use of tobacco; I mean it
consisted partly in that pledge and partly in a red
merino sash, but the red merino sash was the main
part. The boys joined in order to be privileged
to wear it—the pledge part of the matter was of
no consequence. It was so small in importance

that, contrasted with the sash, it was, in effect, non-existent. The organization was weak and impermanent because there were not enough holidays to support it. We could turn out and march and show the red sashes on May Day with the Sunday schools, and on the Fourth of July with the Sunday schools, the independent fire company, and the militia company. But you can't keep a juvenile moral institution alive on two displays of its sash per year. As a private, I could not have held out beyond one procession, but I was Illustrious Grand Worthy Secretary and Royal Inside Sentinel, and had the privilege of inventing the passwords and of wearing a rosette on my sash. Under these conditions, I was enabled to remain steadfast until I had gathered the glory of two displays—May Day and the Fourth of July. Then I resigned straightway, and straightway left the lodge.

I had not smoked for three full months, and no words can adequately describe the smoke appetite that was consuming me. I had been a smoker from my ninth year—a private one during the first two years, but a public one after that—that is to say, after my father's death. I was smoking, and utterly happy, before I was thirty steps from the lodge door. I do not now know what the brand of the cigar was. It was probably not choice, or the previous smoker would not have thrown it away so soon. But I realized that it was the best cigar that was ever made. The previous smoker would have thought the same if he had been without a smoke for three months. I smoked that stub without shame. I could not do it now without shame, because now I am more refined than I was then. But I would smoke it, just the same. I know myself, and I know the human race, well enough to know that.

In those days the native cigar was so cheap that a person who could afford anything could afford cigars. Mr. Garth had a great tobacco factory, and he also had a small shop in the village for the retail sale of his products. He had one brand of cigars which even poverty itself was able to buy. He had had these in stock a good many years, and although they looked well enough on the outside, their insides had decayed to dust and would fly out like a puff of vapor when they were broken in two. This brand was very popular on account of its extreme cheapness. Mr. Garth had other brands which were cheap, and some that were bad, but the supremacy over them enjoyed by this brand was indicated by its name. It was called "Garth's damnedest." We used to trade old newspapers (exchanges) for that brand.

There was another shop in the village where the conditions were friendly to penniless boys. It was kept by a lonely and melancholy little hunchback, and we could always get a supply of cigars by fetching a bucket of water for him from the village pump, whether he needed water or not. One day we found him asleep in his chair—a custom of his —and we waited patiently for him to wake up, which was a custom of ours. But he slept so long, this time, that at last our patience was exhausted and we tried to wake him—but he was dead. I remember the shock of it yet.

In my early manhood, and in middle life, I used to vex myself with reforms, every now and then. And I never had occasion to regret these divergencies, for, whether the resulting deprivations were long or short, the rewarding pleasure which I got out of the vice when I returned to it always paid me for all that it cost. However, I feel sure that I have written about these experiments in the book called *Following the Equator*. By and by I will look and see. Meantime, I will drop the subject and go back to Susy's sketch of me:

From Susy's Biography

After papa had been a pilot on the Mississippi for a time, Uncle Orion Clemens, his brother, was appointed Secretary of the State of Nevada, and papa went with him out to Nevada to be his secretary. Afterwards he became interested in mining in California; then he reported for a newspaper and was on several newspapers. Then he was sent to the Sandwich Islands. After that he came back to America and his friends wanted him to lecture so he lectured. Then he went abroad on the Quaker City, and on board that ship he became equainted with Uncle Charlie (Mr. C. J. Langdon, of Elmira, New York). Papa and Uncle Charlie soon became friends, and when they returned from their journey Grandpa Langdon, Uncle Charlie's father, told Uncle Charlie to invite Mr. Clemens to dine with them at the St. Nicholas Hotel, in New York. Papa accepted the invitation and went to dine at the St. Nicholas with Grandpa and there he met mamma (Olivia Lewis Langdon) first. But they did not meet again until the next August, because papa went away to California, and there wrote "The Inocense Abroad."

I will remark here that Susy is not quite correct as to that next meeting. That first meeting was on the 27th of December, 1867, and the next one was at the house of Mrs. Berry, five days later. Miss Langdon had gone there to help Mrs. Berry receive New Year guests. I went there at ten in the morning to pay a New Year call. I had thirty-four calls on my list, and this was the first one. I continued it during thirteen hours, and put the other thirty-three off till next year.

From Susy's Biography

Mamma was the daughter of Mr. Jervis Langdon, (I don't know whether Grandpa had a middle name or not) and Mrs. Olivia Lewis Langdon, of Elmira, New York. She had one brother and one sister, Uncle Charlie (Charles J. Langdon) and Aunt Susie (Susan Langdon Crane). Mamma loved Grandpa more than any one else in the world. He was her idol and she his; I think mamma's love for grandpa must have very much resembled my love for mamma. Grandpa was a great and good man and we all think of him with respect and love. Mamma was an invalid when she was young, and had to give up study a long time.

She became an invalid at sixteen, through a partial paralysis caused by falling on the ice, and she was never strong again while her life lasted. After that fall she was not able to leave her bed during two years, nor was she able to lie in any position except upon her back. All the great physicians were brought to Elmira, one after another, during that time, but there was no helpful result. In those days both worlds were well acquainted with the name of Doctor Newton, a man who was regarded in both worlds as a quack. He moved through the land in state; in magnificence, like a portent; like a circus. Notice of his coming was spread upon the dead walls in vast colored posters, along with his formidable portrait, several weeks beforehand.

One day Andrew Langdon, a relative of the Langdon family, came to the house and said: "You have tried everybody else; now try Doctor Newton, the quack. He is downtown at the Rathbun House, practicing upon the well-to-do at war prices and upon the poor for nothing. *I saw him* wave his hands over Jake Brown's head and take his crutches away from him and send him about his business as good as new. *I saw him* do the like with some other cripples. *They* may have been 'temporaries' instituted for advertising purposes, and not genuine. But Jake is genuine. Send for Newton."

Newton came. He found the young girl upon her back. Over her was suspended a tackle from the ceiling. It had been there a long time, but unused. It was put there in the hope that by its steady motion she might be lifted to a sitting posture, at intervals, for rest. But it proved a failure. Any attempt to raise her brought nausea and exhaustion, and had to be relinquished. Newton opened the windows—long darkened—and delivered a short fervent prayer; then he put an arm behind her shoulders and said, "Now we will sit up, my child."

The family were alarmed and tried to stop him, but he was not disturbed, and raised her up. She sat several minutes, without nausea or discomfort. Then Newton said, "Now we will walk a few steps, my child." He took her out of bed and supported her while she walked several steps; then he said: "I have reached the limit of my art. She is not cured. It is not likely that she will *ever* be cured. She will never be able to walk far, but after a little daily practice she will be able to walk one or two hundred yards, and she can depend on being able to do *that* for the rest of her life."

His charge was fifteen hundred dollars, and it was easily worth a hundred thousand. For from the day that she was eighteen until she was fifty-six she was always able to walk a couple of hundred yards without stopping to rest; and more than once I saw her walk a quarter of a mile without serious fatigue.

Newton was mobbed in Dublin, in London, and in other places. He was rather frequently mobbed in Europe and in America, but never by the grateful Langdons and Clemenses. I met Newton once, in after years, and asked him what his secret was. He said he didn't know, but thought perhaps some subtle form of electricity proceeded from his body and wrought the cures.

[New York, Wednesday, February 14, 1906

About the accident which prolonged Mr. Clemens's visit at the Langdons'.

From Susy's Biography

Soon papa came back East and papa and mamma were married.

It sounds easy and swift and unobstructed, but that was not the way of it. It did not happen in that smooth and comfortable way. There was a deal of courtship. There were three or four proposals of marriage and just as many declinations. I was roving far and wide on the lecture beat, but I managed to arrive in Elmira every now and then and renew the siege. Once I dug an invitation out of Charley Langdon to come and stay a week. It was a pleasant week, but it had to come to an end. I was not able to invent any way to get the invitation enlarged. No schemes that I could contrive seemed likely to deceive. They did not even deceive *me*, and when a person cannot deceive himself the chances are against his being able to deceive other people. But at last help and good fortune came, and from a most unexpected quarter. It was one of those cases so frequent in the past centuries, so infrequent in our day—a case where the hand of Providence is in it.

I was ready to leave for New York. A democrat wagon stood outside the main gate with my trunk in it, and Barney, the coachman, in the front seat with the reins in his hand. It was eight or nine in the evening, and dark. I bade good-by to the grouped family on the front porch, and Charley and I went out and climbed into the wagon. We took our places back of the coachman on the remaining seat, which was aft toward the end of the wagon, and was only a temporary arrangement for our accommodation, and was not fastened in its place; a fact which—most fortunately for me, we were not aware of. Charley was smoking. Barney touched up the horse with the whip. He made a sudden spring forward. Charley and I went over the stern of the wagon backward. In the darkness the red bud of fire on the end of his cigar described a curve through the air which I can see yet. This was the only visible thing in all that gloomy scenery. I struck exactly on the top of my head and stood up that way for a moment, then crumbled down to the earth unconscious. It was a very good unconsciousness for a person who had not rehearsed the part. It was a cobblestone gutter, and they had been repairing it. My head struck in a dish formed by the conjunction of four cobblestones. That depression was half full of fresh new sand, and this made a competent cushion. My head did not touch any of those cobblestones. I got not a bruise. I was not even jolted. Nothing was the matter with me at all. Charley was considerably battered, but in his solicitude for me he was substantially unaware of it. The whole family swarmed out, Theodore Crane in the van with a flask of brandy. He poured enough of it between my lips to strangle me and make me bark, but it did not abate my unconsciousness. I was taking care of that myself. It was very pleasant to hear the pitying remarks trickling around over me. That was one of the happiest half dozen moments of my life. There was nothing to mar it —except that I had escaped damage. I was afraid that this would be discovered sooner or later, and would shorten my visit. I was such a dead weight that it required the combined strength of Barney and Mr. Langdon, Theodore and Charley, to lug me into the house, but it was accomplished. I was there. I recognized that this was victory. I was there. I was safe to be an incumbrance for an indefinite length of time—but for a length of time, at any rate, and a Providence was in it. They set me up in an armchair in the parlor and sent for the family physician. Poor old creature, it was wrong to rout him out, but it was business, and I was too unconscious to protest. Mrs. Crane— dear soul, she was in this house three days ago, gray and beautiful, and as sympathetic as ever— Mrs. Crane brought a bottle of some kind of liquid fire whose function was to reduce contusions. But I knew that mine would deride it and scoff at it. She poured this on my head and pawed it around with her hand, stroking and massaging, the fierce stuff dribbling down my backbone and marking its way, inch by inch, with the sensation of a forest fire. But *I* was satisfied. When she was getting worn out, her husband, Theodore, suggested that she take a rest and let Livy carry on the assuaging for a while. That was very pleasant. I should have been obliged to recover presently if it hadn't been for that. But under Livy's manipulations—if they had continued—I should probably be unconscious to this day. It was very delightful, those manipulations. So delightful, so comforting, so enchanting, that they even soothed the fire out of that fiendish successor to Perry Davis's "Pain-Killer."

Then that old family doctor arrived and went at the matter in an educated and practical way—that is to say, he started a search expedition for contusions and humps and bumps, and announced that there were none. He said that if I would go to bed and forget my adventure I would be all right in the morning—which was not so. I was *not* all right in the morning. I didn't intend to be all right, and I was far from being all right. But I said I only needed rest and I didn't need that doctor any more.

I got a good three days' extension out of that adventure, and it helped a good deal. It pushed my suit forward several steps. A subsequent visit completed the matter, and we became engaged conditionally; the condition being that the parents should consent.

In a private talk Mr. Langdon called my attention to something I had already noticed—which was that I was an almost entirely unknown person; that no one around about knew me except Charley, and he was too young to be a reliable judge of men; that I was from the other side of the continent, and that only those people out there would be able to furnish me a character, in case I had one—so he asked me for references. I furnished them, and he said we would now suspend our industries and I could go away and wait until he could write to those people and get answers.

In due course answers came. I was sent for and we had another private conference. I had referred him to six prominent men, among them two clergymen (these were all San Franciscans), and he himself had written to a bank cashier who had in earlier years been a Sunday-school superintendent in Elmira and well known to Mr. Langdon. The results were not promising. All those men were frank to a fault. They not only spoke in disapproval of me, but they were quite unnecessarily and exaggeratedly enthusiastic about it. One clergyman (Stebbins) and that ex-Sunday-school superintendent (I wish I could recall his name) added to their black testimony the conviction that I would fill a drunkard's grave. It was just one of those usual long-distance prophecies. There being no time limit, there is no telling how long you may have to wait. I have waited until now, and the fulfillment seems as far away as ever.

The reading of the letters being finished, there was a good deal of a pause, and it consisted largely of sadness and solemnity. I couldn't think of anything to say. Mr. Langdon was apparently in the same condition. Finally he raised his handsome head, fixed his clear and candid eye upon me, and said: "What kind of people are these? Haven't you a friend in the world?"

I said, "Apparently not."

Then he said: "I'll be your friend, myself. Take the girl. I know you better than they do."

Thus dramatically and happily was my fate settled. Afterward, hearing me talking lovingly, admiringly, and fervently of Joe Goodman, he asked me where Goodman lived. I told him out on the Pacific coast. He said: "Why, he seems to be a friend of yours! Is he?"

'I said, "Indeed he is; the best one I ever had."

"Why, then," he said, "what could you have been thinking of? Why didn't you refer me to him?"

I said: "Because he would have lied just as straightforwardly on the other side. The others gave me all the vices; Goodman would have given me all the virtues. You wanted unprejudiced testimony, of course. I knew you wouldn't get it from Goodman. I did believe you would get it from those others, and possibly you did. But it was certainly less complimentary than I was expecting."

The date of our engagement was February 4, 1869. The engagement ring was plain, and of heavy gold. That date was engraved inside of it. A year later I took it from her finger and prepared it to do service as a wedding ring by having the wedding date added and engraved inside of it— February 2, 1870. It was never again removed from her finger for even a moment.

In Italy, a year and eight months ago, when death had restored her vanished youth to her sweet face and she lay fair and beautiful and looking as she had looked when she was girl and bride, they were going to take that ring from her finger to keep for the children. But I prevented that sacrilege. It is buried with her.

In the beginning of our engagement the proofs of my first book, *The Innocents Abroad,* began to arrive, and she read them with me. She also edited them. She was my faithful, judicious, and painstaking editor from that day forth until within three or four months of her death—a stretch of more than a third of a century.

[*New York, Thursday, February 15, 1906*

Susy's biography continued.—Death of Mr. Langdon.—Birth of Langdon Clemens.

From Susy's Biography

Papa wrote mamma a great many beautiful love letters when he was engaged to mamma, but mamma says I am too young to see them yet; I asked papa what I should do for I didn't (know) how I could write a Biography of him without his love letters, papa said that I could write mamma's opinion of them, and that would do just as well. So I'll do as papa says, and mamma says she thinks they are the loveliest love letters that ever were written, she says that Hawthorne's love letters to Mrs. Hawthorne are far inferior to these. Mamma (and papa) were going to board first in Bufalo and grandpa said he would find them a good boarding-house. But he afterwards told mamma that he had bought a pretty house for them, and had it all beautifully furnished, he had also hired a young coachman, Patrick McAleer, and had bought a horse for them, which all would be ready waiting for them, when they should arive in Bufalo; but he wanted to keep it a secret from "Youth," as grandpa called papa. What a delightful surprise it was! Grandpa went down to Bufalo with mamma and papa. And when they drove up to the house, papa said he thought the landlord of such a boarding-house must charge a great deal to those who wanted to live there. And when the secret was told papa was delighted beyond all degree. Mamma has told me the story many times, and I asked her what papa said when grandpa told him that the delightful boarding-house was his home, mamma answered that he was rather embariesed and so delighted he didn't know what to say. About six months after papa and mamma were married grandpa died; it was a terrible blow on mamma, and papa told Aunt Sue he thought Livy would never smile again, she was so broken hearted. Mamma couldn't have had a greater sorrow than that of dear grandpa's death, or any that could equal it exept the death of papa. Mamma helped take care of grandpa during his illness and she couldn't give up hope till the end had realy come.[1]

Surely nothing is so astonishing, so unaccountable, as a woman's endurance. Mrs. Clemens and I went down to Elmira about the 1st of June to help in the nursing of Mr. Langdon. Mrs. Clemens, her sister (Susy Crane), and I did all the nursing both day and night, during two months until the end. Two months of scorching, stifling heat. How much of the nursing did I do? My main watch was from midnight till four in the morning—nearly four hours. My other watch was a midday watch, and I think it was only three hours. The two

---

[1] August 6, 1870.—S. L. C.

sisters divided the remaining seventeen hours of the twenty-four between them, and each of them tried generously and persistently to swindle the other out of a part of her watch. The "on" watch could not be depended upon to call the "off" watch—excepting when I was the "on" watch.

I went to bed early every night, and tried to get sleep enough by midnight to fit me for my work, but it was always a failure. I went on watch sleepy and remained miserably sleepy and wretched straight along through the four hours. I can still see myself sitting by that bed in the melancholy stillness of the sweltering night, mechanically waving a palm-leaf fan over the drawn white face of the patient; I can still recall my noddings, my fleeting unconsciousnesses, when the fan would come to a standstill in my hand and I would wake up with a start and a hideous shock. I can recall all the torture of my efforts to keep awake; I can recall the sense of the indolent march of time, and how the hands of the tall clock seemed not to move at all, but to stand still. Through the long vigil there was nothing to do but softly wave the fan —and the gentleness and monotony of the movement itself helped to make me sleepy. The malady was cancer of the stomach, and not curable. There were no medicines to give. It was a case of slow and steady perishing. At long intervals, the foam of champagne was administered to the patient, but no other nourishment, so far as I can remember.

A bird of a breed not of my acquaintance used to begin a sad and wearisome and monotonous pip-

ing in the shrubbery near the window a full hour
before the dawn, every morning. He had no company; he conducted this torture all alone, and added
it to my stock. He never stopped for a moment.
I have experienced few things that were more maddening than that bird's lamentings. During all that
dreary siege I began to watch for the dawn long
before it came; and I watched for it like the duplicate, I think, of the lonely castaway on an island
in the sea, who watches the horizon for ships and
rescue. When the first faint gray showed through
the window blinds I felt as no doubt that castaway
feels when the dim threads of the looked-for ship
appear against the sky.

I was well and strong, but I was a man and
afflicted with a man's infirmity—lack of endurance.
But neither of those young women was well nor
strong; still, I never found either of them sleepy
or unalert when I came on watch; yet, as I have
said, they divided seventeen hours of watching between them in every twenty-four. It is a marvelous
thing. It filled me with wonder and admiration;
also with shame, for my dull incompetency. Of
course the physicians begged those daughters to
permit the employment of professional nurses, but
they would not consent. The mere mention of such
a thing grieved them so that the matter was soon
dropped, and not again referred to.

All through her life Mrs. Clemens was physically
feeble, but her spirit was never weak. She lived
upon it all her life, and it was as effective as bodily
strength could have been. When our children were

little she nursed them through long nights of sickness, as she had nursed her father. I have seen her sit up and hold a sick child upon her knees and croon to it and sway it monotonously to and fro to comfort it, a whole night long, without complaint or respite. But I could not keep awake ten minutes at a time. My whole duty was to put wood on the fire. I did it ten or twelve times during the night, but had to be called every time, and was always asleep again before I finished the operation, or immediately afterward.

No, there is nothing comparable to the endurance of a woman. In military life she would tire out any army of men, either in camp or on the march. I still remember with admiration that woman who got into the overland stage-coach somewhere on the plains, when my brother and I crossed the continent in the summer of 1861, and who sat bolt upright and cheerful, stage after stage, and showed no wear and tear. In those days, the one event of the day, in Carson City, was the arrival of the overland coach. All the town was usually on hand to enjoy the event. The men would climb down out of the coach doubled up with cramps, hardly able to walk; their bodies worn, their spirits worn, their nerves raw, their tempers at a devilish point; but the women stepped out smiling and apparently unfatigued.

FROM SUSY'S BIOGRAPHY

After grandpapa's death mamma and papa went back to Bufalo; and three months afterward dear little Langdon was born. Mamma named him Langdon after grandpapa, he was a wonderfully beautiful little boy, but very, very delicate. He had wonderful blue eyes, but such a blue that mamma has never been able to describe them to me so that I could see them clearly in my mind's eye. His delicate health was a constant anxiety to mamma, and he was so good and sweet that that must have troubled her too, as I know it did.

[Friday, February 16, 1906

Susy's biography mentions little Langdon.—The change of residence from Buffalo to Hartford.—Mr. Clemens tells of the sale of his Buffalo paper.

FROM SUSY'S BIOGRAPHY

WHILE Langdon was a little baby he used to carry a pencil in his little hand, that was his great plaything; I believe he was very seldom seen without one in his hand. When he was in Aunt Susy's arms and would want to go to mamma he would hold out his hands to her with the backs of his hands out toward her instead of with his palmes out. (About a year and five months) after Langdon was born I was born, and my chief occupation then was to cry, so I must have added greatly to mamma's care. Soon after little Langdon was born (a year) papa and mamma moved to Hartford to live. Their house in Bufalo reminded them too much of dear grandpapa, so they moved to Hartford soon after he died.

Soon after little Langdon was born a friend of mamma's came to visit her (Emma Nigh) [1] and she was taken with the typhoid fever, while visiting mamma. At length she became so delirious, and so hard to take care of that mamma

---
[1] Nye.

had to send to some of her friends in Elmira to come and help take care of her. Aunt Clara came, (Miss Clara L. Spaulding). She is no relation of ours but we call her Aunt Clara because she is such a great friend of mamma's. She came and helped mamma take care of Emma Nigh, but in spite of all the good care that she received, she grew worse and died.

Susy is right. Our year and a half in Buffalo had so saturated us with horrors and distress that we became restless and wanted to change, either to a place with pleasanter associations or with none at all. In accordance with the hard terms of that fearful law—the year of mourning—which deprives the mourner of the society and comradeship of his race when he most needs it, we shut ourselves up in the house and became recluses, visiting no one and receiving visits from no one. There was one exception—a single exception. David Gray—poet, and editor of the principal newspaper—was our intimate friend, through his intimacy and mine with John Hay. David had a young wife and a young baby. The Grays and the Clemenses visited back and forth frequently, and this was all the solace the Clemenses had in their captivity.

When we could endure imprisonment no longer, Mrs. Clemens sold the house and I sold my one-third interest in the newspaper, and we went to Hartford to live. I have some little business sense now, acquired through hard experience and at great expense; but I had none in those days. I had bought Mr. Kinney's share of that newspaper (I think the name was Kinney) at his price—which was twenty-five thousand dollars. Later I found that all that I had bought of real value was the Associated Press privilege. I think we did not make a very large use of that privilege. It runs in my mind that about every night the Associated Press would offer us five thousand words at the usual rate, and that we compromised on five hundred. Still, that privilege was worth fifteen thousand dollars, and was easily salable at that price. I sold my whole share in the paper—including that solitary asset—for fifteen thousand dollars. Kinney (if that was his name) was so delighted at his smartness in selling a property to me for twenty-five thousand that was not worth three-fourths of the money, that he was not able to keep his joy to himself, but talked it around pretty freely and made himself very happy over it. I could have explained to him that what he mistook for his smartness was a poor and driveling kind of thing. If there had been a triumph, if there had been a mental exhibition of a majestic sort, it was not his smartness; it was my stupidity; the credit was all due to me. He was a brisk and ambitious and self-appreciative young fellow, and he left straightway for New York and Wall Street, with his head full of sordid and splendid dreams—dreams of the "get rich quick" order; dreams to be realized through the dreamer's smartness and the other party's stupidity. Kinney had no place in Wall Street. He quickly lost the money he had gouged out of it.

[Tuesday, February 20, 1906

About Rear-Admiral Wilkes.—And meeting Mr. Anson Burlingame in Honolulu.

MRS. MARY WILKES DEAD.

————

FLORENCE, ITALY, Feb. 19.—Mrs. Mary Wilkes, widow of Rear-Admiral Wilkes, U. S. N., is dead, aged eighty-five.

IT is death notices like this that enable me to realize in some sort how long I have lived. They drive away the haze from my life's road and give me glimpses of the beginning of it—glimpses of things which seem incredibly remote.

When I was a boy of ten, in that village on the Mississippi River which at that time was so incalculably far from any place and is now so near to all places, the name of Wilkes, the explorer, was in everybody's mouth, just as Roosevelt's is to-day. What a noise it made, and how wonderful the glory! How far away and how silent it is now! And the glory has faded to tradition. Wilkes had discovered a new world and was another Columbus. That world afterward turned mainly to ice and snow. But it was not *all* ice and snow— and in our late day we are rediscovering it, and the world's interest in it has revived. Wilkes was a marvel in another way, for he had gone wandering about the globe in his ships and had looked with his own eyes upon its furthest corners, its dream-

lands—names and places which exisited rather as
shadows and rumors than as realities. But everybody visits those places now, in outings and summer
excursions, and no fame is to be gotten out of it.

One of the last visits I made in Florence—this
was two years ago—was to Mrs. Wilkes. She had
sent and asked me to come, and it seemed a chapter
out of the romantic and the impossible that I should
be looking upon the gentle face of the sharer in that
long-forgotten glory. We talked of the common
things of the day, but my mind was not present.
It was wandering among the snowstorms and the
ice floes and the fogs and mysteries of the antarctic
with this patriarchal lady's young husband. Nothing remarkable was said; nothing remarkable happened. Yet a visit has seldom impressed me so
much as did this one.

.   .   .   .

Here is a pleasant and welcome letter, which
plunges me back into the antiquities again:

KNOLLWOOD,
WESTFIELD, NEW JERSEY.
February 17, 1906.

MY DEAR MR. CLEMENS:

I should like to tell you how much I thank you for an
article which you wrote once, long ago, (1870 or '71)
about my grandfather, Anson Burlingame.

In looking over the interesting family papers and letters,
which have come into my possession this winter, nothing
has impressed me more deeply than your tribute. I have
read it again and again. I found it pasted into a scrap-

book and apparently it was cut from a newspaper. It is signed with your name.

It seems to bring before one more clearly, than anything I have been told or read, my grandfather's personality and achievements. . . .

Family traditions grow less and less in the telling. Young children are so impatient of anecdotes, and when they grow old enough to understand their value, frequent repetitions, as well as newer interests and associations, seem to have dulled, not the memory, but the spontaneity and joy of telling about the old days—so unless there is something written and preserved, how much is lost to children of the good deeds of their fathers.

Perhaps it will give you a little pleasure to know that after all these years, the words you wrote about "a good man, and a very, very great man" have fallen into the heart of one to whom his fame is very near and precious.

You say "Mr. Burlingame's short history—for he was only forty-seven—reads like a fairy-tale. Its successes, its surprises, its happy situations occur all along, and each new episode is always an improvement upon the one which went before it." That seems to have been very true and it is interesting to hear, although it has the sad ring of Destiny. But how shall I ever thank you for words like these? "He was a true man, a just man, a generous man, in all his ways and by all his instincts a noble man—a man of great brain, a broad, and deep and mighty thinker. He was a great man, a very, very great man. He was imperially endowed by nature, he was faithfully befriended by circumstances, and he wrought gallantly always in whatever station he found himself." How indeed shall I thank you for these words or tell you how deeply they have touched me, and how truly I shall endeavor to teach them to my children.

That your fame may be as sacred as this, is my earnest, grateful wish, not wholly the inevitable, imperishable fame that is laid down for you, but the sweet and precious fame, to your family and friends forever, of the fair attributes you ascribe to my grandfather, which could never have been discerned by one who was not like him in spirit.

With the hope some time of knowing you,

Yours sincerely,

JEAN BURLINGAME BEATTY.

(Mrs. Robert Chetwood Beatty.)

This carries me back forty years, to my first meeting with that wise and just and humane and charming man and great citizen and diplomat, Anson Burlingame. It was in Honolulu. He had arrived in his ship, on his way out on his great mission to China, and I had the honor and profit of his society daily and constantly during many days. He was a handsome and stately and courtly and graceful creature, in the prime of his perfect manhood, and it was a contenting pleasure to look at him. His outlook upon the world and its affairs was as wide as the horizon, and his speech was of a dignity and eloquence proper to it. It dealt in no commonplaces, for he had no commonplace thoughts. He was a kindly man, and most lovable. He was not a petty politician, but a great and magnanimous statesman. He did not serve his country alone, but China as well. He held the balances even. He wrought for justice and humanity. All his ways were clean; all his motives were high and fine.

He had beautiful eyes; deep eyes; speaking eyes;

eyes that were dreamy, in repose; eyes that could beam and persuade like a lover's; eyes that could blast when his temper was up, I judge. Preston S. Brooks, the congressional bully, found this out in his day, no doubt. Brooks had bullied everybody, insulted everybody, challenged everybody, cowed everybody, and was cock of the walk in Washington. But when he challenged the new young Congressman from the West he found a prompt and ardent man at last. Burlingame chose rifles at short range, and Brooks apologized and retired from his bullyship with the laughter of the nation ringing in his ears.

When Mr. Burlingame arrived at Honolulu I had been confined to my room a couple of weeks— by night to my bed, by day to a splint-bottom chair, deep-sunk like a basket. There was another chair, but I preferred this one, because my malady was saddle boils.

When the boatload of skeletons arrived after forty-three days in an open boat on ten days' provisions—survivors of the clipper *Hornet,* which had perished by fire several thousand miles away —it was necessary for me to interview them for the Sacramento *Union,* a journal which I had been commissioned to represent in the Sandwich Islands for a matter of five or six months. Mr. Burlingame put me on a cot and had me carried to the hospital, and during several hours he questioned the skeletons and I set down the answers in my note-book. It took me all night to write out my narrative of the *Hornet* disaster, and—but I will go no further with the subject now. I have already told the rest in some book of mine.

Mr. Burlingame gave me some advice, one day, which I have never forgotten, and which I have lived by for forty years. He said, in substance:

"Avoid inferiors. Seek your comradeships among your superiors in intellect and character; always *climb*."

Mr. Burlingame's son—now editor of *Scribner's Magazine* these many years and soon to reach the foothills that lie near the frontiers of age—was with him there in Honolulu; a handsome boy of nineteen, and overflowing with animation, activity, energy, and the pure joy of being alive. He attended balls and fandangos and *hula hulas* every night—anybody's, brown, half white, white—and he could dance all night and be as fresh as ever the next afternoon. One day he delighted me with a joke which I afterward used in a lecture in San Francisco, and from there it traveled all around in the newspapers. He said, "If a man compel thee to go with him a mile, go *with* him Twain."

When it was new, it seemed exceedingly happy and bright, but it has been emptied upon me upward of several million times since—never by a witty and engaging lad like Burlingame, but always by chuckle-heads of base degree, who did it with offensive eagerness and with the conviction that they were the first in the field. And so it has finally lost its sparkle and bravery, and is become to me a seedy and repulsive tramp whose proper place is in the hospital for the decayed, the friendless, and the forlorn.

[New York, Wednesday, February 21, 1906

Mr. Langdon just escapes being a railway magnate.

BUT I am wandering far from Susy's Biography. I remember that I was about to explain a remark which I had been making about Susy's grandfather Langdon having just barely escaped once the good luck—or the bad luck—of becoming a great railway magnate. The incident has interest for me for more than one reason. Its details came to my knowledge in a chance way in a conversation which I had with my father-in-law when I was arranging a contract with my publisher for *Roughing It*, my second book. I told him the publisher had arrived from Hartford, and would come to the house in the afternoon to discuss the contract and complete it with the signatures. I said I was going to require half the profits over the essential costs of manufacture. He asked if that arrangement would be perfectly fair to both parties, and said it was neither good business nor good morals to make contracts which gave to one side the advantage. I said that the terms which I was proposing were fair to both parties. Then Mr. Langdon after a musing silence said, with something like a reminiscent sorrow in his tone, "When you and the publisher shall have gotten the contract framed to suit you both and no doubts about it are left in your minds, *sign* it—sign it to-day, don't wait till to-morrow."

It transpired that he had acquired this wisdom, which he was giving me gratis, at considerable expense. He had acquired it twenty years earlier, or thereabouts, at the Astor House in New York, where he and a dozen other rising and able business men were gathered together to secure a certain railroad which promised to be a good property by and by, if properly developed and wisely managed. This was the Lehigh Valley Railroad. There were a number of conflicting interests to be reconciled before the deal could be consummated. The men labored over these things the whole afternoon, in a private parlor of that hotel. They dined, then reassembled and continued their labors until after two in the morning. Then they shook hands all around in great joy and enthusiasm, for they had achieved success and had drawn a contract in the rough which was ready for the signatures. The signing was about to begin; one of the men sat at the table with his pen poised over the fateful document, when somebody said: "Oh, we are tired to death. There is no use in continuing this torture any longer. Everything's satisfactory. Let's sign in the morning." All assented, and that pen was laid aside.

Mr. Langdon said: "We got five or ten minutes' additional sleep that night by that postponement, but it cost us several millions apiece, and it was a fancy price to pay. If we had paid out of our existing means, and the price had been a single million apiece, we should have had to sit up, for there wasn't a man among us who could have met the obligation completely. The contract was never signed. We had traded a Bank of England for ten minutes' extra sleep—a very small sleep, an apparently unimportant sleep, but it has kept us tired ever since. When you've got your contract right, this afternoon, sign it."

I followed that advice. It was thirty-five years ago, but it has kept me tired ever since.

[*New York, Thursday, February 22, 1906*

Susy's remarks about her grandfather Langdon.—Mr. Clemens tells about Mr. Atwater, Mr. David Gray, and about meeting David Gray, Jr., at a dinner recently.

I HAVE wandered far from Susy's chat about her grandfather, but that is no matter. In this autobiography it is my purpose to wander whenever I please and come back when I get ready. I have now come back, and we will set down what Susy has to say about her grandfather.

FROM SUSY'S BIOGRAPHY

I mentioned that mamma and papa couldn't stay in their house in Bufalo because it reminded them so much of grandpapa. Mamma received a letter from Aunt Susy in which Aunt Susy says a good deal about grandpapa, and the letter showed so clearly how much every one that knew grandpapa loved and respected him, that mamma let me take it to copy what is in it about grandpapa, and mamma thought it would fit in nicely here.

QUARRY FARM,
April 16, '85

Livy dear, are you not reminded by to-day's report of General Grant of father? You remember how as Judge Smith and others whom father had chosen as executors were going out of the room, he said "Gentlemen I shall live to bury you all"—smiled, and was cheerful. At that time he had far less strength than General Grant seems to have, but that same wonderful courage to battle with the foe. All along there has been much to remind me of father—of his quiet patience—in General Grant. There certainly is a marked likeness in the souls of the two men. Watching, day by day, the reports from the Nation's sick room brings to mind so vividly the days of that summer of 1870. And yet they seem so far away. I seemed as a child, compared with now, both in years and experience. The best and the hardest of life have been since then to me, and I know this is so in your life. All before seems dreamy. I sepose this was because our lives had to be all readjusted to go on without that great power in them. Father was quietly such a power in so many lives beside ours, Livy dear—not in kind or degree the same to any one but oh, a power!

The evening of the last company, I was so struck with the fact that Mr. Atwater stood quietly before father's portrait a long time and turning to me said, "We shall never see his like again," with a tremble and a choking in his voice—this after fifteen years, and from a business friend. And some stranger, a week ago, spoke of his habit of giving, as so remarkable, he having heard of father's generosity. . . .

I remember Mr. Atwater very well. There was nothing citified about him or his ways. He was in

middle age, and had lived in the country all his
life. He had the farmer look, the farmer gait; he
wore the farmer clothes, and also the farmer goatee,
a decoration which had been universal when I was
a boy, but was now become extinct in some of the
Western towns and in all of the Eastern towns and
cities. He was transparently a good and sincere
and honest man. He was a humble helper of Mr.
Langdon, and had been in his employ many years.
His rôle was general utility. If Mr. Langdon's
sawmills needed unscientific but plain common-sense
inspection, Atwater was sent on that service. If Mr.
Langdon's timber rafts got into trouble on account
of a falling river or a rising one, Atwater was sent
to look after the matter. Atwater went on modest
errands to Mr. Langdon's coal mines; also to examine and report upon Mr. Langdon's interests in
the budding coal-oil fields of Pennsylvania. Mr.
Atwater was *always* busy, always moving, always
useful in humble ways, always religious, and always
ungrammatical, except when he had just finished
talking and had used up what he had in stock of
that kind of grammar. He was effective—that is,
he was effective if there was plenty of time. But
he was constitutionally slow, and as he had to discuss all his matters with whomsoever came along, it
sometimes happened that the occasion for his services had gone by before he got them in. Mr. Langdon never would discharge Atwater, though young
Charley Langdon suggested that course now and
then. Young Charley could not *abide* Atwater, because of his provoking dilatoriness and of his com-

fortable contentment in it. But I loved Atwater. Atwater was a treasure to me. When he would arrive from one of his inspection journeys and sit at the table, at noon, and tell the family all about the campaign in delicious detail, leaving out not a single inane, inconsequential, and colorless incident of it, I heard it gratefully; I enjoyed Mr. Langdon's placid patience with it; the family's despondency and despair; and more than all these pleasures together, the vindictiveness in young Charley's eyes and the volcanic disturbances going on inside of him which I could not see, but which I knew were there.

I am dwelling upon Atwater just for love. I have nothing important to say about Atwater—in fact, only one thing to say about him at all. And even that one thing I could leave unmentioned if I wanted to—but I don't want to. It has been a pleasant memory to me for a whole generation. It lets in a fleeting ray of light upon Livy's gentle and calm and equable spirit. Although she could feel strongly and utter her feelings strongly, none but a person familiar with her and with all her moods would ever be able to tell by her language that that language was violent. Young Charley had many and many a time tried to lodge a seed of unkindness against Atwater in Livy's heart, but she was as steadfast in her fidelity as was her father, and Charley's efforts always failed. Many and many a time he brought to her a charge against Atwater which he believed would bring the longed-for bitter word, and at last he scored a success—for "all things come to him who waits."

I was away at the time, but Charley could not wait for me to get back. He was too glad, too eager. He sat down at once and wrote to me while his triumph was fresh and his happiness hot and contenting. He told me how he had laid the whole exasperating matter before Livy and then had asked her, *"Now* what do you say?" And she said, *"Damn* Atwater."

Charley knew that there was no need to explain this to me. He knew I would perfectly understand. He knew that I would know that he was not quoting, but was *translating*. He knew that I would know that his translation was exact, was perfect, that it conveyed the precise length, breadth, weight, meaning, and force of the words which Livy had really used. He knew that I would know that the phrase which she really uttered was, "I disapprove of Atwater."

He was quite right. In her mouth that word "disapprove" was as blighting and withering and devastating as another person's damn.

One or two days ago I was talking about our sorrowful and pathetic brief sojourn in Buffalo, where we became hermits, and could have no human comradeship except that of young David Gray and his young wife and their baby boy. It seems an *age* ago. Last night I was at a large dinner party at Norman Hapgood's palace uptown, and a very long and very slender gentleman was introduced to me—a gentleman with a fine, alert, and intellectual face, with a becoming gold *pince-nez* on his nose and clothed in an evening costume which was perfect from the broad spread of immaculate bosom to the rosetted slippers on his feet. His gait, his bows, and his intonations were those of an English gentleman, and I took him for an earl. I said I had not understood his name, and asked him what it was. He said "David Gray." The effect was startling. His very father stood before me, as I had known him in Buffalo thirty-six years ago. This apparition called up pleasant times in the beer mills of Buffalo with David Gray and John Hay when this David Gray was in his cradle, a beloved and troublesome possession. And this contact kept me in Buffalo during the next hour, and made it difficult for me to keep up my end of the conversation at my extremity of the dinner table. The text of my reveries was: "What was he born for? What was his father born for? What was I born for? What is anybody born for?"

His father was a poet, but was doomed to grind out his living in a most uncongenial occupation—the editing of a daily political newspaper. He was a singing bird in a menagerie of monkeys, macaws, and hyenas. His life was wasted. He had come from Scotland when he was five years old; he had come saturated to the bones with Presbyterianism of the bluest, the most uncompromising and most unlovely shade. At thirty-three, when I was comrading with him, his Presbyterianism was all gone and he had become a frank rationalist and pronounced unbeliever. After a few years news came to me in Hartford that he had had a sunstroke.

By and by the news came that his brain was affected, as a result. After another considerable interval I heard, through Ned House, who had been visiting him, that he was no longer able to competently write either politics or poetry, and was living quite privately and teaching a daily Bible class of young people, and was interested in nothing else. His unbelief had passed away; his early Presbyterianism had taken its place.

This was true. Some time after this I telegraphed and asked him to meet me at the railway station. He came, and I had a few minutes' talk with him—this for the last time. The same sweet spirit of the earlier days looked out of his deep eyes. He was the same David I had known before—great, and fine, and blemishless in character, a creature to adore.

Not long afterward he was crushed and burned up in a railway disaster, at night—and I probably thought then, as I was thinking now, through the gay laughter-and-chatter fog of that dinner table: "What was he born for? What was the use of it?" These tiresome and monotonous repetitions of the human life—where is their value? Susy asked that question when she was a little child. There was nobody then who could answer it; there is nobody yet.

When Mr. Langdon died, on the 6th of August, 1870, I found myself suddenly introduced into what was to me a quite new rôle—that of business man, temporarily.

[Friday, February 23, 1906

Mr. Clemens tells how he became a business man.

DURING the previous year or year and a half, Mr. Langdon had suffered some severe losses through a relative, an annex of the family by marriage, who had paved Memphis, Tennessee, with the wooden pavement so popular in that day. He had done this as Mr. Langdon's agent. Well managed, the contract would have yielded a sufficient profit, but through mismanagement it had merely yielded a large loss. With Mr. Langdon alive, this loss was not a matter of consequence and could not cripple the business. But with Mr. Langdon's brain and hand and credit and high character removed, it was another matter. He was a dealer in anthracite coal. He sold this coal over a stretch of country extending as far as Chicago, and he had important branches of his business in a number of cities. His agents were usually considerably in debt to him, and he was correspondingly in debt to the owners of the mines. His death left three young men in charge of the business—young Charley Langdon, Theodore Crane, and Mr. Slee. He had recently made them partners in the business, by gift. But they were unknown. The business world knew J. Langdon, a name that was a power, but these three young men were ciphers without a unit. Slee turned out afterward to be a very able man and a most capable and persuasive negotiator, but at the time that I speak of his qualities were quite unknown. Mr. Langdon had trained him, and he was well equipped for his headship of the little firm. Theodore Crane was competent in his line—that of head clerk and superintendent of the subordinate clerks. No better man could have been found for that place; but his capacities were limited to that position. He was good and upright and indestructibly honest and honorable, but he had neither desire nor ambition to be anything above chief clerk. He was much too timid for larger work or larger responsibilities. Young Charley was twenty-one, and not any older than his age—that is to say, he was a boy.

A careful statement of Mr. Langdon's affairs showed that the assets were worth eight hundred thousand dollars, and that against them was merely the ordinary obligations of the business. Bills aggregating perhaps three hundred thousand dollars—possibly four hundred thousand—would have to be paid; half in about a month, the other half in about two months. The collections to meet these obligations would come in further along. With Mr. Langdon alive, these debts could be no embarrassment. He could go to the bank in the town, or in New York, and borrow the money without any trouble, but these boys couldn't do that. They could get one hundred and fifty thousand dollars cash, at once, but that was all. It was Mr. Langdon's life insurance. It was paid promptly, but it could not go far—that is it could not go far enough. It did not fall short much—in fact, only fifty thousand dollars, but where to get the fifty thousand dollars was a puzzle. They wrote to Mr. Henry W. Sage, of Ithaca, an old and warm friend and former business partner of Mr. Langdon, and begged him to come to Elmira and give them advice and help. He replied that he would come. Then, to my consternation, the young firm appointed *me* to do the negotiating with him. It was like asking me to calculate an eclipse. I had no idea of how to begin nor what to say. But they brought the big balance sheet to the house and sat down with me in the library and explained, and explained, and explained, until at last I did get a fairly clear idea of what I must say to Mr. Sage.

When Mr. Sage came he and I went to the library to examine that balance sheet, and the firm waited and trembled in some other part of the house. When I got through explaining the situation to Mr. Sage I got struck by lightning again—that is to say, he furnished me a fresh astonishment. He was a man with a straight mouth and a wonderfully firm jaw. He was the kind of man who puts his whole mind on a thing and keeps that kind of a mouth shut and locked all the way through, while the other man states the case. On this occasion I should have been grateful for some slight indication from him, during my long explanation, which might indicate that I was making at least some kind of an impression upon him, favorable or unfavorable. But he kept my heart on the strain all the way through, and I never could catch any hint of what was passing through his mind. But at the finish he spoke out with that robust decision which was a part of his character and said:

"Mr. Clemens, you've got as clear a business head on your shoulders as I have come in contact with for years. What are you an author for? You ought to be a business man."

I knew better, but it was not diplomatic to say so, and I didn't. Then he said:

"All you boys need is my note for fifty thousand dollars, at three months, handed in at the bank, and with that support you will not need the money. If it shall be necessary to extend the note, tell Mr. Arnot it will be extended. The business is all right. Go ahead with it and have no fears. It is my opinion that this note will come back to me without your having extracted a dollar from it, at the end of the three months."

It happened just as he had said. Old Mr. Arnot, the Scotch banker, a very rich and very careful man and life-long friend of Mr. Langdon, watched the young firm and advised it out of his rich store of commercial wisdom, and at the end of the three months the firm was an established and growing concern, and the note was sent back to Mr. Sage without our having needed to extract anything from it. It was a small piece of paper, insignificant in its dimensions, insignificant in the sum which it represented, but formidable was its influence, and formidable was its power, because of the man who stood behind it.

The Sages and the Twichells were very intimate. One or two years later, Mr. Sage came to Hartford on a visit to Joe, and as soon as he had gone away Twichell rushed over to our house, eager to tell me something; something which had astonished him, and which he believed would astonish me. He said:

"Why, Mark, you know, Mr. Sage, one of the best business men in America, says that you have quite extraordinary business talents."

Again I didn't deny it. I would not have had that superstition dissipated for anything. It supplied a long-felt want. We are always more anxious to be distinguished for a talent which we do not possess than to be praised for the fifteen which we do possess.

[*Monday, February 26, 1906*

Susy comes to New York with her mother and father.— Aunt Clara visits them at the Everett House.—Aunt Clara's ill luck with horses.—The omnibus incident in Germany.— Aunt Clara now ill at Hoffman House, result of horse-back accident thirty years ago.—Mr. Clemens takes Susy to see General Grant.—Mr. Clemens's account of his talk with General Grant.—Mr. Clemens gives his first reading in New York—also tells about one in Boston.—Memorial to Mr. Longfellow, and one in Washington.

FROM SUSY'S BIOGRAPHY

PAPA made arrangements to read at Vassar College the 1st of May, and I went with him. We went by way of New York City. Mamma went with us to New York and stayed two days to do some shopping. We started Tuesday, at ½ past two o'clock in the afternoon, and reached New York about ¼ past six. Papa went right

up to General Grants from the station and mamma and I
went to the Everett House. Aunt Clara came to supper
with us up in our room.

This is the same Aunt Clara who has already
been mentioned several times. She had been my
wife's playmate and schoolmate from the earliest
times, and she was about my wife's age, or two or
three years younger—mentally, morally, spiritually,
and in all ways, a superior and lovable personality.

Persons who think there is no such thing as luck—
good or bad—are entitled to their opinion. Clara
Spaulding had the average human being's luck in
all things save one; she was subject to ill luck with
horses. It pursued her like a disease. Every now
and then a horse threw her. Every now and then
carriage horses ran away with her. At intervals
omnibus horses ran away with her. Usually there
was but one person hurt, and she was selected for
that function. In Germany once our little family
started from the inn (in Worms, I think it was)
to go to the station. The vehicle of transportation
was a great long omnibus drawn by a battery of
four great horses. Every seat in the bus was occupied, and the aggregate of us amounted to a good
two dozen persons, possibly one or two more. I
said playfully to Clara Spaulding: "I think you
ought to walk to the station. It isn't right for you
to imperil the lives of such a crowd of inoffensive
people as this." When we had gone a quarter of
a mile and were briskly approaching a stone bridge
which had no protecting railings, the battery broke

and began to run. Outside we saw the long reins dragging along the ground and a young peasant racing after them and occasionally making a grab for them. Presently he achieved success, and none too soon, for the bus had already entered upon the bridge when he stopped the team. The two dozen lives were saved. Nobody offered to take up a collection, but I suggested to our friend and excursion comrade—American consul at a German city —that we get out and tip that young peasant. The consul said, with an enthusiasm native to his character: "Stay right where you are. Leave me to attend to that. His fine deed shall not go unrewarded." He jumped out and arranged the matter, and we continued our journey. Afterward I asked him what he gave the peasant, so that I could pay my half. He told me, and I paid it. It is twenty-eight years ago, yet from that day to this, although I have passed through some stringent seasons, I have never seriously felt or regretted that outlay. It was twenty-three cents.

Clara Spaulding, now Mrs. John B. Stanchfield, is in New York at present, and I went to the Hoffman House yesterday to see her, but it was as I was expecting: she is too ill to see any but physicians and nurses. This illness has its source in a horseback accident which fell to her share thirty years ago and which resulted in broken bones of the foot and ankle. The broken bones were badly set and she always walked with a limp afterward. Some months ago the foot and ankle began to pain her unendurably and it was decided that she must come

to New York and have the bones rebroken and
reset. I saw her in the private hospital about three
weeks after that operation, and the verdict was that
the operation was successful. This turned out to be
a mistake. She came to New York a month or six
weeks ago, and another rebreaking and resetting
was accomplished. A week ago, when I called, she
was able to hobble about the room by help of
crutches, and she was very happy in the conviction
that now she was going to have no more trouble.
But it appears that this dreadful surgery-work must
be done over once more. But she is not fitted for it.
The pain is reducing her strength, and I was told
that it has been for the past three days necessary
to exclude her from contact with all but physicians
and nurses.

From Susy's Biography

We and Aunt Clara were going to the theatre right
after supper, and we expected papa to take us there and
to come home as early as he could. But we got through
dinner and he didn't come, and didn't come, and mamma
got more perplexed and worried, but at last we thought
we would have to go without him. So we put on our
things and started down stairs but before we'd goten half
down we met papa coming up with a great bunch of roses
in his hand. He explained that the reason he was so late
was that his watch stopped and he didn't notice and kept
thinking it an hour earlier than it really was. The roses
he carried were some Col. Fred Grant sent to mamma. We
went to the theatre and enjoyed "Adonis" [word illegible]
acted very much. We reached home about ½ past eleven
o'clock and went right to bed. Wednesday morning we

got up rather late and had breakfast about ½ past nine
o'clock. After breakfast mamma went on shopping and
papa and I went to see papa's agent about some business
matters. After papa had gotten through talking to Cousin
Charlie [Webster], papa's agent, we went to get a friend
of papa's, Major Pond, to go and see a Dog Show with
us. Then we went to see the dogs with Major Pond
and we had a delightful time seeing so many dogs together; when we got through seeing the dogs papa thought
he would go and see General Grant and I went with him—
this was April 29, 1885. Papa went up into General
Grant's room and he took me with him, I felt greatly
honored and delighted when papa took me into General
Grant's room and let me see the General and Col. Grant,
for General Grant is a man I shall be glad all my life
that I have seen. Papa and General Grant had a long
talk together and papa has written an account of his talk
and visit with General Grant for me to put into this
biography.

Susy has inserted in this place that account of
mine—as follows:

[*April 29, 1885*

I called on General Grant and took Susy with me.
The General was looking and feeling far better than he
had looked or felt for some months. He had ventured to
work again on his book that morning—the first time he
had done any work for perhaps a month. This morning's
work was his first attempt at dictating, and it was a thor-
ough success, to his great delight. He had always said
that it would be impossible for him to dictate anything,
but I had said that he was noted for clearness of statement, and as a narrative was simply a statement of con-

secutive facts, he was consequently peculiarly qualified and equipped for dictation. This turned out to be true. For he had dictated two hours that morning to a shorthand writer, had never hesitated for words, had not repeated himself, and the manuscript when finished needed no revision. The two hours' work was an account of Appomattox—and this was such an extremely important feature that his book would necessarily have been severely lame without it. Therefore I had taken a shorthand writer there before, to see if I could not get him to write at least a few lines about Appomattox.[1] But he was at that time not well enough to undertake it. I was aware that of all the hundred versions of Appomattox, not one was really correct. Therefore I was extremely anxious that he should leave behind him the truth. His throat was not distressing him, and his voice was much better and stronger than usual. He was so delighted to have gotten Appomattox accomplished once more in his life—to have gotten the matter off his mind—that he was as talkative as his old self. He received Susy very pleasantly, and then fell to talking about certain matters which he hoped to be able to dictate next day; and he said in substance that, among other things, he wanted to settle once for all a question that had been bandied about from mouth to mouth and from newspaper to newspaper. That question was: "With whom originated the idea of the march to the sea? Was it Grant's, or was it Sherman's idea?" Whether I or some one else (being anxious to get the important fact settled) asked him with whom the idea originated, I don't remember. But I remember his answer. I shall always remember his answer. General Grant said:

"Neither of us originated the idea of Sherman's march to the sea. The enemy did it."

---

[1] I was his publisher. I was putting his *Personal Memoirs* to press at the time.—S. L. C.

He went on to say that the enemy, however, necessarily originated a great many of the plans that the general on the opposite side gets the credit for; at the same time that the enemy is doing that, he is laying open other moves which the opposing general sees and takes advantage of. In this case, Sherman had a plan all thought out, of course. He meant to destroy the two remaining railroads in that part of the country, and that would have finished up that region. But General Hood did not play the military part that he was expected to play. On the contrary, General Hood made a dive at Chattanooga. This left the march to the sea open to Sherman, and so after sending part of his army to defend and hold what he had acquired in the Chattanooga region, he was perfectly free to proceed, with the rest of it, through Georgia. He saw the opportunity, and he would not have been fit for his place if he had not seized it.

"He wrote me" (the General is speaking) "what his plan was, and I sent him word to go ahead. My staff were opposed to the movement." (I think the General said they tried to persuade him to stop Sherman. The chief of his staff, the General said, even went so far as to go to Washington without the General's knowledge and get the ear of the authorities, and he succeeded in arousing their fears to such an extent that they telegraphed General Grant to stop Sherman.)

Then General Grant said, "Out of deference to the government, I telegraphed Sherman and stopped him twenty-four hours; and then, considering that that was deference enough to the government, I telegraphed him to go ahead again."

I have not tried to give the General's language, but only the general idea of what he said. The thing that mainly struck me was his terse remark that the enemy originated the idea of the march to the sea. It struck me because it was so suggestive of the General's epigrammatic fashion—saying a great deal in a single crisp sentence. (This is **my** account, and signed Mark Twain.)

After papa and General Grant had had their **talk, we** went back to the hotel where mamma was, and papa told mamma all about his interview with General Grant. Mamma and I had a nice quiet afternoon together.

That pair of devoted comrades were *always* shutting themselves up together when there was opportunity to have what Susy called "a cozy time." From Susy's nursery days to the end of her life, she and her mother were close friends, intimate friends, passionate adorers of each other. Susy's was a beautiful mind, and it made her an interesting comrade. And with the fine mind she had a heart like her mother's. Susy never had an interest or an occupation which she was not glad to put aside for that something which was in all cases more precious to her—a visit with her mother.

Susy died at the right time, the fortunate time of life, the happy age—twenty-four years. At twenty-four, such a girl has seen the best of life—life as a happy dream. After that age the risks begin; responsibility comes, and with it the cares, the sorrows, and the inevitable tragedy. For her mother's sake, I would have brought her back from the grave if I could, but not for my own.

FROM SUSY'S BIOGRAPHY

Then papa went to read in public; there were a great many authors that read, that Thursday afternoon, beside papa; I would have liked to have gone and heard papa read, but papa said he was going to read in Vassar just what he was planning to read in New York, so I stayed at home with mamma.

I think that that was the first exploitation of a new and devilish invention—the thing called an Authors' Reading. This witch's Sabbath took place in a theater, and began at two in the afternoon. There were nine readers on the list, and I believe I was the only one who was qualified by experience to go at the matter in a sane way. I knew, by my old acquaintanceship with the multiplication table, that nine times ten are ninety, and that consequently the average of time allowed to each of these readers should be restricted to ten minutes. There would be an introducer, and he wouldn't understand his business—this disastrous fact could be counted upon as a certainty. The introducer would be ignorant, windy, eloquent, and willing to hear himself talk. With nine introductions to make, added to his own opening speech—well, I could not go on with these harrowing calculations; I foresaw that there was trouble on hand. I had asked for the sixth place in the list. When the curtain went up and I saw that our half circle of minstrels were all on hand, I made a change in my plan. I judged that in asking for sixth place I had done all that was necessary to establish a fictitious reputation for modesty, and that there could be nothing gained by pushing this reputation to the limit; it had done its work and it was time, now, to leave well enough alone, and do better. So I asked to be moved up to third place, and my prayer was granted.

The performance began at a quarter past two, and I, number three in a list of ten (if we include the introducer), was not called to the bat until a quarter after three. My reading was ten minutes long. When I had selected it originally, it was twelve minutes long, and it had taken me a good hour to find ways of reducing it by two minutes without damaging it. I was through in ten minutes. Then I retired to my seat to enjoy the agonies of the audience. I did enjoy them for an hour or two; then all the cruelty in my nature was exhausted and my native humanity came to the front again. By half past five a third of the house was asleep; another third were dying; and the rest were dead. I got out the back way and went home.

During several years, after that, the Authors' Readings continued. Every now and then we assembled in Boston, New York, Philadelphia, Baltimore, Washington, and scourged the people. It was found impossible to teach the persons who managed these orgies any sense. Also it was found impossible to teach the readers any sense. Once I went to Boston to help in one of these revels which had been instigated in the interest of a memorial to Mr. Longfellow. Howells was always a member of these traveling afflictions, and I was never able to teach him to rehearse his proposed reading by the help of a watch and cut it down to a proper length. He couldn't seem to learn it. He was a bright man in all other ways, but whenever he came to select a reading for one of these carousals his intellect decayed and fell to ruin. I arrived at his house in Cambridge the night before the Longfellow Memorial occasion, and I probably asked him to show me his selection. At any rate, he showed it to me—and I wish I may never attempt the truth again if it wasn't seven thousand words. I made him set his eye on his watch and keep game while I should read a paragraph of it. This experiment proved that it would take me an hour and ten minutes to read the whole of it, and I said, "And mind you, this is not allowing anything for such interruptions as applause—for the reason that after the first twelve minutes there wouldn't be any."

He had a time of it to find something short enough, and he kept saying that he never would find a short enough selection that would be good enough—that is to say, he never would be able to find one that would stand exposure before an audience.

I said: "It's no matter. Better that than a long one—because the audience could stand a bad short one, but couldn't stand a good long one."

We got it arranged at last. We got him down to fifteen minutes, perhaps. But he and Doctor Holmes and Aldrich and I had the only short readings that day out of the most formidable accumulation of authors that had ever thus far been placed in position before the enemy—a battery of sixteen. I think that that was the occasion when we had sixteen. It was in the afternoon, and the place was packed, and the air would have been very bad, only there wasn't any. I can see that mass of people yet, opening and closing their mouths like fishes gasping for breath. It was intolerable.

That graceful and competent speaker, Professor Norton, opened the game with a very handsome speech, but it was a good twenty minutes long. And a good ten minutes of it, I think, were devoted to the introduction of Dr. Oliver Wendell Holmes, who hadn't any more need of an introduction than the Milky Way. Then Doctor Holmes recited—as only Doctor Holmes could recite it—"The Last Leaf," and the house rose as one individual and went mad with worshiping delight. And the house stormed along, and stormed along, and got another poem out of the Doctor as an encore; it stormed again and got a third one—though the storm was not so violent this time as had been the previous outbreaks. By this time Doctor Holmes had, himself, lost a part of his mind, and he actually went on reciting poem after poem until silence had taken the place of encores and he had to do the last encore by himself.

I had learned, by this time, to stipulate for third place on the program. The performance began at two o'clock. My train for Hartford would leave at four o'clock. I would need fifteen minutes for transit to the station. I needed ten minutes for my reading. I did my reading in the ten minutes; I fled at once from the theater, and I came very near not catching that train. I was told afterward that by the time reader number eight stepped forward and trained his gun on the house, the audience were drifting out of the place in groups, shoals, blocks, and avalanches, and that about that time the siege was raised and the conflict given up, with six or seven readers still to hear from.

At the reading in Washington in the spring of '88 there was a crowd of readers. They all came overloaded, as usual. Thomas Nelson Page read forty minutes by the watch, and he was no further down than the middle of the list. We were all due at the White House at half past nine. The President and Mrs. Cleveland were present, and at half past ten they had to go away—the President to attend to some official business which had been arranged to be considered after our White House reception, it being supposed by Mr. Cleveland, who was inexperienced in Authors' Readings, that our reception at the White House would be over by half past eleven, whereas if he had known as much about Authors' Readings as he knew about other kinds of statesmanship, he would have known that we were not likely to get through before time for early breakfast.

[*Monday, March 5, 1906*

Mrs. Clemens's warning to Mr. Clemens when he attends the Cleveland reception at the White House.—Describes the Paris house in which they lived in 1893—also room in Villa Viviani—also dining-room in house at Riverdale.—Tells how Mr. Clemens was "dusted off" after the various dinners—and the card system of signals.—Letter from Mr. Gilder regarding Mr. Cleveland's sixty-ninth birthday.—Mason.

I WAS always heedless. I was born heedless, and therefore I was constantly, and quite unconsciously, committing breaches of the minor proprieties, which brought upon me humiliations which ought to have humiliated me, but didn't, because I didn't know any-thing had happened. But Livy knew; and so the humiliations fell to her share, poor child, who had not earned them and did not deserve them. She always said I was the most difficult child she had. She was very sensitive about me. It distressed her to see me do heedless things which could bring me under criticism, and so she was always watchful and alert to protect me from the kind of transgressions which I have been speaking of.

When I was leaving Hartford for Washington, upon the occasion referred to, she said: "I have written a small warning and put it in a pocket of your dress vest. When you are dressing to go to the Authors' Reception at the White House you will naturally put your fingers in your vest pockets, according to your custom, and you will find that little note there. Read it carefully and do as it tells you. I cannot be with you, and so I delegate my sentry duties to this little note. If I should give you the warning by word of mouth, now, it would pass from your head and be forgotten in a few minutes."

It was President Cleveland's first term. I had never seen his wife—the young, the beautiful, the good-hearted, the sympathetic, the fascinating. Sure enough, just as I had finished dressing to go to the White House I found that little note, which I had long ago forgotten. It was a grave little note, a serious little note, like its writer, but it made me laugh. Livy's gentle gravities often produced that effect upon me, where the expert humorist's best joke would have failed, for I do not laugh easily.

When we reached the White House and I was shaking hands with the President, he started to say something, but I interrupted him and said, "If Your Excellency will excuse me, I will come back in a moment; but now I have a very important matter to attend to, and it must be attended to at once." I turned to Mrs. Cleveland, the young, the beautiful, the fascinating, and gave her my card, on which I had written *"He did not"*—and I asked her to sign her name below those words.

She said: "He did not? He did not what?"

"Oh," I said, "never mind. We cannot stop to discuss that now. This is urgent. Won't you please sign your name?" (I handed her a fountain pen.)

"Why," she said, "I cannot commit myself in that way. Who is it that didn't?—and what is it that he didn't?"

"Oh," I said, "time is flying, flying, flying! Won't you take me out of my distress and sign your name to it? It's all right. I give you my word it's all right."

She looked nonplused, but hesitatingly and mechanically she took the pen and said: "I will sign it. I will take the risk. But you must tell me all about it, right afterward, so that you can be arrested before you get out of the house in case there should be anything criminal about this."

Then she signed; and I handed her Mrs. Clemens's note, which was very brief, very simple, and to the point. It said, *"Don't wear your arctics in the White House."* It made her shout; and at my request she summoned a messenger and we sent that card at once to the mail on its way to Mrs. Clemens in Hartford.

> He did not.
> Frances F. Cleveland,
>
> Mr. Samuel L. Clemens.
>
> Hartford, Conn.

During 1893 and '94 we were living in Paris, the first half of the time at the Hotel Brighton, in the rue de Rivoli, the other half in a charming mansion in the rue de l'Université, on the other side of the Seine, which, by good luck, we had gotten hold of through another man's ill luck. This was Pomeroy, the artist. Illness in his family had made it necessary for him to go to the Riviera. He was paying thirty-six hundred dollars a year for the house, but allowed us to have it at twenty-six hundred. It was a lovely house; large, rambling, quaint, charmingly furnished and decorated; built upon no particular plan; delightfully rambling, uncertain, and full of surprises. You were always getting lost in it, and finding nooks and corners and rooms which you didn't know were there and whose presence you had not suspected before. It was built by a rich French artist; and he had also furnished it and decorated it himself. The studio was coziness itself. We used it as drawing-room, sitting-room, living-room, dancing-room—we used it for everything. We couldn't get enough of it. It is odd that it should have been so cozy, for it was forty feet long, forty feet high, and thirty feet wide, with a vast fireplace on each side in the middle, and a musicians' gallery at one end. But we had, before this, found out that under the proper conditions spaciousness and coziness do go together most affectionately and congruously. We had found it out a year or two earlier, when we were living in the Villa Viviani three miles outside the walls of Florence. That house had a room in it which was forty feet square and forty feet high, and at first we couldn't endure it. We called it the Mammoth Cave; we called it the skating-rink; we called it the Great Sahara; we called it all sorts of names intended to convey our disrespect. We had to pass through it to get from one end of the house to the other, but we passed straight through and did not loiter—and yet before long, and without our knowing how it happened, we found ourselves infesting that vast place day and night, and preferring it to any other part of the house.

Four or five years ago, when we took a house on the banks of the Hudson, at Riverdale, we drifted from room to room on our tour of inspection, always with a growing doubt as to whether we wanted that house or not. But at last when we arrived in a dining-room that was sixty feet long, thirty feet wide, and had two great fireplaces in it, that settled it.

But I have wandered. What I was proposing to talk about was quite another matter—to wit: In that pleasant Paris house Mrs. Clemens gathered little dinner companies together once or twice a week, and it goes without saying that in these circumstances my defects had a large chance for display. *Always,* always without fail, as soon as the guests were out of the house, I saw that I had been miscarrying again. Mrs. Clemens explained to me the various things which I had been doing and which should have been left undone. The children had a name for this performance. They called it "dusting off papa."

At last I had an inspiration. It is astonishing that it had not occurred to me earlier. I said: "Why, Livy, you know that dusting me off *after* these dinners is not the wise way. You could dust me off after every dinner for a year and I should always be just as competent to do the forbidden thing at each succeeding dinner as if you had not said a word, because in the meantime I have forgotten all these instructions. I think the correct way is for you to dust me off immediately before the guests arrive, and then I can keep some of it in my head and things will go better."

She recognized that that was wisdom and that it was a very good idea. Then we set to work to arrange a system of signals to be delivered by her to me during dinner; signals which would indicate definitely which particular crime I was now engaged in, so that I could change to another. The children got a screen arranged so that they could be behind it during the dinner and listen for the signals and entertain themselves with them. The system of signals was very simple, but it was very effective. If Mrs. Clemens happened to be so busy, at any time, talking with her elbow neighbor that she overlooked something that I was doing, she was sure to get a low-voiced hint from behind that screen in these words:

"Blue card, mamma"; or, "Red card, mamma"—"Green card, mamma"—so that I was under double and triple guard. What the mother didn't notice the children detected for her.

As I say, the signals were quite simple, but very effective. At a hint from behind the screen, Livy would look down the table and say, in a voice full of interest, if not of counterfeited apprehension, "What did you do with the blue card that was on the dressing table——"

That was enough. I knew what was happening— that I was talking the lady on my right to death and never paying any attention to the one on my left. The blue card meant "Let the lady on your right have a reprieve; destroy the one on your left"; so I would at once go to talking vigorously to the lady on my left. It wouldn't be long till there would be another hint, followed by a remark from Mrs. Clemens which had in it an apparently casual reference to a red card, which meant, "Oh, **are you** going to sit there all the evening and never say anything? Do wake up and talk." So I woke up and drowned the table with talk. We had a number of cards, of different colors, each meaning a definite thing, each calling attention to some crime or other in my common list; and that system was exceedingly useful. It was entirely successful. It was like Buck Fanshaw's riot. It broke up the riot before it got a chance to begin. It headed off crime after crime all through the dinner, and I always came out at the end successful, triumphant, with large praises owing to me, and I got them on the spot.

It is a far call back over the accumulation of years to that night in the White House when Mrs. Cleveland signed the card. Many things have happened since then. The Cleveland family have been born since then. Ruth, the first-born, whom I never knew, but with whom I corresponded when she was a baby, lived only a few years.

To-day comes this letter, and it brings back the Clevelands, and the past, and my lost little correspondent.

March 3, 1906

Editorial Department,
The Century Magazine,
Union Square, New York.

My dear Mr. Clemens:

President Finley and I are collecting letters to Ex-President Cleveland from his friends, appropriate to his 69th birthday.

If the plan appeals to you, will you kindly send a sealed greeting under cover to me at the above address, and I will send it, and the other letters, South to him in time for him to get them, all together, on the 18th of the present month.

Yours sincerely,

R. W. GILDER.

MR. SAMUEL L. CLEMENS.

When the little Ruth was about a year or a year and a half old, Mason, an old and valued friend of mine, was consul-general at Frankfort-on-the-Main. I had known him well in 1867, '68, and '69, in America, and I and mine had spent a good deal of time with him and his family in Frankfort in 1892-93. He was a thoroughly competent, diligent, and conscientious official. Indeed, he possessed these qualities in so large a degree that among American consuls he might fairly be said to be monumental, for at that time our consular service was largely—and I think I may say mainly—in the hands of ignorant, vulgar, and incapable men who had been political heelers in America, and had been taken care of by transference to consulates, where they could be supported at the government's expense instead of being transferred to the poorhouse, which would have been cheaper and more patriotic. Mason, in '78, had been consul-general in Frankfort several years—four, I think. He had come from Marseilles with a great record. He had been consul there during thirteen years, and one part of his record was heroic. There had been a desolating cholera epidemic, and Mason was the only representative of any foreign country who stayed at his post and saw it through. And during that time he not only represented his own country, but he represented all the other countries in Christendom and did their work, and did it well and was praised for it in words of no uncertain sound. This great record of Mason's had saved him from official decapitation straight along while Republican Presidents occupied the chair, but now it was occupied by a Democrat. Mr. Cleveland was not seated in it—he was not yet inaugurated—before he was deluged with applications from Democratic politicians desiring the appointment of a thousand or so politically useful Democrats to Mason's place. A year or two later Mason wrote me and asked me if I couldn't do something to save him from destruction.

[Tuesday, March 6, 1906

Mr. Clemens makes Baby Ruth intercede in behalf of Mr. Mason, and he is retained in his place.—Mr. Clemens's letter to ex-President Cleveland.—Mr. Cleveland as sheriff, in Buffalo.—As Mayor, he vetoes ordinance of railway corporation.—Mr. Clemens and Mr. Cable visit Governor Cleveland at Capitol, Albany.—Mr. Clemens sits on the bells and summons sixteen clerks.

I WAS very anxious to keep him in his place, but at first I could not think of any way to help him, for I was a mugwump. We, the mugwumps, a little company made up of the unenslaved of both parties, the very best men to be found in the two great parties—that was our idea of it—voted sixty thousand strong for Mr. Cleveland in New York and elected him. Our principles were high and very definite. We were not a party; we had no candidates; we had no axes to grind. Our vote laid upon the man we cast it for no obligation of any kind. By our rule we could not ask for office; we could not accept office. When voting, it was our duty to vote for the best man, regardless of his party name. We had no other creed. Vote for the best man—that was creed enough.

Such being my situation, I was puzzled to know how to try to help Mason and at the same time save my mugwump purity undefiled. It was a delicate place. But presently, out of the ruck of confusions in my mind, rose a sane thought, clear and bright—to wit: since it was a mugwump's duty to do his best to put the best man in office, necessarily it must be a mugwump's duty to *keep* the best man in when he was already there. My course was easy now. It might not be quite delicate for a mugwump to approach the President directly, but I could approach him indirectly, with all delicacy, since in that case not even courtesy would require him to take notice of an application which no one could prove had ever reached him.

Yes, it was easy and simple sailing now. I could lay the matter before Ruth, in her cradle, and wait for results. I wrote the little child, and said to her all that I have just been saying about mugwump principles and the limitations which they put upon me. I explained that it would not be proper for me to apply to her father in Mr. Mason's behalf, but I detailed to her Mr. Mason's high and honorable record and suggested that she take the matter in her own hands and do a patriotic work, which I felt some delicacy about venturing upon myself. I asked her to forget that her father was only President of the United States, and her subject and servant; I asked her not to put her application in the form of a command, but to modify this, and give it the fictitious and pleasanter form of a mere request——that it would be no harm to let him gratify himself with the superstition that he was independent and could do as he pleased in the matter. I begged her to put stress, and plenty of it, upon the proposition that to keep Mason in his place would be a benefaction to the nation; to enlarge upon that, and keep still about all other considerations.

In due time I received a letter from the President, written with his own hand, signed by his own hand, acknowledging Ruth's intervention and thanking me for enabling him to save to the country the services of so good and well tried a servant as Mason, and thanking me, also, for the detailed fullness of Mason's record, which could leave no doubt in anyone's mind that Mason was in his right place and ought to be kept there.

In the beginning of Mr. Cleveland's second term a very strong effort to displace Mason was made, and Mason wrote me again. He was not hoping that we would succeed this time, because the assault upon his place was well organized, determined, and exceedingly powerful, but he hoped I would try again and see what I could do. I was not disturbed. It seemed to me that he did not know Mr. Cleveland or he would not be disturbed himself. I believed I knew Mr. Cleveland, and that he was not the man to budge an inch from his duty in any circumstances, and that he was a Gibraltar against whose solid bulk a whole Atlantic of assaulting politicians would dash itself in vain.

I wrote Ruth Cleveland once more. Mason remained in his place and I think he would have remained in it without Ruth's intercession. There have been other Presidents since, but Mason's record has protected him, and the many and powerful efforts to dislodge him have all failed. Also, he has been complimented with promotions. He was promoted from consul-general in Frankfort to consul-general at Berlin, our highest consular post in Germany. A year ago he was promoted another step—to the consul-generalship in Paris, and he holds that place yet.

Ruth, the child, remained not long on earth to help make it beautiful and to bless the home of her parents. But, little creature as she was, she did high service for her country, as I have shown, and it is right that this should be recorded and remembered.

In accordance with the suggestion made in Gilder's letter (as copied in yesterday's talk) I have written the following note to ex-President Cleveland:

HONORED SIR:—

Your patriotic virtues have won for you the homage of half the nation and the enmity of the other half. This places your character as a citizen upon a summit as high as Washington's. The verdict is unanimous and unassailable. The votes of both sides are necessary in cases like these, and the votes of the one side are quite as valuable as are the votes of the other. Where the votes are all in a man's favor the verdict is against him. It is sand, and history will wash it away. But the verdict for you is rock, and will stand.

S. L. CLEMENS.

As of date March 18, 1906.

When Mr. Cleveland was a member of a very strong and prosperous firm of lawyers, in Buffalo, just before the 'seventies, he was elected to the mayoralty. Presently a formidably rich and powerful railway corporation worked an ordinance through the city government whose purpose was to take possession of a certain section of the city inhabited altogether by the poor, the helpless, and the inconsequential, and drive those people out. Mr. Cleveland vetoed the ordinance. The other members of his law firm were indignant and also terrified. To them the thing which he had done meant disaster to their business. They waited upon him and begged him to reconsider his action. He declined to do it. They insisted. He still declined. He said that his official position imposed upon him a duty which he could not honorably avoid; therefore he should be loyal to it; that the helpless situation of these inconsequential citizens made it his duty to stand by them and be their friend, since they had no other; that he was sorry if this conduct of his must bring disaster upon the firm, but that he had no choice; his duty was plain, and he would stick to the position which he had taken. They intimated that this would lose him his place in the firm. He said he did not wish to be a damage to the co-partnership, therefore they could remove his name from it, and without any hard feeling on his part.

During the time that we were living in Buffalo in '70 and '71, Mr. Cleveland was sheriff, but I never happened to make his acquaintance, or even see him. In fact, I suppose I was not even aware of his existence. Fourteen years later, he was become the greatest man in the state. I was not living in the state at the time. He was Governor, and was about to step into the post of President of the United States. At that time I was on the public highway in company with another bandit, George W. Cable. We were robbing the public with readings from our works during four months—and in the course of time we went to Albany to levy tribute, and I said, "We ought to go and pay our respects to the Governor."

So Cable and I went to that majestic Capitol building and stated our errand. We were shown into the Governor's private office, and I saw Mr. Cleveland for the first time. We three stood chatting together. I was born lazy, and I comforted myself by turning the corner of a table into a sort of seat. Presently the Governor said: "Mr. Clemens, I was a fellow citizen of yours in Buffalo a good many months, a good while ago, and during those months you burst suddenly into a mighty fame, out of a previous long-continued and no doubt proper obscurity—but I was a nobody, and you wouldn't notice me nor have anything to do with me. But now that I have become somebody, you have changed your style, and you come here to shake hands with me and be sociable. How do you explain this kind of conduct?"

"Oh," I said, "it is very simple, Your Excellency. In Buffalo you were nothing but a sheriff. I was in society. I couldn't afford to associate with sheriffs. But you are a Governor, now, and you are on your way to the Presidency. It is a great difference, and it makes you worth while."

There appeared to be about sixteen doors to that spacious room. From each door a young man now emerged, and the sixteen lined up and moved forward and stood in front of the Governor with an aspect of respectful expectancy in their attitude. No one spoke for a moment. Then the Governor said: "You are dismissed, gentlemen. Your services are not required. Mr. Clemens is sitting on the bells."

There was a cluster of sixteen bell-buttons on the corner of the table against which I had been lounging.

[*Wednesday, March 7, 1906*

Susy's biography.—Susy and her father escort Mrs. Clemens to train, then go over Brooklyn Bridge.—On the

way to Vassar they discuss German profanity.—Mr.
Clemens tells of the sweet and profane German nurse.—
The arrival at Vassar and the dreary reception—told by
Susy—the reading, etc. Mr. Clemens's opinion of girls.—
He is to talk to the Barnard girls this afternoon.

FROM SUSY'S BIOGRAPHY

THE next day mamma planned to take the four-o'clock
car back to Hartford. We rose quite early that morning
and went to the Vienna Bakery and took breakfast there.
From there we went to a German bookstore and bought
some German books for Clara's birthday.

Then mamma and I went to do some shopping and
papa went to see General Grant. After we had finnished
doing our shopping we went home to the hotel together.
When we entered our rooms in the hotel we saw on the
table a vase full of exquisett red roses. Mamma who is
very fond of flowers exclaimed "Oh I wonder who could
have sent them." We both looked at the card in the midst
of the roses and saw that it was written on in papa's handwriting, it was written in German. "Liebes Geshchenk on
die Mamma." [I am sure I didn't say "on"—that is
Susy's spelling, not mine.—S. L. C.] Mamma was delighted. Papa came home and gave mamma her ticket;
and after visiting a while with her went to see Major
Pond and mamma and I sat down to our lunch. After
lunch most of our time was taken up with packing, and
at about three o'clock we went to escort mamma to the
train. We got on board the train with her and stayed
with her about five minutes and then we said good-bye to
her and the train started for Hartford. It was the first
time I had ever beene away from home without mamma
in my life, although I was 13 yrs. old. Papa and I drove
back to the hotel and got Major Pond and then went to

see the Brooklyn Bridge we went across it to Brooklyn on the cars and then walked back across it from Brooklyn to New York. We enjoyed looking at the beautiful scenery and we could see the bridge moove under the intense heat of the sun. We had a perfectly delightful time, but were pretty tired when we got back to the hotel.

The next morning we rose early, took our breakfast and took an early train to Poughkeepsie. We had a very pleasant journey to Poughkeepsie. The Hudson was magnificent—shrouded with beautiful mist. When we arrived at Poughkeepsie it was raining quite hard; which fact greatly dissapointed me because I very much wanted to see the outside of the buildings of Vasser College and as it rained that would be impossible. It was quite a long drive from the station to Vasser College and papa and I had a nice long time to discuss and laugh over German profanity. One of the German phrases papa particularly enjoys is "O heilige maria Mutter Jesus!" Jean has a German nurse, and this was one of her phrases, there was a time when Jean exclaimed "Ach Gott!" to every trifle, but when mamma found it out she was shocked and instantly put a stop to it.

It brings that pretty little German creature vividly before me—a sweet and innocent and plump little creature, with peachy cheeks; a clear-souled little maiden and without offense, notwithstanding her profanities, and she was loaded to the eyebrows with them. She was a mere child. She was not fifteen yet. She was just from Germany, and knew no English. She was always scattering her profanities around, and they were such a satisfaction to me that I never dreamed of such a thing as modifying her.

For my own sake, I had no disposition to tell on her. Indeed, I took pains to keep her from being found out. I told her to confine her religious expressions to the children's quarters, and urged her to remember that Mrs. Clemens was prejudiced against pieties on week days. To the children, the little maid's profanities sounded natural and proper and right because they had been used to that kind of talk in Germany, and they attached no evil importance to it. It grieves me that I have forgotten those vigorous remarks. I long hoarded them in my memory as a treasure. But I remember one of them still, because I heard it so many times. The trial of that little creature's life was the children's hair. She would tug and strain with her comb, accompanying her work with her misplaced pieties. And when finally she was through with her triple job she always fired up and exploded her thanks toward the sky, where they belonged, in this form: "Gott sei Dank! Ich bin schon fertig mit'm Gott verdammtes Haar!" (I believe I am not quite brave enough to translate it.)

From Susy's Biography

We at length reached Vasser College and she looked very finely, her buildings and her grounds being very beautiful. We went to the front doore and rang the bell. The young girl who came to the doore wished to know who we wanted to see. Evidently we were not expected. Papa told her who we wanted to see and she showed us to the parlor. We waited, no one came; and waited, no one came, still no one came. It was beginning to seem pretty awkard, "Oh well this is a pretty piece of business," papa exclaimed. At length we heard footsteps coming down the long corridor and Miss C, (the lady who had invited papa) came into the room. She greeted papa very pleasantly and they had a nice little chatt together. Soon the lady principal also entered and she was very pleasant and agreable. She showed us to our rooms and said she would send for us when dinner was ready. We went into our rooms, but we had nothing to do for half an hour exept to watch the rain drops as they fell upon the window panes. At last we were called to dinner, and I went down without papa as he never eats anything in the middle of the day. I sat at the table with the lady principal and enjoyed very much seing all the young girls trooping into the dining-room. After dinner I went around the College with the young ladies and papa stayed in his room and smoked. When it was supper time papa went down and ate supper with us and we had a very delightful supper. After supper the young ladies went to their rooms to dress for the evening. Papa went to his room and I went with the lady principal. At length the guests began to arive, but papa still remained in his room until called for. Papa read in the chapell. It was the first time I had ever heard him read in my life—that is in public. When he came out on the stage I remember the people behind me exclaimed "Oh how queer he is! Isn't he funny!" I thought papa was very funny, although I did not think him queer. He read "A Trying Situation" and "The Golden Arm," a ghost story that he heard down South when he was a little boy. "The Golden Arm" papa had told me before, but he had startled me so that I did not much wish to hear it again. But I had resolved this time to be prepared and not to let myself be startled, but still papa did, and very very much; he startled the whole roomful of people and they jumped as one man. The other story was also very funny and interesting and I enjoyed the evening inexpressibly much.

After papa had finished reading we all went down to the collation in the dining-room, and after that there was dancing and singing. Then the guests went away and papa and I went to bed. The next morning we rose early, took an early train for Hartford and reached Hartford at ½ past 2 o'clock. We were very glad to get back.

How charitably she treats that ghastly experience! It is a dear and lovely disposition, and a most valuable one, that can brush away indignities and discourtesies and seek and find the pleasanter features of an experience. Susy had that disposition, and it was one of the jewels of her character that had come to her straight from her mother. It is a feature that was left out of me at birth. And at seventy I have not yet acquired it. I did not go to Vassar College professionally, but as a guest—as a guest, and gratis. Aunt Clara (Mrs. Stanchfield) was a graduate of Vassar and it was to please her that I inflicted that journey upon Susy and myself. The invitation had come to me from both the lady mentioned by Susy and the president of the college—a sour old saint who has probably been gathered to his fathers long ago; and I hope they enjoy him; I hope they enjoy his society. I think I can get along without it, in either end of the next world.

We arrived at the college in that soaking rain, and Susy has described, with just a suggestion of dissatisfaction, the sort of reception we got. Susy had to sit in her damp clothes half an hour while we waited in the parlor; then she was taken to a fireless room and left to wait there again, as she has stated. I do not remember that president's name, and I am sorry. He did not put in an appearance until it was time for me to step upon the platform in front of that great garden of young and lovely blossoms. He caught up with me and advanced upon the platform with me and was going to introduce me. I said in substance, "You have allowed me to get along without your help thus far, and if you will retire from the platform I will try to do the rest without it." I did not see him any more, but I detest his memory.

Of course my resentment did not extend to the students, and so I had an unforgetable good time talking to them. And I think they had a good time, too, for they responded as one man, to use Susy's unimprovable phrase.

Girls are charming creatures. I shall have to be twice seventy years old before I change my mind as to that. I am to talk to a crowd of them this afternoon, students of Barnard College (the sex's annex to Columbia University), and I think I shall have just as pleasant a time with those lassies as I had with the Vassar girls twenty-one years ago.

[*Thursday, March 8, 1906*

Letter from brother of Captain Tonkray.—Mr. Clemens replied that original of "Huckleberry Finn" was Tom Blankenship.—Tom's father Town Drunkard.—Describes Tom's character.—Death of Injun Joe.—Storm which came that night.—Incident of the Episcopal sextons and their reforms.—Mr. Dawson's school in Hannibal.—Arch Fuqua's great gift.

FOR thirty years, I have received an average of a dozen letters a year from strangers who remember me, or whose fathers remember me as boy and young man. But these letters are almost always disappointing. I have not known these strangers nor their fathers. I have not heard of the names they mention; the reminiscences to which they call my attention have had no part in my experience; all of which means that these strangers have been mistaking me for somebody else. But at last I have the refreshment, this morning, of a letter from a man who deals in names that were familiar to me in my boyhood. The writer incloses a newspaper clipping which has been wandering through the press for four or five weeks, and he wants to know if his brother, Captain Tonkray, was really the original of "Huckleberry Finn."

"HUCKLEBERRY FINN" DEAD

ORIGINAL OF MARK TWAIN'S FAMOUS CHARACTER HAD LED QUIET LIFE IN IDAHO

(By Direct Wire to the *Times*.)

WALLACE, (IDAHO), Feb. 2.—(Exclusive dispatch.) Capt. A. O. Tonkray, commonly known as "Huckleberry Finn," said to be the original of Mark Twain's famous character, was found dead in his room at Murray this morning from heart failure.

Capt. Tonkray, a native of Hannibal, Mo., was 65 years

old. In early life, he ran on steamboats on the Mississippi and the Missouri rivers, in frequent contact with Samuel L. Clemens, and tradition has it "Mark Twain" later used Tonkray as his model for "Huckleberry Finn." He came to Murray in 1884 and had been living a quiet life since.

I have replied that "Huckleberry Finn" was Tom Blankenship. As this writer evidently knew the Hannibal of the 'forties, he will easily recall Tom Blankenship. Tom's father was at one time Town Drunkard, an exceedingly well-defined and unofficial office of those days. He succeeded General—(I forget the General's name) [1] and for a time he was sole and only incumbent of the office; but afterward Jimmy Finn proved competency and disputed the place with him, so we had two town drunkards at one time—and it made as much trouble in that village as Christendom experienced in the fourteenth century, when there were two Popes at the same time.

In *Huckleberry Finn* I have drawn Tom Blankenship exactly as he was. He was ignorant, unwashed, insufficiently fed; but he had as good a heart as ever any boy had. His liberties were totally unrestricted. He was the only really independent person—boy or man—in the community, and by consequence he was tranquilly and continuously happy, and was envied by all the rest of us. We liked him; we enjoyed his society. And as his society was forbidden us by our parents, the prohibition trebled and quadrupled its value, and there-

---

[1] Gaines.

fore we sought and got more of his society than of any other boy's. I heard, four years ago, that he was justice of the peace in a remote village in Montana, and was a good citizen and greatly respected.

During Jimmy Finn's term he was not exclusive; he was not finical; he was not hypercritical; he was largely and handsomely democratic—and slept in the deserted tanyard with the hogs. My father tried to reform him once, but did not succeed. My father was not a professional reformer. In him the spirit of reform was spasmodic. It only broke out now and then, with considerable intervals between. Once he tried to reform Injun Joe. That also was a failure. It was a failure, and we boys were glad. For Injun Joe, drunk, was interesting and a benefaction to us, but Injun Joe, sober, was a dreary spectacle. We watched my father's experiments upon him with a good deal of anxiety, but it came out all right and we were satisfied. Injun Joe got drunk oftener than before, and became intolerably interesting.

I think that in *Tom Sawyer* I starved Injun Joe to death in the cave. But that may have been to meet the exigencies of romantic literature. I can't remember now whether the real Injun Joe died in the cave or out of it, but I do remember that the news of his death reached me at a most unhappy time—that is to say, just at bedtime on a summer night, when a prodigious storm of thunder and lightning accompanied by a deluging rain that turned the streets and lanes into rivers caused me to repent and resolve to lead a better life. I can remember those awful thunder-bursts and the white glare of the lightning yet, and the wild lashing of the rain against the windowpanes. By my teachings I perfectly well knew what all that wild rumpus was for—Satan had come to get Injun Joe. I had no shadow of doubt about it. It was the proper thing when a person like Injun Joe was required in the under world, and I should have thought it strange and unaccountable if Satan had come for him in a less spectacular way. With every glare of lightning I shriveled and shrank together in mortal terror, and in the interval of black darkness that followed I poured out my lamentings over my lost condition, and my supplications for just one more chance, with an energy and feeling and sincerity quite foreign to my nature.

But in the morning I saw that it was a false alarm and concluded to resume business at the old stand and wait for another reminder.

The axiom says, "History repeats itself." A week or two ago my nephew, by marriage, Edward Loomis, dined with us, along with his wife, my niece (*née* Julie Langdon). He is vice-president of the Delaware and Lackawanna Railway system. The duties of his office used to carry him frequently to Elmira, New York; the exigencies of his courtship carried him there still oftener, and so in the course of time he came to know a good many of the citizens of that place. At dinner he mentioned a circumstance which flashed me back over about sixty years and landed me in that little bedroom on that tempestuous night. He said Mr. Buckly was sexton of the Episcopal church in Elmira, and had been for many years the competent superintendent of all the church's worldly affairs, and was regarded by the whole congregation as a stay, a blessing, a priceless treasure. But he had a couple of defects—not large defects, but they seemed large when flung against the background of his profoundly religious character: he drank a good deal, and he could outswear a brakeman. A movement arose to persuade him to lay aside these vices, and after consulting with his pal, who occupied the same position as himself in the other Episcopal church, and whose defects were duplicates of his own and had inspired regret in the congregation whom he was serving, they concluded to try for reform—not wholesale, but half at a time. They took the liquor pledge and waited for results. During nine days the results were entirely satisfactory, and they were recipients of many compliments and much congratulation. Then on New Year's Eve they had business a mile and a half out of town, just beyond the New York State line. Everything went well with them that evening in the barroom of the inn—but at last the celebration of the occasion by those villagers came to be of a burdensome nature. It was a bitter cold night and the multitudinous hot toddies that were circulating began, by and by, to exert a powerful influence upon the new prohibitionists. At last Buckly's friend remarked, "Buckly, does it occur to you that we are outside the diocese?" That ended reform No. 1.

Then they took a chance in reform No. 2. For a while that one prospered and they got much applause.

One morning this stepnephew of mine, Loomis, met Buckly on the street and said: "You have made a gallant struggle against those defects of yours. I am aware that you failed on No. 1, but I am also aware that you are having better luck with No. 2."

"Yes," Buckly said, "No. 2 is all right and sound up to date, and we are full of hope."

Loomis said: "Buckly, of course you have your troubles like other people, but they never show on the outside. I have never seen you when you were not cheerful. Are you always cheerful? Really always cheerful?"

"Well, no," he said. "No, I can't say that I am always cheerful, but— Well, you know that kind of a night that comes; you wake up way in the night and the whole world is sunk in gloom and there are storms and earthquakes and all sorts of disasters in the air threatening and you get cold and chill; and when that happens to me I recognize how sinful I am and it goes all clear to my heart and wrings it and I have such terrors and terrors —oh, they are indescribable, those terrors that assail and thrill me, and I slip out of bed and get on my knees and pray and pray and pray and promise that I will be good, etc. And then, you know, in the morning the sun shines out so lovely and the birds sing and the whole world is so beautiful, and—b' god! I rally!"

Now I will quote a brief paragraph from this letter which I have received from Mr. Tonkray. He says:

You no doubt are at a loss to know who I am. I will tell you. In my younger days I was a resident of Hannibal, Mo., and you and I were schoolmates attending Mr. Dawson's school along with Sam and Will Bowen and Andy Fuqua and others whose names I have forgotten. I was then about the smallest boy in school, for my age, and they called me little Aleck Tonkray for short.

I don't remember Aleck Tonkray, but I knew those other people as well as I knew the town drunkards. I remember Dawson's schoolhouse perfectly. If I wanted to describe it I could save myself the trouble by conveying the description of it to these pages from *Tom Sawyer*. I can remember the drowsy and inviting summer sounds that used to float in through the open windows from that distant boy-Paradise, Cardiff Hill, and mingle with the murmurs of the studying pupils and make them the more dreary by the contrast. I remember Andy Fuqua, the oldest pupil—a man of twenty-five. I remember the youngest pupil, Nannie Owsley, a child of seven. I remember George RoBards, eighteen or twenty years old, the only pupil who studied Latin. I remember vaguely the rest of the twenty-five boys and girls. I remember Mr. Dawson very well. I remember his boy, Theodore, who was as good as he could be. In fact he was inordinately good, extravagantly good, offensively good, detestably good—and he had pop-eyes—and I would have drowned him if I had had a chance.

In that school we were all about on an equality, and, so far as I remember, the passion of envy had no place in our hearts, except in the case of Arch Fuqua—the other one's brother. Of course we all went barefoot in the summertime. Arch Fuqua was about my own age—ten or eleven. In the winter we could stand him, because he wore shoes then, and his great gift was hidden from our sight and we were enabled to forget it. But in the summertime he was a bitterness to us. He was our envy, for he could double back his big toe and let it fly and you could hear it snap thirty yards. There was not another boy in the school that could approach this feat. He had not a rival as regards a physical distinction—except in Theodore Eddy, who could work his ears like a horse. But he was no real rival, because you couldn't hear him work his ears; so all the advantage lay with Arch Fuqua.

[*Friday, March 9, 1906*

Mr. Clemens tells of several of his schoolmates in Mr. Dawson's Hannibal school: George RoBards and Mary Moss; John RoBards, who traveled far; John Garth and Helen Kercheval.—Mr. Kercheval's slave woman and his apprentice saved Mr. Clemens from drowning in Bear Creek.—Meredith, who became a guerrilla chief in Civil War.—Will and Sam Bowen, Mississippi pilots—died of yellow fever.

I AM talking of a time sixty years ago and up-ward. I remember the names of some of those schoolmates, and, by fitful glimpses, even their faces rise before me for a moment—only just long enough to be recognized; then they vanish. I catch glimpses of George RoBards, the Latin pupil—slender, pale, studious, bending over his book and absorbed in it, his long straight black hair hanging down below his jaws like a pair of curtains on the sides of his face. I can see him give his head a toss and flirt one of the curtains back around his head—to get it out of his way, apparently; really to show off. In that day it was a great thing among the boys to have hair of so flexible a sort that it could be flung back in that way, with a flirt of the head. George RoBards was the envy of us all. For there was no hair among us that was so competent for this exhibition as his. My hair was a dense ruck of short curls, and so was my brother Henry's. We tried all kinds of devices to get these crooks straightened out so that they would flirt, but we never succeeded. Sometimes, by soaking our heads and then combing and brushing our hair down tight and flat to our skulls, we could get it straight, temporarily, and this gave us a comforting moment of joy. But the first time we gave it a flirt it all shriveled into curls again and our happiness was gone.

George was a fine young fellow in all ways. He and Mary Moss were sweethearts and pledged to eternal constancy, from a time when they were merely children. But Mr. Lakenan arrived now and became a resident. He took an important position in the little town at once, and maintained it. He

brought with him a distinguished reputation as a
lawyer. He was educated, cultured; he was grave
even to austerity; he was dignified in his conversation and deportment. He was a rather oldish
bachelor—as bachelor oldishness was estimated in
that day. He was a rising man. He was con-
templated with considerable awe by the community,
and as a catch he stood at the top of the market.
That blooming and beautiful thing, Mary Moss,
attracted his favor. He laid siege to her and won.
Everybody said she accepted him to please her
parents, not herself. They were married. And
everybody again, testifying, said he continued her
schooling all by himself, proposing to educate her
up to standard and make her a meet companion
for him. These things may have been true. They
may not have been true. But they were interesting.
That is the main requirement in a village like that.
George went away, presently, to some far-off region
and there he died—of a broken heart, everybody
said. That could be true, for he had good cause.
He would go far before he would find another Mary
Moss.

How long ago that little tragedy happened!
None but the white heads know about it now. Lakenan is dead these many years, but Mary still lives,
and is still beautiful, although she has grandchildren. I saw her and one of her married daughters
when I went out to Missouri four years ago to receive an honorary LL.D. from Missouri University.

John RoBards was the little brother of George,

a wee chap with silky golden curtains to his face
which dangled to his shoulders and below, and
could be flung back ravishingly. When he was
twelve years old he crossed the plains with his
father amid the rush of the gold seekers of '49;
and I remember the departure of the cavalcade
when it spurred westward. We were all there to
see and to envy. And I can still see that proud
little chap sailing by on a great horse, with his
long locks streaming out behind. We were all on
hand to gaze and envy when he returned, two years
later, in unimaginable glory—for he had traveled.
None of us had ever been forty miles from home.
But he had crossed the continent. He had been
in the gold mines, that fairyland of our imagination. And he had done a still more wonderful thing.
He had been in ships—in ships on the actual ocean;
in ships on three actual oceans. For he had sailed
down the Pacific and round the Horn among ice-
bergs and through snowstorms and wild wintry
gales, and had sailed on and turned the corner and
flown northward in the trades and up through the
blistering equatorial waters—and there in his brown
face were the proofs of what he had been through.
We would have sold our souls to Satan for the
privilege of trading places with him.

I saw him when I was out on that Missouri trip
four years ago. He was old then—though not
quite so old as I—and the burden of life was upon
him. He said his granddaughter, twelve years old,
had read my books and would like to see me. It
was a pathetic time, for she was a prisoner in her

room and marked for death. And John knew that she was passing swiftly away. Twelve years old —just her grandfather's age when he rode away on that great journey. In her I seemed to see that boy again. It was as if he had come back out of that remote past and was present before me in his golden youth. Her malady was heart disease, and her brief life came to a close a few days later.

Another of those schoolboys was John Garth. And one of the prettiest of the schoolgirls was Helen Kercheval. They grew up and married. He became a prosperous banker and a prominent and valued citizen; and a few years ago he died, rich and honored. *He died.* It is what I have to say about so many of those boys and girls. The widow still lives, and there are grandchildren. I saw John's tomb when I made that Missouri visit.

Mr. Kercheval had an apprentice in the early days when I was nine years old, and he had also a slave woman who had many merits. But I can't feel either very kindly or forgivingly toward either that good apprentice boy or that good slave woman, for they saved my life. One day when I was playing on a loose log which I supposed was attached to a raft—but it wasn't—it tilted me into Bear Creek. And when I had been under water twice and was coming up to make the third and fatal descent, my fingers appeared above the water and that slave woman seized them and pulled me out. Within a week I was in again, and that apprentice had to come along just at the wrong time, and he plunged in and dived, pawed around on the bottom and found me, and dragged me out, emptied the water out of me, and I was saved again. I was drowned seven times after that before I learned to swim—once in Bear Creek and six times in the Mississippi. I do not now know who the people were who interfered with the intentions of a Providence wiser than themselves, but I hold a grudge against them yet.

Another schoolmate was John Meredith, a boy of a quite uncommonly sweet and gentle disposition. He grew up, and when the Civil War broke out he became a sort of guerrilla chief on the Confederate side, and I was told that in his raids upon Union families in the country parts of Monroe County—in earlier times the friends and familiars of his father—he was remorseless in his devastations and sheddings of blood. It seems almost incredible that this could have been that gentle comrade of my school days; yet it can be true, for Robespierre when he was young was like that. John has been in his grave many and many a year.

Will Bowen was another schoolmate, and so was his brother, Sam, who was his junior by a couple of years. Before the Civil War broke out both became St. Louis and New Orleans pilots. While Sam was still very young he had a curious adventure. He fell in love with a girl of sixteen, only child of a very wealthy German brewer. He wanted to marry her, but he and she both thought that the papa would not only not consent, but would shut his door against Sam. The old man was not so disposed, but they were not aware of that. He had his eye upon them, and it was not a hostile eye. That indiscreet young couple got to living together surreptitiously. Before long the old man died. When the will was examined it was found that he had left the whole of his wealth to Mrs. Samuel A. Bowen. Then the poor things made another mistake. They rushed down to the French suburb, Carondelet, and got a magistrate to marry them and date the marriage back a few months. The old brewer had some nieces and nephews and cousins, and different kinds of assets of that sort, and they traced out the fraud and proved it and got the property. This left Sam with a girl wife on his hands and the necessity of earning a living for her at the pilot wheel. After a few years Sam and another pilot were bringing a boat up from New Orleans when the yellow fever broke out among the few passengers and the crew. Both pilots were stricken with it and there was nobody to take their place at the wheel. The boat was landed at the head of Island 82 to wait for succor. Death came swiftly to both pilots—and there they lie buried, unless the river has cut the graves away and washed the bones into the stream, a thing which has probably happened long ago.

[*Monday, March 12, 1906*

Mr. Clemens comments on the killing of six hundred Moros—men, women and children—in a crater bowl near Jolo in the Philippines—our troops commanded by General Wood.—Contrasts this "battle" with various other details of our military history.—The newspapers' attitude toward the announcements.—The President's message of congratulation,

WE will stop talking about my schoolmates of sixty years ago, for the present, and return to them later. They strongly interest me, and I am not going to leave them alone permanently. Strong as that interest is, it is for the moment pushed out of the way by an incident of to-day, which is still stronger. This incident burst upon the world last Friday in an official cablegram from the commander of our forces in the Philippines to our government at Washington. The substance of it was as follows:

A tribe of Moros, dark-skinned savages, had fortified themselves in the bowl of an extinct crater not many miles from Jolo; and as they were hostiles, and bitter against us because we have been trying for eight years to take their liberties away from them, their presence in that position was a menace. Our commander, Gen. Leonard Wood, ordered a reconnoissance. It was found that the Moros numbered six hundred, counting women and children; that their crater bowl was in the summit of a peak or mountain twenty-two hundred feet above sea level, and very difficult of access for Christian troops and artillery. Then General Wood ordered a surprise, and went along himself to see the order carried out. Our troops climbed the heights by devious and difficult trails, and even took some artillery with them. The kind of artillery is not specified, but in one place it was hoisted up a sharp acclivity by tackle a distance of some three hundred feet. Arrived at the rim of the crater, the battle began. Our soldiers numbered five hundred and forty. They were assisted by auxiliaries consisting of a detachment of native constabulary in our pay —their numbers not given—and by a naval detachment, whose numbers are not stated. But apparently the contending parties were about equal as to number—six hundred men on our side, on the edge of the bowl; six hundred men, women, and children in the bottom of the bowl. Depth of the bowl, 50 feet.

General Wood's order was, "Kill or capture the six hundred."

The battle began—it is officially called by that name—our forces firing down into the crater with their artillery and their deadly small arms of precision; the savages furiously returning the fire, probably with brickbats—though this is merely a surmise of mine, as the weapons used by the savages are not nominated in the cablegram. Heretofore the Moros have used knives and clubs mainly; also ineffectual trade-muskets when they had any.

The official report stated that the battle was fought with prodigious energy on both sides during a day and a half, and that it ended with a complete victory for the American arms. The completeness of the victory is established by this fact: that of the six hundred Moros not one was left alive. The brilliancy of the victory is established by this other fact, to wit: that of our six hundred heroes only fifteen lost their lives.

General Wood was present and looking on. His order had been, "Kill *or* capture those savages." Apparently our little army considered that the "or" left them authorized to kill *or* capture according to taste, and that their taste had remained what it has been for eight years, in our army out there—the taste of Christian butchers.

The official report quite properly extolled and magnified the "heroism" and "gallantry" of our troops, lamented the loss of the fifteen who perished, and elaborated the wounds of thirty-two of our men who suffered injury, and even minutely and faithfully described the nature of the wounds, in the interest of future historians of the United States. It mentioned that a private had one of his elbows scraped by a missile, and the private's name was mentioned. Another private had the end of his nose scraped by a missile. His name was also mentioned—by cable, at one dollar and fifty cents a word.

Next day's news confirmed the previous day's report and named our fifteen killed and thirty-two wounded *again,* and once more described the wounds and gilded them with the right adjectives.

Let us now consider two or three details of our military history. In one of the great battles of the Civil War 10 per cent of the forces engaged on the two sides were killed and wounded. At Waterloo, where four hundred thousand men were present on the two sides, fifty thousand fell, killed and wounded, in five hours, leaving three hundred and fifty thousand sound and all right for further adventures. Eight years ago, when the pathetic comedy called the Cuban War was played, we summoned two hundred and fifty thousand men. We fought a number of showy battles, and when the war was over we had lost two hundred and sixty-eight men out of our two hundred and fifty thousand, in killed and wounded in the field, and just *fourteen times as many* by the gallantry of the army doctors in the hospitals and camps. We did not exterminate the Spaniards—far from it. In each engagement we left an average of *2 per cent* of the enemy killed or crippled on the field.

Contrast these things with the great statistics which have arrived from that Moro crater! There, with six hundred engaged on each side, we lost fifteen men killed outright, and we had thirty-two wounded—counting that nose and that elbow. The enemy numbered six hundred—including women and children—and we abolished them utterly, leaving not even a baby alive to cry for its dead mother. *This is incomparably the greatest victory that was ever achieved by the Christian soldiers of the United States.*

Now then, how has it been received? The splendid news appeared with splendid display heads in every newspaper in this city of four million and thirteen thousand inhabitants, on Friday morning. But there was not a single reference to it in the editorial columns of any one of those newspapers. The news appeared again in all the evening papers of Friday, and again those papers were editorially silent upon our vast achievement. Next day's additional statistics and particulars appeared in all the morning papers, and still without a line of editorial rejoicing or a mention of the matter in any way. These additions appeared in the evening papers of that same day (Saturday) and again without a word of comment. In the columns devoted to correspondence, in the morning and evening papers of Friday and Saturday, nobody said a word about the "battle." Ordinarily those columns are teeming with the passions of the citizen; he lets no incident go by, whether it be large or small, without pouring out his praise or blame, his joy or his indignation, about the matter in the correspondence column. But, as I have said, during those two days he was as silent as the editors themselves. So far as I can find out, there was only one person among our eighty millions who allowed himself the privilege of a public remark on this great occasion —that was the President of the United States. All day Friday he was as studiously silent as the rest. But on Saturday he recognized that his duty required him to say something, and he took his pen and performed that duty. If I know President Roosevelt—and I am sure I do—this utterance cost him more pain and shame than any other that ever issued from his pen or his mouth. I am far from blaming him. If I had been in his place my official duty would have compelled me to say what he said. It was a convention, an old tradition, and he had to be loyal to it.　There was no help for it.　This is what he said:

WOOD, MANILA:

I congratulate you and the officers and men of your command upon the brilliant feat of arms wherein you and they so well upheld the honor of the American flag.

(Signed)　THEODORE ROOSEVELT.

His whole utterance is merely a convention.　Not a word of what he said came out of his heart.　He knew perfectly well that to pen six hundred helpless and weaponless savages in a hole like rats in a trap and massacre them in detail during a stretch of a day and a half, from a safe position on the heights above, was no brilliant feat of arms—and would not have been a brilliant feat of arms even if Christian America, represented by its salaried soldiers, had shot them down with bibles and the Golden Rule instead of bullets.　He knew perfectly well that our uniformed assassins had *not* upheld the honor of the American flag, but had done as they have been doing continuously for eight years in the Philippines—that is to say, they had dishonored it.

The next day, Sunday—which was yesterday—the cable brought us additional news—still more splendid news—still more honor for the flag.　The first display head shouts this information at us in stentorian capitals: "WOMEN SLAIN IN MORO SLAUGHTER."

"Slaughter" is a good word.　Certainly there is

not a better one in the Unabridged Dictionary for this occasion.

The next display line says:

"With Children They Mixed in Mob in Crater, and All Died Together."

They were mere naked savages, and yet there is a sort of pathos about it when that word *children* falls under your eye, for it always brings before us our perfectest symbol of innocence and helplessness; and by help of its deathless eloquence color, creed, and nationality vanish away and we see only that they are children—merely children. And if they are frightened and crying and in trouble, our pity goes out to them by natural impulse. We see a picture. We see the small forms. We see the terrified faces. We see the tears. We see the small hands clinging in supplication to the mother; but we do not see those children that we are speaking about. We see in their places the little creatures whom we know and love.

The next heading blazes with American and Christian glory like to the sun in the zenith:

"Death List is Now 900."

I was never so enthusiastically proud of the flag till now!

The next heading explains how safely our daring soldiers were located. It says:

"Impossible to Tell Sexes Apart in Fierce Battle on Top of Mount Dajo."

The naked savages were so far away, down in the bottom of that trap, that our soldiers could not tell the breasts of a woman from the rudimentary paps of a man—so far away that they couldn't tell a toddling little child from a black six-footer. *This was by all odds the least dangerous battle that Christian soldiers of any nationality were ever engaged in.*

The next heading says:

"Fighting for Four Days."

So our men were at it four days instead of a day and a half. It was a long and happy picnic with nothing to do but sit in comfort and fire the Golden Rule into those people down there and imagine letters to write home to the admiring families, and pile glory upon glory. Those savages fighting for their liberties had the four days, too, but it must have been a sorrowful time for them. Every day they saw two hundred and twenty-five of their number slain, and this provided them grief and mourning for the night—and doubtless without even the relief and consolation of knowing that in the meantime they had slain four of their enemies and wounded some more on the elbow and the nose.

The closing heading says:

"Lieutenant Johnson Blown from Parapet by Exploding Artillery Gallantly Leading Charge."

Lieutenant Johnson had pervaded the cablegrams from the first. He and his wound have sparkled around through them like the serpentine thread of fire that goes excursioning through the black crisp fabric of a fragment of burnt paper. It reminds one of Gillette's comedy farce of a few years ago, "Too Much Johnson." Apparently Johnson was the only wounded man on our side whose wound was worth anything as an advertisement. It has made a great deal more noise in the world than has any similar event since "Humpty Dumpty" fell off the wall and got injured. The official dispatches do not know which to admire most, Johnson's adorable wound or the nine hundred murders. The ecstasies flowing from army headquarters on the other side of the globe to the White House, at one dollar and a half a word, have set fire to similar ecstasies in the President's breast. It appears that the immortally wounded was a Rough Rider under Lieutenant-Colonel Theodore Roosevelt at San Juan Hill—that twin of Waterloo—when the colonel of the regiment, the present Major-General Dr. Leonard Wood, went to the rear to bring up the pills and missed the fight. The President has a warm place in his heart for anybody who was present at that bloody collision of military solar systems, and so he lost no time in cabling to the wounded hero, "How are you?" And got a cable answer, "Fine, thanks." This is historical. This will go down to posterity.

Johnson was wounded in the shoulder with a slug. The slug was in a shell—for the account says the damage was caused by an exploding shell which blew Johnson off the rim. The people down in the hole had no artillery; therefore it was our artillery that blew Johnson off the rim. And so it is now a matter of historical record that the only officer of ours who acquired a wound of advertising dimensions got it at our hands, and not the enemies'. It seems more than probable that if we had placed our soldiers out of the way of our own weapons, we should have come out of the most extraordinary battle in all history without a scratch.

[*Wednesday, March 14, 1906*

Moro slaughter continued.—Luncheon for Geo. Harvey. —Opinions of the guests as to Moro fight.—Cable from General Wood explaining and apologizing.—What became of the wounded?—President Roosevelt's joy over the splendid achievement.—McKinley's joy over capture of Aguinaldo.

THE ominous paralysis continues. There has been a slight sprinkle—an exceedingly slight sprinkle —in the correspondence columns, of angry rebukes of the President for calling this cowardly massacre a "brilliant feat of arms" and for praising our butchers for "holding up the honor of the flag" in that singular way; but there is hardly a ghost of a whisper about the feat of arms in the editorial columns of the papers.

I hope that this silence will continue. It is about as eloquent and as damaging and effective as the most indignant words could be, I think. When a man is sleeping in a noise, his sleep goes placidly on; but if the noise stops, the stillness wakes him. This silence has continued five days now. Surely it must be waking the drowsy nation. Surely the nation must be wondering what it means. A five-day silence following a world-astonishing event has not happened on this planet since the daily newspaper was invented.

At a luncheon party of men convened yesterday to God-speed George Harvey, who is leaving to-day for a vacation in Europe, all the talk was about the brilliant feat of arms; and no one had anything to say about it that either the President or Major-General Dr. Wood or the damaged Johnson would regard as complimentary, or as proper comment to put into our histories. Harvey said he believed that the shock and shame of this episode would eat down deeper and deeper into the hearts of the nation and fester there and produce results. He believed it would destroy the Republican party and President Roosevelt. I cannot believe that the prediction will come true, for the reason that prophecies which promise valuable things, desirable things, good things, worthy things, never come true. Prophecies of this kind are like wars fought in a good cause—they are so rare that they don't count.

Day before yesterday the cable note from the happy General Doctor Wood was still all glorious. There was still proud mention and elaboration of what was called the "desperate hand-to-hand fight," Doctor Wood not seeming to suspect that he was giving himself away, as the phrase goes—since if there was any very desperate hand-to-hand fighting it would necessarily happen that nine hundred hand-to-hand fighters, if really desperate, would surely be able to kill more than fifteen of our men before their last man and woman and child perished.

Very well, there was a new note in the dispatches

yesterday afternoon—just a faint suggestion that Doctor Wood was getting ready to lower his tone and begin to apologize and explain. He announces that he assumes full responsibility for the fight. It indicates that he is aware that there is a lurking disposition here amid all this silence to blame somebody. He says there was "no wanton destruction of women and children in the fight, though many of them were killed by force of necessity because the Moros used them as shields in the hand-to-hand fighting."

This explanation is better than none; indeed, it is considerably better than none. Yet if there was so much hand-to-hand fighting there must have arrived a time, toward the end of the four days' butchery, when only one native was left alive. We had six hundred men present; we had lost only fifteen; why did the six hundred kill that remaining man—or woman, or child?

Doctor Wood will find that explaining things is not in his line. He will find that where a man has the proper spirit in him and the proper force at his command, it is easier to massacre nine hundred unarmed animals than it is to explain why he made it so remorselessly complete. Next he furnishes us this sudden burst of unconscious humor, which shows that he ought to edit his reports before he cables them:

"Many of the Moros feigned death and butchered the American hospital men who were relieving the wounded."

We have the curious spectacle of hospital men

going around trying to relieve the wounded savages
—for what reason? The savages were all mas-
sacred. The plain intention was to massacre them
all and leave none alive. Then where was the use
in furnishing mere temporary relief to a person
who was presently to be exterminated? The dispatches call this battue a "battle." In what way
was it a battle? It has no resemblance to a battle.
In a battle there are always as many as five wounded
men to one killed outright. When this so-called
battle was over, there were certainly not fewer than
two hundred wounded savages lying on the field.
What became of them? Since not one savage was
left alive!

The inference seems plain. We cleaned up our
four days' work and made it complete by butcher-
ing those helpless people.

The President's joy over this achievement brings
to mind an earlier presidential ecstasy. When the
news came, in 1901, that Colonel Funston had pene-
trated to the refuge of the patriot, Aguinaldo, in
the mountains, and had captured him by the use
of these arts, to wit: by forgery, by lies, by dis-
guising his military marauders in the uniform of
the enemy, by pretending to be friends of Aguinaldo's and by disarming suspicion by cordially
shaking hands with Aguinaldo's officers and in that
moment shooting them down—when the cablegram
announcing this "brilliant feat of arms" reached the
White House, the newspapers said that that meek-
est and mildest and gentlest of men, President
McKinley, could not control his joy and gratitude,

but was obliged to express it in motions resembling
a dance.

*Mr. Clemens talks to the West Side Young Men's Chris-
tian Association in the Majestic Theater.—Patrick's funeral.—Luncheon next day at the Hartford Club.—Mr.
Clemens meets eleven of his old friends.—They tell many
stories.—Mr. Twichell's story on board the "Kanawha,"
about Richard Croker's father.—The Mary Ann story!—
Decoration Day and the fiery major and Mr. Twichell's
interrupted prayer.*

YESTERDAY, in the afternoon, I talked to the West
Side Young Men's Christian Association in the Majestic Theater. The audience was to have been
restricted to the membership, or at least to the
membership's sex, but I had asked for a couple of
stage boxes and had invited friends of mine of both
sexes to occupy them. There was trouble out at
the doors and I became afraid that these friends
would not get in. My secretary volunteered to go
out and see if she could find them and rescue them
from the crowd. She was a pretty small person for
such a service, but maybe her lack of dimensions
was in her favor, rather than against it. She plowed
her way through the incoming masculine wave and
arrived outside, where she captured the friends,
and also had an adventure. Just as the police were
closing the doors of the theater and announcing
to the crowd that the place was full and no more

could be admitted, a flushed and excited man crowded his way to the door and got as much as his nose in, but there the officer closed the door and the man was outside. He and my secretary were for the moment the center of attention—she because of her solitariness in that sea of masculinity, and he because he had been defeated before folks, a thing which we all enjoy, even when we are West Side Young Christians and ought to let on that we don't. The man looked down at my secretary—anybody can do that without standing on a chair—and he began pathetically—I say *began* pathetically; the pathos of his manner and his words was confined to his beginning. He began on my secretary, then shifted to the crowd for a finish. He said, "I have been a member of this West Side Young Men's Christian Association in good standing for seven years, and have always done the best I could, yet never once got any reward." He paused half an instant, shot a bitter glance at the closed door, and added, with deep feeling, "It's just my God damned luck."

I think it damaged my speech for my secretary. The speech was well enough—certainly better than the report of it in the papers—but in spite of her compliments, I knew there was nothing in it so good as what she had heard outside; and by the delight which she exhibited in that outsider's eloquence I knew that she knew it.

I will insert here a passage from the newspaper report, because it refers to Patrick.

DEFINITION OF A GENTLEMAN

Mark Twain went on to speak of the man who left $10,000 to disseminate his definition of a gentleman. He denied that he had ever defined one, but said if he did he would include the mercifulness, fidelity, and justice the Scripture read at the meeting spoke of. He produced a letter from William Dean Howells, and said:

"He writes he is just sixty-nine, but I have known him longer than that. 'I was born to be afraid of dying, not of getting old,' he says. Well, I'm the other way. It's terrible getting old. You gradually lose your faculties and fascinations and become troublesome. People try to make you think you are not. But I know I'm troublesome.

"Then he says no part of life is so enjoyable as the eighth decade. That's true. I've just turned it, and I enjoy it very much. 'If old men were not so ridiculous'— Why didn't he speak for himself? 'But,' he goes on, 'they are ridiculous, and they are ugly.' I never saw a letter with so many errors in it. Ugly! I was never ugly in my life! Forty years ago I was not so good-looking. A looking glass then lasted me three months. Now I can wear it out in two days.

" 'You've been up in Hartford burying poor old Patrick. I suppose he was old, too,' says Mr. Howells. No, he was not old. Patrick came to us thirty-six years ago—a brisk, lithe young Irishman. He was as beautiful in his graces as he was in his spirit, and he was as honest a man as ever lived. For twenty-five years he was our coachman, and if I were going to describe a gentleman in detail I would describe Patrick.

"At my own request I was his pallbearer with our old gardener. He drove me and my bride so long ago. As the little children came along he drove them, too. He was all the world to them, and for all in my house he had the same feelings of honor, honesty, and affection.

"He was sixty years old, ten years younger than I. Howells suggests he was old. He was not old. He had the same gracious and winning ways to the end. Patrick was a gentleman, and to him I would apply the lines:

" 'So may I be courteous to men, faithful to friends,
   True to my God, a fragrance in the path I trod.' "

At the funeral I saw Patrick's family. I had seen no member of it for a good many years. The children were men and women. When I had seen them last they were little creatures. So far as I could remember I had not seen them since as little chaps they joined with ours, and with the children of the neighbors, in celebrating Christmas Eve around a Christmas tree in our house, on which occasion Patrick came down the chimney (apparently) disguised as Saint Nicholas, and performed the part to the admiration of the little and the big alike.

John, our old gardener, was a fellow pallbearer with me. The rest were Irish coachmen and laborers—old friends of Patrick. The cathedral was half filled with people.

I spent the night at Twichell's house, that night, and at noon next day at the Hartford Club I met, at a luncheon, eleven of my oldest friends—Charley Clarke, editor of the *Courant;* Judge Hammersley of the Supreme Court; Colonel Cheney; Sam Dunham; Twichell; Rev. Dr. Parker; Charles E. Perkins; Archie Welsh. A deal of pretty jolly reminiscing was done, interspersed with mournings over beloved members of the old comradeship whose names have long ago been carved upon their gravestones.

Several things were told on Twichell illustrative of his wide catholicity of feeling and conduct, and I was able to furnish something in this line myself. Three or four years ago, when Sir Thomas Lipton came over here to race for the *America* cup, I was invited to go with Mr. Rogers and a half a dozen other worldlings in Mr. Rogers's yacht, the *Kanawha,* to see the race. Mr. Rogers is fond of Twichell and wanted to invite him to go also, but was afraid to do it because he thought Twichell would be uncomfortable among those worldlings. I said I didn't think that would be the case. I said Twichell was chaplain in a fighting brigade all through the Civil War, and was necessarily familiar with about all the different kinds of worldlings that could be started; so Mr. Rogers told me—though with many misgivings—to invite him, and that he would do his best to see that the worldlings should modify their worldliness and pay proper respect and deference to Twichell's cloth.

When Twichell and I arrived at the pier at eight in the morning, the launch was waiting for us. All the others were on board. The yacht was anchored out there, ready to sail. Twichell and I went aboard and ascended to the little drawing-room on the upper deck. The door stood open, and as we approached we heard hilarious laughter and talk proceeding from that place, and I recognized that the worldlings were having a worldly good time. But as Twichell appeared in the door all that hilarity ceased as suddenly as if it had been shut off with an electric button, and the gay faces of the worldlings at once put on a most proper and impressive solemnity. The last word we had heard from these people was the name of Richard Croker, the celebrated Tammany leader, all-round blatherskite and chief pillager of the municipal till. Twichell shook hands all around and broke out with:

"I heard you mention Richard Croker. I knew his father very well indeed. He was head teamster in our brigade in the Civil War—the Sickles brigade —a fine man—as fine a man as a person would want to know. He was always splashed over with mud, of course, but that didn't matter. The man inside the muddy clothes was a whole man; and he was educated, he was highly educated. He was a man who had read a great deal. And he was a Greek scholar; not a mere surface scholar, but a real one; used to read aloud from his Greek Testament, and when he hadn't it handy he could recite from it from memory, and he did it well and with spirit. Presently I was delighted to see that every now and then he would come over of a Sunday morning and sit under the trees in our camp with our boys and listen to my ministrations. I couldn't refrain from introducing myself to him—that is, I couldn't refrain from speaking to him about this, and I said: 'Mr. Croker, I want to tell you what a pleasure it is to see you come and sit with my boys and listen to me. For I know what it must cost you to do this, and I want to express my admiration for a man who can put aside his religious prejudices and manifest the breadth and tolerance that you have manifested.' He flushed, and said with eloquent emphasis, 'Mr. Twichell, do you take me for a God damned papist?' "

Mr. Rogers said to me, aside, "This relieves me from my burden of uneasiness."

Twichell, with his big heart, his wide sympathies, and his limitless benignities and charities and generosities, is the kind of person that people of all ages and both sexes fly to for consolation and help in time of trouble. He is always being levied upon by this kind of persons. Years ago—many years ago—a soft-headed young donkey who had been reared under Mr. Twichell's spiritual ministrations sought a private interview—a very private interview—with him, and said:

"Mr. Twichell, I wish you would give me some advice. It is a very important matter with me. It lies near my heart and I want to proceed wisely. Now it is like this: I have been down to the Bermudas on the first vacation I have ever had in my life, and there I met a most charming young lady, native of that place, and I fell in love with her, Mr. Twichell. I fell in love with her, oh so deeply! Well, I can't describe it, Mr. Twichell. I can't describe it. I have never had such feelings before, and they just consume me; they burn me up. When I got back here I found I couldn't think of anybody but that girl. I wanted to write to her, but I was afraid. I was afraid. It seemed too bold. I ought to have taken advice, perhaps— but really I was not myself. I *had* to write—I couldn't help it. So I wrote to her. I wrote to her as guardedly as my feelings would allow— but I had the sense all the time that I was too bold—I was too bold—she wouldn't like it. I— Well, sometimes I would almost think maybe she would answer; but then there would come a colder wave and I would say, 'No, I shall never hear from her—she will be offended.' But at last, Mr. Twichell, a letter *has* come. I don't know how to contain myself. I want to write again, but I may spoil it—I may spoil it—and I want your advice. Tell me if I had better venture. Now here she has written—here is her letter, Mr. Twichell. She says this: she says—she says—'You say in your letter you wish it could be your privilege to see me half your time. How would you like it to see me *all* the time?' What do you think of that, Mr. Twichell? How does that strike you? Do you think she is not offended? Do you think that that indicates a sort of a shadowy leaning toward me? Do you think it, Mr. Twichell? Could you say that?"

"Well," Twichell said, "I would not like to be too sanguine. I would not like to commit myself too far. I would not like to put hopes into your mind which could fail of fruition, but, on the whole —on the whole—daring is a good thing in these cases. Sometimes daring—a bold front—will ac- complish things that timidity would fail to accomplish. I think I would write her—guardedly of course—but write her."

"Oh, Mr. Twichell, oh, you don't know how happy you do make me! I'll write her right away. But I'll be guarded. I'll be careful—careful."

Twichell read the rest of the letter—saw that this girl was just simply throwing herself at this young fellow's head and was going to capture him by fair means or foul, but capture him. But he sent the young fellow away to write the guarded letter.

In due time he came with the girl's second letter and said: "Mr. Twichell, will you read that? Now read that. How does that strike you? Is she kind of leaning my way? I wish you could say so, Mr. Twichell. You see there, what she says. She says —'You offer to send me a present of a ring—' I did it, Mr. Twichell! I declare it was a bold thing —but—but—I couldn't help it. I did that intrepid thing—and that is what she says: 'You offer to send me a ring. But my father is going to take a little vacation excursion in the New England states and he is going to let me go with him. If you should send the ring here it might get lost. We shall be in Hartford a day or two. Won't it be safer to wait till then and you put it on my finger yourself?'

"What do you think of that, Mr. Twichell? How does it strike you? Is she leaning? Is she leaning?"

"Well," Twichell said, "I don't know about that. I must not be intemperate. I must not say things too strongly, for I might be making a mistake. But I think—I think—on the whole I think she is leaning—I do—I think she is leaning—"

"Oh, Mr. Twichell, it does my heart so much good to hear you say that! Mr. Twichell, if there was anything I could do to show my gratitude for those words—well, you see the condition I am in— and to have you say that—"

Twichell said: "Now wait a minute—now let's not make any mistake here. Don't you know that this is a most serious position? It can have the most serious results upon two lives. You know there is such a thing as a mere passing fancy that sets a person's soul on fire for the moment. That person thinks it is love, and that it is permanent love—that it is real love. Then he finds out, by and by, that it was but a momentary insane passion—and then perhaps he has committed himself for life, and he wishes he was out of that predicament. Now let us make sure of this thing. I believe that if you try, and conduct yourself wisely and cautiously—I don't feel sure, but I believe that if you conduct yourself wisely and cautiously you can beguile that girl into marrying you."

"Oh, Mr. Twichell, I can't express—"

"Well, never mind expressing anything. What I am coming at is this: let us make sure of our position. If this is *real* love, go ahead! If it is nothing but a passing fancy, drop it right here, for both your sakes. Now tell me, is it real love? If it is real love how do you arrive at that conclusion? Have you some way of proving to your entire satisfaction that this *is* real, genuine, lasting, permanent love?"

"Mr. Twichell, I can tell you this. You can just judge for yourself. From the time that I was a baby in the cradle up, Mr. Twichell, I have had to sleep close to my mother, with a door open between, because I have always been subject to the most horrible nightmares, and when they break out my mother has to come running from her bed and appease me and comfort me and pacify me. Now then, Mr. Twichell, from the cradle up, whenever I got hit with those nightmare convulsions I have always sung out, 'Mamma, Mamma, Mamma.' Now I sing out, 'Mary Ann, Mary Ann, Mary Ann.' "

So they were married. They moved to the West and we know nothing more about the romance.

Fifteen or twenty years ago, Decoration Day happened to be more like the Fourth of July for temperature than like the 30th of May. Twichell was orator of the day. He pelted his great crowd of old Civil War soldiers for an hour in the biggest church in Hartford, while they mourned and sweltered. Then they marched forth and joined the procession of other old soldiers and tramped through clouds of dust to the cemetery and began to distribute the flags and the flowers—a tiny flag and a small basket of flowers to each military grave. This industry went on and on and on, everybody breathing dust—for there was nothing else to breathe; everybody streaming with perspiration; everybody tired and wishing it was over. At last there was but one basket of flowers left, only one grave still undecorated. A fiery little major, whose patience was all gone, was shouting:

"Corporal Henry Jones, Company C, Fourteenth Connecticut Infantry—"

No response. Nobody seemed to know where that corporal was buried.

The major raised his note a degree or two higher:

"Corporal Henry Jones, Company C, Fourteenth Connecticut Infantry. Doesn't anybody know where that man is buried?"

No response. Once, twice, three times, he shrieked again, with his temper ever rising higher and higher:

"Corporal Henry Jones, Company C, Fourteenth Connecticut Infantry. Doesn't anybody know where that man is buried?"

No response. Then he slammed the basket of flowers on the ground and said to Twichell, "Proceed with the finish."

The crowd massed themselves together around Twichell with uncovered heads, the silence and solemnity interrupted only by subdued sneezings, for these people were buried in the dim cloud of dust. After a pause Twichell began an impressive prayer, making it brief to meet the exigencies of the occasion. In the middle of it he made a pause. The drummer thought he was through, and let fly a rub-a-dub-dub—and the little major stormed out, "*Stop* that drum!" Twichell tried again. He got almost to the last word safely, when somebody trod on a dog and the dog let out a howl of anguish that could be heard beyond the frontier. The major said, "God damn that dog!"—and Twichell said, "Amen."

Schoolmates of sixty years ago: Mary Miller, one of Mr. Clemens's first sweethearts—Artimisia Briggs, another—Mary Lacy, another—Jimmie McDaniel, to whom Mr. Clemens told his first humorous story.—Mr. Richmond, Sunday-school teacher, afterwards owner of Tom Sawyer's cave, which is now being ground into cement.—Hickman, the showy young captain.—Reuel Gridley, and the sack of flour incident.—The Levin Jew boys called Twenty-two. —George Butler, nephew of Ben Butler.—The incident of getting into bed with Will Bowen to catch the measles, and the successful and nearly fatal case which resulted.

WE will return to those school children of sixty years ago. I recall Mary Miller. She was not my first sweetheart, but I think she was the first one that furnished me a broken heart. I fell in love with her when she was eighteen and I nine—but she scorned me, and I recognized that this was a cold world. I had not noticed that temperature before. I believe I was as miserable as a grown man could be. But I think that this sorrow did not remain with me long. As I remember it, I soon transferred my worship to Artimisia Briggs, who was a year older than Mary Miller. When I revealed my passion to her she did not scoff at it. She did not make fun of it. She was very kind and gentle about it. But she was also firm, and said she did not want to be pestered by children.

And there was Mary Lacy. She was a school-mate. But she also was out of my class because of her advanced age. She was pretty wild and de-termined and independent. She was ungovernable, and was considered incorrigible. But that was all a mistake. She married, and at once settled down and became in all ways a model matron and was as highly respected as any matron in the town. Four years ago she was still living, and had been married fifty years.

Jimmie McDaniel was another schoolmate. His age and mine about tallied. His father kept the candy shop and he was the most envied little chap in the town—after Tom Blankenship—for, although we never saw him eating candy, we supposed that it was, nevertheless, his ordinary diet. He pre-tended that he never ate it, didn't care for it be-cause there was nothing forbidden about it—there was plenty of it and he could have as much of it as he wanted. Still, there was circumstantial evi-dence that suggested that he only scorned candy in public to show off, for he had the worst teeth in town. He was the first human being to whom I ever told a humorous story, so far as I can re-member. This was about Jim Wolfe and the cats; and I gave him that tale the morning after that memorable episode. I thought he would laugh his remaining teeth out. I had never been so proud and happy before, and I have seldom been so proud and happy since. I saw him four years ago when I was out there. He was working in a cigar-mak-ing shop. He wore an apron that came down to his knees and a beard that came nearly half as far, and yet it was not difficult for me to recognize him. He had been married fifty-four years. He had many children and grandchildren and great-grandchildren, and also even posterity, they all said —thousands—yet the boy to whom I had told the cat story when we were fourteen years old was still present in that cheerful little old man.

Artimisia Briggs got married not long after refusing me. She married Richmond, the stone mason, who was my Methodist Sunday-school teacher in the earliest days, and he had one distinction which I envied him: He was a very kindly and considerate Sunday-school teacher, and patient and compassionate, so he was the favorite teacher with us little chaps. In that school they had slender oblong pasteboard blue tickets, each with a verse from the Testament printed on it, and you could get a blue ticket by reciting two verses. By reciting five verses you could get three blue tickets, and you could trade these at the bookcase and borrow a book for a week. I was under Mr. Richmond's spiritual care every now and then for two or three years, and he was never hard upon me. I always recited the same five verses every Sunday. He was always satisfied with the performance. He never seemed to notice that these were the same five foolish virgins that he had been hearing about every Sunday for months. I always got my tickets and exchanged them for a book. They were pretty dreary books, for there was not a bad boy in the entire bookcase. They were *all* good boys and good girls and drearily uninteresting, but they were better society than none, and I was glad to have their company and disapprove of it.

Twenty years ago Mr. Richmond had become possessed of Tom Sawyer's cave in the hills three miles from town, and had made a tourist resort of it. In 1849, when the gold-seekers were streaming through our little town of Hannibal, many of our grown men got the gold fever, and I think that all the boys had it. On the Saturday holidays in summertime we used to borrow skiffs whose owners were not present and go down the river three miles to the cave hollow, and there we staked out claims and pretended to dig gold, panning out half a dollar a day at first; two or three times as much, later, and by and by whole fortunes, as our imaginations became inured to the work. Stupid and unprophetic lads! We were doing this in play and never suspecting. Why, that cave hollow and all the adjacent hills were made of gold!—but we did not know it. We took it for dirt. We left its rich secret in its own peaceful possession and grew up in poverty and went wandering about the world struggling for bread—and this because we had not the gift of prophecy. That region was all dirt and rocks to us, yet all it needed was to be ground up and scientifically handled and it was gold. That is to say, the whole region was a cement mine— and they make the finest kind of Portland cement there now, five thousand barrels a day, with a plant that cost $2,000,000.

Several months ago a telegram came to me from

there saying that Tom Sawyer's cave was now be-ing ground into cement. Would I like to say any-thing about it in public? But I had nothing to say. I was sorry we lost our cement mine, but it was not worth while to talk about it at this late day, and, to take it all around, it was a painful subject, anyway. There are seven miles of Tom Sawyer's cave—that is to say, the lofty ridge which conceals that cave stretches down the bank of the Mississippi seven miles to the town of Saverton.

For a little while Reuel Gridley attended that school of ours. He was an elderly pupil; he was perhaps twenty-two or twenty-three years old. Then came the Mexican War and he volunteered. A company of infantry was raised in our town and Mr. Hickman, a tall, straight, handsome athlete of twenty-five, was made captain of it and had a sword by his side and a broad yellow stripe down the leg of his gray uniform pants. And when that company marched back and forth through the streets in its smart uniform—which it did several times a day for drill—its evolutions were attended by all the boys whenever the school hours permitted. I can see that marching company yet, and I can almost feel again the consuming desire that I had to join it. But they had no use for boys of twelve and thirteen, and before I had a chance in another war the desire to kill people to whom I had not been introduced had passed away.

I saw the splendid Hickman in his old age. He seemed about the oldest man I had ever seen—an amazing and melancholy contrast with the showy young captain I had seen preparing his warriors for carnage so many, many years before. Hickman is dead—it is the old story. As Susy said, "What is it all for?"

Reuel Gridley went away to the wars and we heard of him no more for fifteen or sixteen years. Then one day in Carson City, while I was having a difficulty with an editor on the sidewalk—an editor better built for war than I was—I heard a voice say: "Give him the best you've got, Sam. I'm at your back." It was Reuel Gridley. He said he had not recognized me by my face, but by my drawling style of speech.

He went down to the Reese River mines about that time and presently he lost an election bet in his mining camp, and by the terms of it he was obliged to buy a fifty-pound sack of self-rising flour and carry it through the town, preceded by music, and deliver it to the winner of the bet. Of course the whole camp was present and full of fluid and enthusiasm. The winner of the bet put up the sack at auction for the benefit of the United States Sanitary Fund, and sold it. The purchaser put it up for the Fund and sold it. The excitement grew and grew. The sack was sold over and over again for the benefit of the Fund. The news of it came to Virginia City by telegraph. It produced great enthusiasm, and Reuel Gridley was begged by telegraph to bring the sack and have an auction in Virginia City. He brought it. An open barouche was provided, also a brass band. The sack was sold over and over again at Gold Hill, then was brought up to Virginia City toward night and sold—and sold again, netting twenty or thirty thousand dollars for the Sanitary Fund. Gridley carried it across California, selling it at various towns. He sold it for large sums in Sacramento and in San Francisco. He brought it East, sold it in New York and in various other cities, finally carried it out to a great fair at St. Louis, went on selling it, finally made it up into small cakes and sold those at a dollar apiece. First and last, the sack of flour which had originally cost five dollars, perhaps, netted more than two hundred thousand dollars for the Sanitary Fund. Reuel Gridley has been dead these many, many years—it is the old story.

In that school were the first Jews I had ever seen. It took me a good while to get over the awe of it. To my fancy they were clothed invisibly in the damp and cobwebby mold of antiquity. They carried me back to Egypt, and in imagination I moved among the Pharaohs and all the shadowy celebrities of that remote age. The name of the boys was Levin. We had a collective name for them which was the only really large and handsome witticism that was ever born on those premises. We called them Twenty-two—and even when the joke was old and had been worn threadbare we always followed it with the explanation, to make sure that it would be understood, "Twice Levin—twenty-two."

There were other boys whose names remain with me. Irving Ayres—but no matter; he's dead.

George Butler, whom I remember as a child of seven wearing a blue leather belt with a brass buckle, and hated and envied by all the boys on account of it. He was a nephew of General Ben Butler and fought gallantly at Ball's Bluff and in several other actions of the Civil War. He is dead, long and long ago.

Will Bowen (dead long ago), Ed Stevens (dead long ago) and John Briggs were special mates of mine. John is still living.

In 1845, when I was ten years old, there was an epidemic of measles in the town and it made a most alarming slaughter among the little people. There was a funeral almost daily, and the mothers of the town were nearly demented with fright. My mother was greatly troubled. She worried over Pamela and Henry and me, and took constant and extraordinary pains to keep us from coming into contact with the contagion. But upon reflection I believed that her judgment was at fault. It seemed to me that I could improve upon it if left to my own devices. I cannot remember now whether I was frightened about the measles or not, but I clearly remember that I grew very tired of the suspense I suffered on account of being continually under the threat of death. I remember that I got so weary of it and so anxious to have the matter settled one way or the other, and promptly, that this anxiety spoiled my days and my nights. I had no pleasure in them. I made up my mind to end this suspense and settle this matter one way or the other and be done with it. Will Bowen was dangerously ill with the measles and I thought I would go down there and catch them. I entered the house by the front way and slipped along through rooms and halls, keeping sharp watch against discovery, and at last I reached Will's bedroom in the rear of the house on the second floor and got into it uncaptured. But that was as far as my victory reached. His mother caught me there a moment later and snatched me out of the house and gave me a most competent scolding and drove me away. She was so scared that she could hardly get her words out, and her face was white. I saw that I must manage better next time, and I did. I hung about the lane at the rear of the house and watched through cracks in the fence until I was convinced that the conditions were favorable. Then I slipped through the back yard and up the back way and got into the room and into the bed with Will Bowen without being observed. I don't know how long I was in the bed. I only remember that Will Bowen, as society, had no value for me, for he was too sick to even notice that I was there. When I heard his mother coming I covered up my head, but that device was a failure. It was dead summertime—the cover was nothing more than a limp blanket or sheet, and anybody could see that there were two of us under it. It didn't remain two very long. Mrs. Bowen snatched me out of that bed and conducted me home herself, with a grip on my collar which she never loosened until she delivered me into my mother's hands along with her opinion of that kind of a boy.

It was a good case of measles that resulted. It brought me within a shade of death's door. It brought me to where I no longer felt any interest in anything, but, on the contrary, felt a total absence of interest—which was most placid and tranquil and sweet and delightful and enchanting. I have never enjoyed anything in my life any more than I enjoyed dying that time. I was, in effect, dying. The word had been passed and the family notified to assemble around the bed and see me off. I knew them all. There was no doubtfulness in my vision. They were all crying, but that did not affect me. I took but the vaguest interest in it, and that merely because I was the center of all this emotional attention and was gratified by it and felt complimented.

When Doctor Cunningham had made up his mind that nothing more could be done for me he put bags of hot ashes all over me. He put them on my breast, on my wrists, on my ankles; and so, very much to his astonishment—and doubtless to my regret—he dragged me back into this world and set me going again.

[*Wednesday, March 21, 1906*

Mental telegraphy.—Letter from Mr. Jock Brown.— Search for Dr. John Brown's letters a failure.—Mr. Twichell and his wife, Harmony, have an adventure in Scotland.—Mr. Twichell's picture of a military execution. —Letter relating to foundation of the Players' Club.— The mismanagement which caused Mr. Clemens to be expelled from the club.—He is now an honorary member.

CERTAINLY mental telegraphy is an industry which is always silently at work—oftener than otherwise, perhaps, when we are not suspecting that it is affecting our thought. A few weeks ago when

I was dictating something about Dr. John Brown of Edinburgh and our pleasant relations with him during six weeks there, and his pleasant relations with our little child, Susy, he had not been in my mind for a good while—a year, perhaps—but he has often been in my mind since, and his name has been frequently upon my lips and as frequently falling from the point of my pen. About a fortnight ago I began to plan an article about him and about Marjorie Fleming, whose first biographer he was, and yesterday I began the article. To-day comes a letter from his son Jock, from whom I had not previously heard for a good many years. He has been engaged in collecting his father's letters for publication. This labor would naturally bring me into his mind with some frequency, and I judge that his mind telegraphed his thoughts to me across the Atlantic. I imagine that we get most of our thoughts out of somebody else's head, by mental telegraphy— and not always out of heads of acquaintances, but, in the majority of cases, out of the heads of strangers; strangers far removed—Chinamen, Hindus, and all manner of remote foreigners whose language we should not be able to understand, but whose thoughts we can read without difficulty.

> 7 GREENHILL PLACE,
> EDINBURGH,
> *8th March, 1906.*

DEAR MR. CLEMENS:

I hope you remember me, Jock, son of Dr. John Brown. At my father's death I handed to Dr. J. T. Brown all the letters I had to my father, as he intended to write his life, being his cousin and life-long friend. He did write a memoir, published after his death in 1901, but he made no use of the letters and it was little more than a critique of his writings. If you care to see it I shall send it. Among the letters which I got back in 1902 were some from you and Mrs. Clemens. I have now got a large number of letters written by my father between 1830 and 1882 and intend publishing a selection in order to give the public an idea of the man he was. This I think they will do. Miss E. T. MacLaren is to add the necessary notes. I now write to ask you if you have letters from him and if you will let me see them and use them. I enclose letters from yourself and Mrs. Clemens which I should like to use, 15 sheets typewritten. Though I did not write as I should to you on the death of Mrs. Clemens, I was very sorry to hear of it through the papers, and as I now read these letters, she rises before me, gentle and lovable as I knew her. I do hope you will let me use her letter, it is most beautiful. I also hope you will let me use yours. . . .

I am

Yours very sincerely,

JOHN BROWN.

We have searched for Doctor John's letters, but without success. I do not understand this. There ought to be a good many, and none should be missing, for Mrs. Clemens held Doctor John in such love and reverence that his letters were sacred things in her eyes and she preserved them and took watchful care of them. During our ten years' absence in Europe many letters and like memorials became scattered and lost, but I think it unlikely that

Doctor John's have suffered this fate. I think we shall find them yet.

These thoughts about Jock bring back to me the Edinburgh of thirty-three years ago, and the thought of Edinburgh brings to my mind one of Rev. Joe Twichell's adventures. A quarter of a century ago Twichell and Harmony, his wife, visited Europe for the first time, and made a stay of a day or two in Edinburgh. They were devotees of Scott, and they devoted that day or two to ransacking Edinburgh for things and places made sacred by contact with the Magician of the North. Toward midnight, on the second night, they were returning to their lodgings on foot; a dismal and steady rain was falling, and by consequence they had George Street all to themselves. Presently the rainfall became so heavy that they took refuge from it in a deep doorway, and there in the black darkness they discussed with satisfaction all the achievements of the day. Then Joe said:

"It has been hard work, and a heavy strain on the strength, but we have our reward. There isn't a thing connected with Scott in Edinburgh that we haven't seen or touched—not one. I mean the things a stranger *could* have access to. There is *one* we haven't seen, but it's not accessible—a private collection of relics and memorials of Scott of great interest, but I do not know where it is. I can't get on the track of it. I wish we could, but we can't. We've got to give the idea up. It would be a grand thing to have a sight of that collection, Harmony."

A voice out of the darkness said, "Come upstairs and I will show it to you."

And the voice was as good as its word. The voice belonged to the gentleman who owned the collection. He took Joe and Harmony upstairs, fed them and refreshed them; and while they examined the collection he chatted and explained. When they left at two in the morning they realized that they had had the star time of their trip.

Joe has always been on hand when anything was going to happen—except once. He got delayed in some vexatious and unaccountable way, or he would have been blown up at Petersburg when the mined defenses of that place were flung heavenward in the Civil War.

When I was in Hartford the other day he told me about another of his long string of providential opportunities. I think he thinks Providence is always looking out for him when interesting things are going to happen. This was the execution of some deserters during the Civil War. When we read about such things in history we always have the same picture—blindfolded men kneeling with their heads bowed; a file of stern and alert soldiers fronting them with their muskets ready; an austere officer in uniform standing apart who gives sharp terse orders: "Make ready. Take aim. Fire." There is a belch of flame and smoke, the victims fall forward, expiring, the file shoulders arms, wheels, marches erect and stiff-legged off the field, and the incident is closed.

Joe's picture is different. And I suspect that it

is the true one—the common one. In this picture the deserters requested that they might be allowed to stand, not kneel; that they might not be blindfolded, but permitted to look the firing file in the eye. These requests were granted. The men stood erect and soldierly; they kept their color, they did not blench; their eyes were steady. But these things could not be said of any other of the persons present. A general of brigade sat upon his horse, white-faced—white as a corpse. The officer commanding the squad was white-faced—white as a corpse. The firing file were white-faced and their forms wobbled so that the wobble was transmitted to their muskets when they took aim. The officer of the squad could not command his voice, and his tone was weak and poor, not brisk and stern. When the file had done its deadly work it did not march away martially erect and stiff-legged. It wobbled.

This picture commends itself to me as being the truest one that any one has yet furnished of a military execution.

In searching for Doctor Brown's letters—a failure—we have made a find which we were not expecting. Evidently it marks the foundation of the Players' Club, and so it has value for me.

DALY'S THEATRE,
NEW YORK, *Jan. 2, 1888.*

Mr. Augustin Daly will be very much pleased to have Mr. S. L. Clemens meet Mr. Booth, Mr. Barrett and Mr. Palmer and a few friends at lunch on Friday next, January 6th (at one o'clock in Delmonico's) to discuss the formation of a new club which it is thought will claim your interest.

R.S.V.P.

All the founders, I think, were present at that luncheon—among them Booth, Barrett, Palmer, General Sherman, Bispham, Aldrich, and the rest. I do not recall the other names. I think Laurence Hutton states in one of his books that the club's name—The Players'—had been already selected and accepted before this luncheon took place, but I take that to be a mistake. I remember that several names were proposed, discussed, and abandoned at the luncheon; that finally Thomas Bailey Aldrich suggested that compact and simple name, The Players'; and that even that happy title was not immediately accepted. However, the discussion was very brief. The objections to it were easily routed and driven from the field, and the vote in its favor was unanimous.

I lost my interest in the club three years ago—for cause—but it has lately returned to me, to my great satisfaction. Mr. Booth's bequest was a great and generous one—but he left two. The other one was not much of a benefaction. It was a relative of his who needed a support. As secretary he governed the club and its board of managers like an autocrat from the beginning until three or four months ago, when he retired from his position superannuated. From the beginning, I left my dues and costs to be paid by my business agent in Hartford—Mr. Whitmore. He attended to all business of mine. I interested myself in none of it. When we went to Europe in '91 I left a written order in the secretary's office continuing Whitmore in his function of paymaster of my club dues. Nothing happened until a year had gone by. Then a bill for dues reached me in Europe. I returned it to the secretary and reminded him of my order, which had not been changed. Then for a couple of years the bills went to Whitmore, after which a bill came to me in Europe. I returned it with the previous remarks repeated. But about every two years the sending of bills to me would be resumed. I sent them back with the usual remarks. Twice the bills were accompanied by offensive letters from the secretary. These I answered profanely. At last we came home, in 1901. No bills came to me for a year. Then we took a residence at Riverdale-on-the-Hudson, and straightway came a Players' bill for dues. I was aweary, aweary, and I put it in the waste basket. Ten days later the bill came again, and with it a shadowy threat. I waste-basketed it. After another ten days the bill came once more, and this time the threat was in a concreted condition. It said very peremptorily that if the bill were not paid within a week I would be expelled from the club and posted as a delinquent. This went the way of its predecessors, into the waste basket. On the named day I was posted as expelled.

Robert Reid, David Munro, and other special friends in the club were astonished and put themselves in communication with me to find out what this strange thing meant. I explained to them. They wanted me to state the case to the management and require a reconsideration of the decree of expulsion, but I had to decline that proposition. And therefore things remained as they were until a few months ago, when the ancient secretary retired from the autocracy. The boys thought that my return to the club would be plain and simple sailing now, but I thought differently. I was no longer a member. I could not become a member without consenting to be voted for by the board, like any other candidate, and I would not do that. The management had expelled me upon the mere statement of a clerk that I was a delinquent. They had not asked me to testify in my defense. They might properly argue from that that I had not all of a sudden become a rascal, and that I might be able to explain the situation if asked. The board's whole proceeding had been like *all* the board's proceedings from the beginning—arbitrary, insolent, stupid. That board's proper place, from the beginning, was the idiot asylum. I could not allow myself to be voted for again, because from my view of the matter I had never lawfully and legitimately ceased to be a member. However, a way fair and honorable to all concerned was easily found to bridge the separating crack. I was made an honorary member, and I have been glad to resume business at the old stand.

[*Friday, March 22, 1906*

Susy's biography.—Langdon's illness and death.—Susy tells of interesting men whom her father met in England

and Scotland—Dr. John Brown, Mr. Charles Kingsley,
Mr. Henry M. Stanley, Sir Thomas Hardy, Mr. Henry
Irving, Robert Browning, Sir Charles Dilke, Charles Reade,
William Black, Lord Houghton, Frank Buckland, Tom
Hughes, Anthony Trollope, Tom Hood, Doctor Macdon-
ald, and Harrison Ainsworth.—Mr. Clemens tells of meet-
ing Lewis Carroll—of luncheon at Lord Houghton's.—
Letters from Mr. and Mrs. Clemens to Doctor Brown.—
Mr. Clemens's regret that he did not take Mrs. Clemens
for a last visit to Doctor Brown.

FROM SUSY'S BIOGRAPHY

I STOPPED in the middle of mamma's early history to tell
about our tripp to Vassar because I was afraid I would
forget about it, now I will go on where I left off. Some
time after Miss Emma Nigh died papa took mamma and
little Langdon to Elmira for the summer. When in Elmira Langdon began to fail but I think mamma did not
know just what was the matter with him.

I was the cause of the child's illness. His mother
trusted him to my care and I took him for a long
drive in an open barouche for an airing. It was a
raw, cold morning, but he was well wrapped about
with furs and, in the hands of a careful person,
no harm would have come to him. But I soon
dropped into a reverie and forgot all about my
charge. The furs fell away and exposed his bare
legs. By and by the coachman noticed this, and
I arranged the wraps again, but it was too late.
The child was almost frozen. I hurried home with
him. I was aghast at what I had done, and I feared

the consequences. I have always felt shame for that treacherous morning's work and have not allowed myself to think of it when I could help it. I doubt if I had the courage to make confession at that time. I think it most likely that I have never confessed until now.

FROM SUSY'S BIOGRAPHY

At last it was time for papa to return to Hartford, and Langdon was real sick at that time, but still mamma decided to go with him, thinking the journey might do him good. But after they reached Hartford he became very sick, and his trouble prooved to be diptheeria. He died about a week after mamma and papa reached Hartford. He was burried by the side of grandpa at Elmira, New York. [Susy rests there with them.—S. L. C.] After that, mamma became very very ill, so ill that there seemed great danger of death, but with a great deal of good care she recovered. Some months afterward mamma and papa [and Susy, who was perhaps fourteen or fifteen months old at the time.—S. L. C.] went to Europe and stayed for a time in Scotland and England. In Scotland mamma and papa became very well equanted with Dr. John Brown, the author of "Rab and His Friends," and he met, but was not so well equanted with, Mr. Charles Kingsley, Mr. Henry M. Stanley, Sir Thomas Hardy grandson of the Captain Hardy to whom Nellson said "Kiss me Hardy," when dying on shipboard, Mr. Henry Irving, Robert Browning, Sir Charles Dilke, Mr. Charles Reade, Mr. William Black, Lord Houghton, Frank Buckland, Mr. Tom Hughes, Anthony Trollope, Tom Hood, son of the poet—and mamma and papa were quite well equanted with Dr. Macdonald and family, and papa met Harison Ainsworth.

I remember all these men very well indeed, except the last one. I do not recall Ainsworth. By my count, Susy mentions fourteen men. They are all dead except Sir Charles Dilke and Mr. Tom Hughes.

We met a great many other interesting people, among them Lewis Carroll, author of the immortal *Alice*—but he was only interesting to look at, for he was the stillest and shyest full-grown man I have ever met except "Uncle Remus." Doctor Macdonald and several other lively talkers were present, and the talk went briskly on for a couple of hours, but Carroll sat still all the while except that now and then he answered a question. His answers were brief. I do not remember that he elaborated any of them.

At a dinner at Smalley's we met Herbert Spencer. At a large luncheon party at Lord Houghton's we met Sir Arthur Helps, who was a celebrity of world-wide fame at the time, but is quite forgotten now. Lord Elcho, a large, vigorous man, sat at some distance down the table. He was talking earnestly about Godalming. It was a deep and flowing and unarticulated rumble, but I got the Godalming pretty clearly every time it broke free of the rumble, and as all the strength was on the first end of the word it startled me every time, because it sounded so like swearing. In the middle of the luncheon Lady Houghton rose, remarked to the guests on her right and on her left in a matter-of-fact way, "Excuse me, I have an engagement," and without further ceremony she went off to meet it. This would have been doubtful etiquette in America. Lord Houghton told a number of delightful stories. He told them in French, and I lost nothing of them but the nubs.

I will insert here one or two of the letters referred to by Jock Brown in the letter which I received from him a day or two ago, and which we copied into yesterday's record:

June 22, 1876.

DEAR DOCTOR BROWN:

Indeed I was a happy woman to see the familiar handwriting. I do hope that we shall not have to go so long again without a word from you. I wish you could come over to us for a season; it seems as if it would do you good, you and yours would be so very welcome.

We are now where we were two years ago, on the farm on the top of a high hill where my sister spends her summers. The children are grown fat and hearty, feeding chickens and ducks twice a day, and are keenly alive to all the farm interests. Mr. J. T. Fields was with us with his wife a short time ago, and you may be sure we talked most affectionately of you. We do so earnestly desire that you may continue to improve in health; do let us know of your welfare as often as possible. Love to your sister. Kind regards to your son please.

As ever affectionately your friend,
LIVY L. CLEMENS.

DEAR DOCTOR BROWN:

We had grown so very anxious about you that it was a great pleasure to see the dear, familiar handwriting again, but the contents of the letter did make us *inexpressibly sad.*

We have talked so much since about your coming to see us. Would not the change do you good? Could you not trust yourself with us? We would do everything to make you comfortable and happy that we could, and you have so many admirers in America that would be so happy and proud to welcome you. Is it not possible for you to come? Perhaps the entire change would give you a new and healthier lease of life.

Our children are both well and happy; I wish that you could see them. Susie is very motherly to the little one. Mr. Clemens is hard at work on a new book now. He has a new book of sketches recently out, which he is going to send you in a few days; most of the sketches are old, but some few are new.

Oh Doctor Brown how can you speak of your life as a wasted one? What you have written has alone done an *immense* amount of good, and I know for I speak from experience that one must get good every time they meet and chat with you. I receive good every time I even *think* of you. Can a life that produces such an effect on others be a wasted life? I feel that while you live the world is sweeter and better. You ask if Clara is "queer and wistful and commanding," like your Susie. We think she is more queer, (more quaint) perhaps more commanding, but not nearly so wistful in her ways as "your Susie." . . . I must leave a place for Mr. C. Do you think about coming to us. Give my love to your sister and your son.

Affectionately,

LIVY L. CLEMENS.

·

DEAR DOCTOR, if you and your son Jock only *would* run over here! What a welcome we would give you! and besides, you would forget cares and the troubles that come of them. To forget pain is to be painless; to forget care is to be rid of it; to go abroad is to accomplish both. Do try the prescription!

> Always with love,
> SAML. L. CLEMENS.

P.S. Livy, you haven't *signed* your letter. Don't forget *that*. S. L. C.

P.P.S. I hope you will excuse Mr. Clemens's P.S. to me; it is characteristic for him to put it right on the letter. *Livy* L. C.

(S. L. C. to Dr. Brown's Son, Jock.)

> HARTFORD, *June 1, 1882.*

MY DEAR MR. BROWN:

I was three thousand miles from home, at breakfast in New Orleans, when the damp morning paper revealed the sorrowful news among the cable dispatches. There was no place in America, however remote, or however rich or poor or high or humble, where words of mourning for your honoured father were not uttered that morning, for his works had made him known and loved all over the land. To Mrs. Clemens and me, the loss is a personal one, and our grief the grief which one feels for one who was peculiarly near and dear. Mrs. Clemens has never ceased to express regret that we came away from England the last time without going to see him, and often we have since projected a voyage across the Atlantic for the sole purpose of taking him by the hand and looking into his kind eyes once more before he should be called to his rest.

We both thank you greatly for the Edinburgh papers which you sent. My wife and I join in affectionate re-membrances and greetings to yourself and your aunt, and in the sincere tender of our sympathies.

> Faithfully yours,
> S. L. CLEMENS.

P.S. Our Susy is still "Megalopis." He gave her that name.

Can you spare us a photograph of your father? We have none but the one taken in group with ourselves.

It was my fault that she never saw Doctor John in life again. How many crimes I committed against that gentle and patient and forgiving spirit! I always told her that if she died first, the rest of my life would be made up of self-reproaches for the tears I had made her shed. And she always replied that if I should pass from life first, she would never have to reproach herself with having loved me the less devotedly or the less constantly because of those tears. We had this conversation again, and for the thousandth time, when the night of death was closing about her—though we did not suspect that.

In the letter last quoted above, I say, "Mrs. Clemens has never ceased to express regret that we came away from England the last time without going to see him." I think that that was intended to convey the impression that *she* was a party concerned in our leaving England without going to see him. It is not so. She urged me, she begged me, she implored me to take her to Edinburgh to see Doctor John—but I was in one of my devil moods, and I would not do it. I would not do it because I should have been obliged to continue the courier in service until we got back to Liverpool. It seemed to me that I had endured him as long as I could. I wanted to get aboard ship and be done with him. How childish it all seems now! And how brutal—that I could not be moved to confer upon my wife a precious and lasting joy because it would cause me a small inconvenience. I have known few meaner men than I am. By good fortune this feature of my nature does not often get to the surface, and so I doubt if any member of my family except my wife ever suspected how much of that feature there was in me. I suppose it never failed to arrive at the surface when there was opportunity, but it was as I have said—the opportunities have been so infrequent that this worst detail of my character has never been known to any but two persons— Mrs. Clemens, who suffered from it, and I, who suffer from the remembrance of the tears it caused her.

[Friday, March 23, 1906

Some curious letter superscriptions which have come to Mr. Clemens.—Our inefficient postal system under Post-master-General Key.—Reminiscences of Mrs. Harriet Beecher Stowe.—Story of Rev. Charlie Stowe's little boy.

A GOOD many years ago Mrs. Clemens used to keep as curiosities some of the odd and strange superscriptions that decorated letters that came to me from strangers in out-of-the-way corners of the earth. One of these superscriptions was the work of Dr. John Brown, and the letter must have been the first one he wrote me after we came home from Europe in August or September, '74. Evidently the

Doctor was guessing at our address from memory, for he made an amusing mess of it. The superscription was as follows:

> Mr. S. L. Clemens,
> (Mark Twain),
> Hartford, N. Y.
> Near Boston, U. S. A.

Now then comes a fact which is almost incredible, to wit: the New York Post Office, which did not contain a single salaried idiot who could not have stated promptly who the letter was for and to what town it should go, actually sent that letter to a wee little hamlet hidden away in the remotenesses of the vast State of New York—for what reason? Because that lost and never previously heard-of hamlet was named Hartford. The letter was returned to the New York Post Office from that hamlet. It was returned innocent of the suggestion, "Try Hartford, Connecticut," although the hamlet's postmaster knew quite well that that was the Hartford the writer of the letter was seeking. Then the New York Post Office opened the envelope, got Doctor John's address out of it, then inclosed it in a fresh envelope and sent it back to Edinburgh. Doctor John then got my address from Menzies, the publisher, and sent the letter to me again. He also inclosed the former envelope—the one that had had the adventures—and his anger at our postal system was like the fury of an angel. He came the nearest to being bitter and offensive than ever he came in his life, I suppose. He said that in Great Britain it was the postal department's boast that by no ingenuity could a man so disguise and conceal a Smith or a Jones or a Robinson in a letter address that the department couldn't find that man, whereas —then he let fly at our system, which was apparently designed to defeat a letter's attempts to get to its destination when humanly possible.

Doctor John was right about our department— at that time. But that time did not last long. I think Postmaster-General Key was in office then. He was a new broom, and he did some astonishing sweeping for a while. He made some cast-iron rules which worked great havoc with the nation's correspondence. It did not occur to him—rational things seldom occurred to him—that there were several millions of people among us who seldom wrote letters; who were utterly ignorant of postal rules, and who were quite sure to make blunders in writing letter addresses whenever blunders were possible, and that it was the government's business to do the very best it could by the letters of these innocents and help them get to their destinations, instead of inventing ways to block the road. Key suddenly issued some boiler-iron rules—one of them was that a letter must go to the place named on the envelope, and the effort to find its man must stop there. He must not be searched for. If he wasn't at the place indicated the letter must be returned to the sender. In the case of Doctor John's letter the Post Office had a wide discretion—not so very wide, either. It must go to a Hartford. That Hartford must be near Boston; it must also be in the State of New York. It went to the Hartford that was farthest from Boston, but it filled the requirement of being in the State of New York—and it got defeated.

Another rule instituted by Key was that letter superscriptions could not end with "Philadelphia"— or "Chicago," or "San Francisco," or "Boston," or "New York," but, in every case, must add the *state*, or go to the Dead Letter Office. Also, you could not say "New York, N. Y.," you must add the word *City* to the first "New York" or the letter must go to the Dead Letter Office.

During the first thirty days of the dominion of this singular rule sixteen hundred thousand tons of letters, more or less, went to the Dead Letter Office from the New York Post Office alone. The Dead Letter Office could not contain them and they had to be stacked up outside the building. There was not room outside the building inside the city, so they were formed into a rampart around the city; and if they had had it there during the Civil War we should not have had so much trouble and uneasiness about an invasion of Washington by the Confederate armies. They could neither have climbed over or under that breastwork nor bored nor blasted through it. Mr. Key was soon brought to a more rational frame of mind.

Then a letter arrived for me inclosed in a fresh envelope. It was from a village priest in Bohemia or Galicia, and was boldly addressed:

MARK TWAIN
SOMEWHERE.

It had traveled over several European countries; it had met with hospitality and with every possible assistance during its wide journey; it was ringed all over, on both sides, with a chain-mail mesh of postmarks—there were nineteen of them altogether. And one of them was a New York postmark. The postal hospitalities had ceased at New York—within three hours and a half of my home. There the letter had been opened, the priest's address ascertained, and the letter had then been returned to him, as in the case of Dr. John Brown.

Among Mrs. Clemens's collection of odd addresses was one on a letter from Australia, worded thus:

MARK TWAIN
GOD KNOWS WHERE.

That superscription was noted by newspapers [1]
here and there and yonder while it was on its travels,
and doubtless suggested another odd superscription
invented by some stranger in a far-off land—and
this was the wording of it:

MARK TWAIN,
SOMEWHERE,
(TRY SATAN).

That stranger's trust was not misplaced. Satan
courteously sent it along.

This morning's mail brings another of these nov-
elties. It comes from France—from a young English girl—and is addressed:

MARK TWAIN,
c/o PRESIDENT ROOSEVELT,
THE WHITE HOUSE,
WASHINGTON,
AMERICA, U. S. A.

It was not delayed, but came straight along bearing the Washington postmark of yesterday.

In a diary which Mrs. Clemens kept for a little
while, a great many years ago, I find various mentions of Mrs. Harriet Beecher Stowe, who was a
near neighbor of ours in Hartford, with no fences
between. And in those days she made as much
use of our grounds as of her own, in pleasant
weather. Her mind had decayed and she was a

---

[1] This letter was originally mailed in New York by Brander
Matthews and Francis Wilson.

pathetic figure. She wandered about all the day long in the care of a muscular Irishwoman. Among the colonists of our neighborhood the doors always stood open in pleasant weather. Mrs. Stowe entered them at her own free will, and as she was always softly slippered and generally full of animal spirits, she was able to deal in surprises, and she liked to do it. She would slip up behind a person who was deep in dreams and musings and fetch a war whoop that would jump that person out of his clothes. And she had other moods. Sometimes we would hear gentle music in the drawing-room and would find her there at the piano singing ancient and melancholy songs with infinitely touching effect.

Her husband, old Professor Stowe, was a picturesque figure. He wore a broad slouch hat. He was a large man, and solemn. His beard was white and thick and hung far down on his breast. His nose was enlarged and broken up by a disease which made it look like a cauliflower. The first time our little Susy ever saw him she encountered him on the street near our house and came flying wide-eyed to her mother and said, "Santa Claus has got loose."

[*Monday, March 26, 1906*

Mr. Clemens comments on newspaper clipping.—Tells Mr. Howells the scheme of this autobiography.—Tells the newspaper account of girl who tried to commit suicide. —Newspapers in remote villages and in great cities con-

trasted.—Remarks about Capt. E. L. Marsh and Dick Higham.—Higbie's letter, and "Herald" letter to Higbie.

BABY ADVICE IN A CAR

OLD MAN GOT IT, FIVE-YEAR-OLD GAVE IT, MOTHER SAID, "SHUT UP"

A benevolent-looking old man clung to a strap in a crowded Broadway car bound uptown Saturday afternoon. In a corner seat in front of him huddled a weak-looking little woman who clasped a baby to her breast. Beside her sat another child, a girl perhaps five years old, who seemed to be attracted by the old man's kindly face, for she gazed at him and the baby with her bright, intelligent eyes opened wide. He smiled at her interest and said to her:

"My! What a nice baby! Just such a one as I was looking for. I am going to take it."

"You can't," declared the little girl, quickly. "She's my sister."

"What! Won't you give her to me?"

"No, I won't."

"But," he insisted, and there was real wistfulness in his tones, "I haven't a baby in my home."

"Then write to God. He'll send you one," said the child confidently.

The old man laughed. So did the other passengers. But the mother evidently scented blasphemy.

"Tillie," said she, "shut up and behave yourself!"

That is a scrap which I have cut from this morning's *Times*. It is very prettily done, charmingly done; done with admirable ease and grace—with the ease and grace that are born of feeling and sympathy, as well as of practice with the pen. Every now and then a newspaper reporter astonishes me with felicities like this. I was a newspaper reporter myself forty-four years ago, and during three subsequent years—but as I remember it I and my comrades never had time to cast our things in a fine literary mold. That scrap will be just as touching and just as beautiful three hundred years hence as it is now.

I intend that this autobiography shall become a model for all future autobiographies when it is published, after my death, and I also intend that it shall be read and admired a good many centuries because of its form and method—a form and method whereby the past and the present are constantly brought face to face, resulting in contrasts which newly fire up the interest all along like contact of flint with steel. Moreover, this autobiography of mine does not select from my life its showy episodes, but deals merely in the common experiences which go to make up the life of the average human being, and the narrative must interest the average human being because these episodes are of a sort which he is familiar with in his own life, and in which he sees his own life reflected and set down in print. The usual, conventional autobiographer seems to particularly hunt out those occasions in his career when he came into contact with celebrated persons, whereas his contacts with the uncelebrated were just as interesting to him, and would be to his reader, and were vastly more numerous than his collisions with the famous.

Howells was here yesterday afternoon, and I

told him the whole scheme of this autobiography
and its apparently systemless system—only apparently systemless, for it is not that. It is a deliberate
system, and the law of the system is that I shall
talk about the matter which for the moment interests me, and cast it aside and talk about something else the moment its interest for me is exhausted. It is a system which follows no charted
course and is not going to follow any such course.
It is a system which is a complete and purposed
jumble—a course which begins nowhere, follows no
specified route, and can never reach an end while
I am alive, for the reason that if I should talk
to the stenographer two hours a day for a hundred
years, I should still never be able to set down a
tenth part of the things which have interested me
in my lifetime. I told Howells that this autobiography of mine would live a couple of thousand years
without any effort and would then take a fresh start
and live the rest of the time.

He said he believed it would, and asked me if I
meant to make a library of it.

I said that that was my design, but that if I
should live long enough the set of volumes could
not be contained merely in a city, it would require
a state, and that there would not be any multi-
billionaire alive, perhaps, at any time during its
existence who would be able to buy a full set, except
on the installment plan.

Howells applauded, and was full of praises and
indorsement, which was wise in him and judicious.
If he had manifested a different spirit I would have

thrown him out of the window. I like criticism, but it must be my way.

Day before yesterday there was another of those happy literary efforts of the reporters, and I meant to cut it out and insert it to be read with a sad pleasure in future centuries, but I forgot and threw the paper away. It was a brief narrative, but well stated. A poor little starved girl of sixteen, clothed in a single garment, in midwinter (albeit properly speaking this is spring), was brought in her pendent rags before a magistrate by a policeman, and the charge against her was that she had been found trying to commit suicide. The judge asked her why she was moved to that crime, and she told him, in a low voice broken by sobs, that her life had become a burden which she could no longer bear; that she worked sixteen hours a day in a sweat shop; that the meager wage she earned had to go toward the family support; that her parents were never able to give her any clothes or enough to eat; that she had worn this same ruined garment as long back as she could remember; that her poor companions were her envy because often they had a penny to spend for some pretty trifle for themselves; that she could not remember when she had had a penny for such a purpose. The court, the policemen, and the other spectators cried with her —a sufficient proof that she told her pitiful tale convincingly and well. And the fact that I also was moved by it, at second hand, is proof that that reporter delivered it from his heart through his pen, and did his work well.

In the remote parts of the country the weekly village newspaper remains the same curious production it was when I was a boy, sixty years ago, on the banks of the Mississippi. The metropolitan daily of the great city tells us every day about the movements of Lieutenant-General So-and-so and Rear-Admiral So-and-so, and what the Vanderbilts are doing. These great dailies keep us informed of Mr. Carnegie's movements and sayings; they tell us what President Roosevelt said yesterday and what he is going to do to-day. They tell us what the children of his family have been saying, just as the princelings of Europe are daily quoted—and we notice that the remarks of the Roosevelt children are distinctly princely in that the things they say are rather notably not worth while.

Now the court circular of the remote village newspaper has always dealt, during these sixty years, with the comings and goings and sayings of *its* local princelings. They have told us during all those years, and they still tell us, what the principal grocery man is doing and how he has bought a new stock; they tell us that relatives are visiting the ice-cream man, that Miss Smith has arrived to spend a week with the Joneses, and so on, and so on. And all that record is just as intensely interesting to the villagers as is the record I have just been speaking of, of the doings and sayings of the colossally conspicuous personages of the United States. This shows that human nature is all alike; it shows that we like to know what the big people are doing, so that we can envy them. It shows that the big personage of a village bears the same proportion to the little people of the village that the President of the United States bears to the nation. It shows that *conspicuousness* is the only thing necessary in a person to command our interest and, in a larger or smaller sense, our worship. We recognize that there are *no* trivial occurrences in life if we get the right focus on them. In a village they are just as prodigious as they are when the subject is a personage of national importance.

THE SWANGOS

(From The Hazel Green (Ky.) Herald.)

Dr. Bill Swango is able to be in the saddle again.

Aunt Rhod Swango visited Joseph Catron and wife Sunday.

Mrs. Shiloh Swango attended the auction at Maytown Saturday.

W. W. Swango has a nice bunch of cattle ready for the Mount Sterling market.

James Murphy bought ten head of cattle from W. W. Swango last week.

Mrs. John Swango of Montgomery County visited Shiloh Swango and family last week.

Mrs. Sarah Ellen Swango, wife of Wash, the noted turkey trader of Valeria, was the guest of Mrs. Ben Murphy Saturday and Sunday.

Now that is a very genuine and sincere and honest account of what the Swangos have been doing lately in the interior of Kentucky. We see at a glance what a large place that Swango tribe hold in the admiration and worship of the villagers of Hazel Green, Kentucky. In this account, change Swango to *Vanderbilt;* then change it to *Carnegie;* next time change it to *Rockefeller;* next time change it to the *President;* next time to the *Mayor of New York.*

CAPT. E. L. MARSH

FORMER ELMIRAN WHO DIED AT DES MOINES, IOWA, RECENTLY

Captain E. L. Marsh, aged sixty-four years, died at Des Moines, Iowa, a week ago Friday—February 23—after a long illness. The deceased was born in Enfield, Tompkins county, N. Y., in 1842, later came to Elmira to live with his parents and in 1857 left Elmira to locate in Iowa, where he has lived the greater part of the time since, the only exception being brief times of residence in the south and east. He enlisted in Company D, of the Second Iowa at Des Moines, and was elected a captain in that regiment. He served throughout the war with marked courage and efficiency. After the war Captain Marsh went to New Orleans, where he remained during most of the reconstruction period and then went to New York, where he engaged in paving business for several years. He went back to Des Moines in 1877 and resided there during the almost thirty years since. He engaged in the real estate business there with great success. He was married in 1873 and is survived by his wife and two children. Captain Marsh was a member of the Loyal Legion, Commandery of Iowa, and was senior vice commander of the order for Iowa. He was a member of the G. A. R., also, and a member of the Congregational church. Captain Marsh was the son of Mr. and Mrs. Sheppard Marsh, and Mrs. Marsh was twin sister of the late Mrs. Jervis Langdon of this city. Captain Marsh was a very dear and close friend of his cousin, General Charles J. Langdon, of Elmira.

This clipping from a Des Moines, Iowa, newspaper arrives this morning. Ed Marsh was a cousin of my wife, and I remember him very well. He was present at our wedding thirty-six years ago, and was a handsome young bachelor. Aside from my interest in him as a cousin of my young bride, he had another interest for me in the fact that in his company of the Second Iowa Infantry was Dick Higham. Five years before the war, Dick, a good-natured, simple-minded, winning lad of seventeen, was an apprentice in my brother's small printing-office in Keokuk, Iowa. He had an old musket and he used to parade up and down with it in the office, and he said he would rather be a soldier than anything else. The rest of us laughed at him and said he was nothing but a disguised girl, and that if he were confronted by the enemy he would drop his gun and run.

But we were not good prophets. By and by when President Lincoln called for volunteers Dick joined the Second Iowa Infantry, about the time that I was thrown out of my employment as Mississippi River pilot and was preparing to become an imitation soldier on the Confederate side in Ralls County, Missouri. The Second Iowa was moved down to the neighborhood of St. Louis and went into camp there. In some way or other it disgraced itself—and if I remember rightly the punishment

decreed was that it should never unfurl its flag
again until it won the privilege by gallantry in
battle. When General Grant, by and by—February,
'62—was ordering the charge upon Fort Donelson,
the Second Iowa begged for the privilege of leading
the assault, and got it. Ed Marsh's company, with
Dick in it serving as a private soldier, moved up the
hill and through and over the felled trees and other
obstructions in the forefront of the charge, and Dick
fell with a bullet through the center of his forehead
—thus manfully wiping from the slate the chaffing
prophecy of five or six years before. Also, what
was left of the Second Iowa finished that charge
victorious, with its colors flying and never more to
be furled in disgrace.

Ed Marsh's sister also was at our wedding. She
and her brother bore for each other an almost
idolatrous love, and this endured until about a year
ago. About the time of our marriage that sister
married a blatherskite by the name of Talmage
Brown. He was a smart man and intemperately religious. Through his smartness he acquired a large
fortune, and in his will, made shortly before his
death, he appointed Ed Marsh as one of the executors. The estate was worth a million dollars or
more, but its affairs were in a very confused condition. Ed Marsh and the other one or two executors performed their duty faithfully, and without
remuneration. It took them years to straighten out
the estate's affairs, but they accomplished it. During
the succeeding years all went pleasantly. But at
last, about a year ago, some relatives of the late

Talmage Brown persuaded the widow to bring suit against Ed Marsh and his fellow executors for a large sum of money which it was pretended they had either stolen or had wasted by mismanagement. That severed the devoted relationship which had existed between the brother and sister throughout their lives. The mere bringing of the suit broke Ed Marsh's heart, for he was a thoroughly honorable man and could not bear even the breath of suspicion. He took to his bed and the case went to court. He had no word of blame for his sister, and said that no one was to blame but the Browns. They had poisoned her mind. The case was heard in court. Then the judge threw it out with many indignant comments. But the news of the rehabilitation reached Marsh too late to save him. He did not rally. He has been losing ground gradually for the past two months, and now at last the end has come.

This morning arrives a letter from my ancient silver-mining comrade, Calvin H. Higbie, a man whom I have not seen nor had communication with for forty-four years. Higbie figures in a chapter of mine in *Roughing It*, where the tale is told of how we discovered a rich blind lead in the Wide West Mine in Aurora—or, as we called that region then, Esmeralda—and how, instead of making our ownership of that exceedingly rich property permanent by doing ten days' work on it, as required by the mining laws, he went off on a wild-goose chase to hunt for the mysterious cement mine; and how I went off nine miles to Walker River to nurse

Captain John Nye through a violent case of spasmodic rheumatism or blind staggers, or some malady
of the kind; and how Cal and I came wandering
back into Esmeralda one night just in time to be
too late to save our fortune from the jumpers.[1]

I will insert here this letter, and as it will not
see the light until Higbie and I are in our graves,
I shall allow myself the privilege of copying his
punctuation and his spelling, for to me they are
a part of the man. He is as honest as the day is
long. He is utterly simple-minded and straightfor-
ward, and his spelling and his punctuation are as
simple and honest as he is himself. He makes no
apology for them, and no apology is needed. They
plainly state that he is not educated, and they as
plainly state that he makes no pretense to being
educated.

GREENVILLE, PLUMAS CO., CALIFORNIA
March 15— 1906.

SAML. L. CLEMENS.
NEW YORK CITY, N.Y.

MY DEAR SIR—

Two or three parties have ben after me to write up
my recolections of Our associations in Nevada, in the early
60's and have come to the conclusion to do so, and have
ben jocting down incidents that came to mind, for several
years. What I am in dout is, the date you came to Aurora,
Nevada- allso, the first trip you made over thee Sieras to
California, after coming to Nev. allso as near as possable

---

[1] *Roughing It* is dedicated to Higbie.

date, you tended sick man, on, or near Walker River, when our mine was jumped, dont think for a moment that I intend to steal any of your Thunder, but onely to mention some instances that you failed to mention, in any of your articles, Books &c. that I ever saw. I intend to submit the articles to you so that you can see if anything is objectionabl, if so to erase, same, & add anything in its place you saw fit.

I was burned out a few years since, and all old data, went up in smoke, is the reason I ask for above dates. have ben sick more or less for 2 or 3 years, unable to earn anything to speak of, & the finances are getting pretty low, and I will admit that it is mainly for the purpose of Earning a little money, that my first attempt at writing will be made- and I should be so pleased to have your candid opinion, of its merits, and what in your wisdom in such matters. would be its value for publication. I enclose a coppy of Herald in answer to enquiry I made, if such an article was desired.

Hoping to hear from you as soon as convenient, I remain with great respect,

Yours &c

C. H. HIGBIE.

[Copy.]

NEW YORK, Mar. 6-'06

C. H. HIGBIE,
    GREENVILLE- CAL.

DrSir

I should be glad indeed to receive your account of your experiences with Mark Twain, if they are as interesting as I should imagine they would be the Herald would be quite willing to pay you verry well for them, of course, it would be impassible for me to set a price on the matter until I had an opertunity of examining it. if you will kindly send it on, with the privilege of our authenticating it through Mr. Clemens, I shall be more than pleased, to give you a quick decision and make you an offer as it seems worth to us. however, if you have any particular sum in mind which you think should be the price I would suggest that you communicate with me to that effect.

Yours truly

New York Herald,
By Geo. R. Miner.
Sunday Editor.

I have written Higbie and asked him to let me do his literary trading for him. He can shovel sand better than I can—as will appear in the next chapter —but I can beat him all to pieces in the art of fleecing a publisher.

[Tuesday, March 27, 1906

Higbie's spelling.—Mr. Clemens's scheme for getting Higbie a job at the Pioneer.—In 1863 Mr. Clemens goes to Virginia City to be sole reporter on "Territorial Enterprise."—Mr. Clemens tries his scheme for finding employment for the unemployed, on a young St. Louis reporter, with great success. Also worked the scheme for his nephew, Mr. Samuel E. Moffett.

I HAVE allowed Higbie to assist the *Herald* man's spelling and make it harmonize with his own. He has done it well and liberally and without prejudice.

To my mind he has improved it, for I have had an aversion to good spelling for sixty years and more, merely for the reason that when I was a boy there was not a thing I could do creditably except spell according to the book. It was a poor and mean distinction, and I early learned to disenjoy it. I suppose that this is because the ability to spell correctly is a talent, not an acquirement. There is some dignity about an acquirement, because it is a product of your own labor. It is wages earned, whereas to be able to do a thing merely by the grace of God, and not by your own effort, transfers the distinction to our heavenly home—where possibly it is a matter of pride and satisfaction, but it leaves you naked and bankrupt.

Higbie was the first person to profit by my great and infallible scheme for finding work for the unemployed. I have tried that scheme, now and then, for forty-four years. So far as I am aware it has always succeeded, and it is one of my high prides that I invented it, and that in basing it upon what I conceived to be a fact of human nature I estimated that fact of human nature accurately.

Higbie and I were living in a cotton-domestic lean-to at the base of a mountain. It was very cramped quarters, with barely room for us and the stove—wretched quarters, indeed, for every now and then, between eight in the morning and eight in the evening, the thermometer would make an excursion of fifty degrees. We had a silver-mining claim under the edge of a hill half a mile away, in partnership with Bob Howland and Horatio Phillips, and we used to go there every morning, carrying with us our luncheon, and remain all day picking and blasting in our shaft, hoping, despairing, hoping again, and gradually but surely running out of funds. At last, when we were clear out and still had struck nothing, we saw that we must find some other way of earning a living. I secured a place in a near-by quartz mill to screen sand with a long-handled shovel. I hate a long-handled shovel. I never could learn to swing it properly. As often as any other way the sand didn't reach the screen at all, but went over my head and down my back, inside of my clothes. It was the most detestable work I have ever engaged in, but it paid ten dollars a week and board—and the board was worth while, because it consisted not only of bacon, beans, coffee, bread, and molasses, but we had stewed dried apples every day in the week just the same as if it were Sunday. But this palatial life, this gross and luxurious life, had to come to an end, and there were two sufficient reasons for it. On my side, I could not endure the heavy labor; and on the company's side, they did not feel justified in paying me to shovel sand down my back; so I was discharged just at the moment that I was going to resign.

If Higbie had taken that job all would have been well and everybody satisfied, for his great frame would have been competent. He was muscled like a giant. He could handle a long-handled shovel like an emperor, and he could work patiently and contentedly twelve hours on a stretch without ever hastening his pulse or his breath. Meantime, he had found nothing to do, and was somewhat discouraged. He said, with an outburst of pathetic longing, "If I could only get a job at the Pioneer!"

I said, "What kind of a job do you want at the Pioneer?"

He said, "Why, laborer. They get five dollars a day."

I said, "If that's all you want I can arrange it for you."

Higbie was astonished. He said, "Do you mean to say that you know the foreman there and could get me a job and yet have never said anything about it?"

"No," I said, "I don't know the foreman."

"Well," he said, "who is it you know? How is it you can get me the job?"

"Why," I said, "that's perfectly simple. If you will do as I tell you to do, and don't try to improve on my instructions, you shall have the job before night."

He said, eagerly, "I'll obey the instructions, I don't care what they are."

"Well," I said, "go there and say that you want work as a laborer; that you are tired of being idle; that you are not used to being idle, and can't stand it; that you just merely want the refreshment of work and require nothing in return."

He said, "Nothing?"

I said, "That's it—nothing."

"No wages at all?"

"No, no wages at all."

"Not even board?"

"No, not even board. You are to work for nothing. Make them understand that—that you are perfectly willing to work for nothing. When they look at that figure of yours that foreman will understand that he has drawn a prize. You'll get the job."

Higbie said, indignantly, "Yes, a hell of a job."

I said: "You said you were going to do it, and now you are already criticizing. You have said you would obey my instructions. You are always as good as your word. Clear out, now, and get the job."

He said he would.

I was pretty anxious to know what was going to happen—more anxious than I would have wanted him to find out. I preferred to seem entirely confident of the strength of my scheme, and I made good show of that confidence. But really I was very anxious. Yet I believed that I knew enough of human nature to know that a man like Higbie would not be flung out of that place without reflection when he was offering those muscles of his for nothing. The hours dragged along and he didn't return. I began to feel better and better. I began to accumulate confidence. At sundown he did at last arrive and I had the joy of knowing that my invention had been a fine inspiration and was successful.

He said the foreman was so astonished at first that he didn't know how to take hold of the proposition, but that he soon recovered and was evidently very glad that he was able to accommodate Higbie and furnish him the refreshment he was pining for.

Higbie said, "How long is this to go on?"

I said: "The terms are that you are to stay right there; do your work just as if you were getting the going wages for it. You are never to make any complaint; you are never to indicate that you would like to have wages or board. This will go on one, two, three, four, five, six days, according to the make of that foreman. Some foremen would break down under the strain in a couple of days. There are others who would last a week. It would be difficult to find one who could stand out a whole fortnight without getting ashamed of himself and offering you wages. Now let's suppose that this is a fortnight foreman. In that case you will not be there a fortnight. Because the men will spread it around that the very ablest laborer in this camp is so fond of work that he is willing and glad to do it without pay. You will be regarded as the latest curiosity. Men will come from the other mills to have a look at you. You could charge admission and get it, but you mustn't do that. Stick to your colors. When the foremen of the other mills cast their eyes upon this bulk of yours and perceive that you are worth two ordinary men they'll offer you half a man's wages. You are not to accept until you report to your foreman. Give him an opportunity to offer you the same. If he doesn't do it, then you are free to take up with that other man's offer. Higbie, you'll be foreman of a mine or a mill inside of three weeks, and at the best wages going."

It turned out just so—and after that I led an easy life, with nothing to do, for it did not occur to me to take my own medicine. I didn't want a job as long as Higbie had one. One was enough for so small a family—and so during many succeeding weeks I was a gentleman of leisure, with books and newspapers to read and stewed dried apples every day for dinner the same as Sunday, and I wanted no better career than this in this life. Higbie supported me handsomely, never once complained of it, never once suggested that I go out and try for a job at no wages and keep myself.

That would be in 1862. I parted from Higbie about the end of '62—or possibly it could have been the beginning of '63—and went to Virginia City, for I had been invited to come there and take William H. Wright's place as sole reporter on the *Territorial Enterprise* and do Wright's work for three months while he crossed the plains to Iowa to visit his family. However, I have told all about this in *Roughing It*.

I have never seen Higbie since, in all these forty-four years.

Shortly after my marriage, in 1870, I received a letter from a young man in St. Louis who was possibly a distant relative of mine—I don't remember now about that—but his letter said that he was anxious and ambitious to become a journalist—and would I send him a letter of introduction to some St. Louis newspaper and make an effort to get him a place as a reporter? It was the first time I had had an opportunity to make a new trial of my great scheme. I wrote him and said I would get him a place on any newspaper in St. Louis; he could choose the one he preferred, but he must promise me to faithfully follow out the instructions which I should give him. He replied that he would follow out those instructions to the letter and with enthusiasm. His letter was overflowing with gratitude—premature gratitude. He asked for the instructions. I sent them. I said he must not use a letter of introduction from me or from anyone else. He must go to the newspaper of his choice and say that he was idle, and weary of being idle, and wanted work—that he was pining for work, longing for work—that he didn't care for wages, didn't want wages, but would support himself; he wanted work, nothing but work, and not work of a particular kind, but any kind of work they would give him to do. He would sweep out the editorial rooms; he would keep the inkstands full, and the mucilage bottles; he would run errands; he would make himself useful in every way he could.

I suspected that my scheme would not work with everybody—that some people would scorn to labor for nothing and would think it matter for self-contempt; also that many persons would think me a fool to suggest such a project; also that many persons would not have character enough to go into the scheme in a determined way and test it. I was interested to know what kind of a candidate this one was, but of course I had to wait some time to find out. I had told him he must never ask for wages; he must never be beguiled into making that mistake; that sooner or later an offer of wages would come from somewhere, and in that case he must go straight to his employer and give him the opportunity to offer him the like wages, in which case he must stay where he was—that as long as he was in anybody's employ he must never ask for an advance of wages; that would always come from somewhere else if he proved his worthiness.

The scheme worked again. That young fellow chose his paper, and during the first few days he did the sweeping out and other humble work, and kept his mouth shut. After that the staff began to take notice of him. They saw that they could employ him in lots of ways that saved time and effort for them at no expense. They found that he was alert and willing. They began presently to widen his usefulness. Then he ventured to risk another detail of my instructions; I had told him not to be in a hurry about it, but to make his popularity secure first. He took up that detail now. When he was on his road between office and home, and when he was out on errands, he kept his eyes open, and whenever he saw anything that could be useful in the local columns he wrote it out, then went over it and abolished adjectives, went over it again and extinguished other surplusages, and finally when he got it boiled down to the plain facts with the ruffles and other embroideries all gone, he laid it on the city editor's desk. He scored several successes, and saw his stuff go into the paper unpruned. Presently the city editor when short of help sent him out on an assignment. He did his best with it, and with good results. This happened with more and more frequency. It brought him into contact with all the reporters of all the newspapers. He made friends with them and presently one of them told him of a berth that was vacant, and that he could get it and the wages too. He said he must see his own employers first about it. In strict accordance with my instructions he carried the offer to his own employers, and the thing happened which was to be expected. They said they could pay that wage as well as any other newspaper—stay where he was.

This young man wrote me two or three times a year and he always had something freshly encouraging to report about my scheme. Now and then he would be offered a raise by another newspaper. He carried the news to his own paper; his own paper stood the raise every time and he remained there. Finally he got an offer which his employers could not meet and then they parted. This offer was a salary of three thousand a year, to be managing editor on a daily in a Southern city of considerable importance, and it was a large wage for that day and region. He held that post three years. After that I never heard of him any more.

About 1886 my nephew, Samuel E. Moffett, a youth in the twenties, lost his inherited property and found himself obliged to hunt for something to do by way of making a living. He was an extraordinary young fellow in several ways. A nervous malady had early unfitted him for attending school in any regular way, and he had come up without a school education—but this was no great harm for him, for he had a prodigious memory and a powerful thirst for knowledge. At twelve years he had picked up, through reading and listening, a large and varied treasury of knowledge, and I remember one exhibition of it which was very offensive to me. He was visiting in our house and I was trying to build a game out of historical facts drawn from all the ages. I had put in a good deal of labor on this game, and it was hard labor, for the facts were not in my head. I had to dig them painfully out of the books. The boy looked over my work, found that my facts were not accurate and the game, as it stood, not usable. Then he sat down and built the whole game out of his memory. To me it was a wonderful performance, and I was deeply offended.

As I have said, he wrote me from San Francisco in his early twenties, and said he wanted to become a journalist, and would I send him some letters of introduction to the newspaper editors of that city? I wrote back and put him strictly under those same old instructions. I sent him no letter of introduction and forbade him to use one furnished by anybody else. He followed the instructions strictly. He went to work in the *Examiner,* a property of William R. Hearst. He cleaned out the editorial rooms and carried on the customary drudgeries required by my scheme. In a little while he was on the editorial staff at a good salary. After two or three years the salary was raised to a very

good figure indeed. After another year or two he
handed in his resignation—for in the meantime he
had married and was living in Oakland, or one of
those suburbs, and did not like the travel to and
fro between the newspaper and his home in the late
hours of the night and the morning. Then he was
told to stay in Oakland, write his editorials there
and send them over, and the large salary was continued. By and by he was brought to New York
to serve on Mr. Hearst's New York paper, and
when he finally resigned from that employment he
had been in Mr. Hearst's employ sixteen years without a break. Then he became an editorial writer
on the New York *World* with the privilege of living out of town and sending his matter in. His
wage was eight thousand dollars a year. A couple
of years ago *Collier's Weekly* offered him an easy
berth and one which was particularly desirable in
his case, since it would deal mainly with historical
matters, past and present—and that was an industry
which he liked. The salary was to be ten thousand
dollars. He came to me for advice, and I told
him to accept, which he did. When Mr. Pulitzer
found that he was gone from the *World* he was
not pleased with his managing editor for letting
him go, but his managing editor was not to blame.
He didn't know that Moffett was going until he received his resignation. Pulitzer offered Moffett a
billet for twenty years, this term to be secured in
such a way that it could not be endangered by Pulitzer's death, and to this offer was added the extraordinary proposition that Moffett could name his

own salary. But of course Moffett remains with Collier, his agreement with *Collier's* having been already arrived at satisfactorily to both parties.

[*Wednesday, March 28, 1906*

Orion Clemens's personality.—His adventure at the house of Doctor Meredith.—Death of Mr. Clemens's father, just after having been made county judge.

My brother's experience was another conspicuous example of my scheme's efficiency. I will talk about that by and by. But for the moment my interest suddenly centers itself upon his personality, moved thereto by this passing mention of him— and so I will drop other matters and sketch that personality. It is a very curious one. In all my seventy years I have not met the twin of it.

Orion Clemens was born in Jamestown, Fentress County, Tennessee, in 1825. He was the family's first-born and antedated me ten years. Between him and me came a sister, Margaret, who died, aged nine, in 1839 in that village of Florida, Missouri, where I was born; and Pamela, mother of Samuel E. Moffett, who was an invalid all her life and died in the neighborhood of New York a year ago, aged about seventy-five. Also there was a brother, Benjamin, who died in 1842, aged ten.

Orion's boyhood was spent in that wee little log hamlet of Jamestown up there among the knobs— so called—of East Tennessee, among a very sparse population of primitives who were as ignorant of the outside world and as unconscious of it as the other wild animals were that inhabited the forest around. The family migrated to Florida, Missouri, then moved to Hannibal, Missouri, when Orion was ten years old. When he was fifteen or sixteen he was sent to St. Louis and there he learned the printer's trade. One of his characteristics was eagerness. He woke with an eagerness about some matter or other every morning; it consumed him all day; it perished in the night and he was on fire with a fresh new interest next morning before he could get his clothes on. He exploited in this way three hundred and sixty-five red-hot new eagernesses every year of his life—until he died sitting at a table with a pen in his hand, in the early morning, jotting down the conflagration for that day and preparing to enjoy the fire and smoke of it until night should extinguish it. He was then seventy-two years old. But I am forgetting another characteristic, a very pronounced one. That was his deep glooms, his despondencies, his despairs; these had their place in each and every day along with the eagernesses. Thus his day was divided—no, not divided, mottled—from sunrise to midnight with alternating brilliant sunshine and black cloud. Every day he was the most joyous and hopeful man that ever was, I think, and also every day he was the most miserable man that ever was.

While he was in his apprenticeship in St. Louis he got well acquainted with Edward Bates, who was afterward in Mr. Lincoln's first Cabinet. Bates was a very fine man, an honorable and upright man,

and a distinguished lawyer. He patiently allowed
Orion to bring to him each new project; he discussed
it with him and extinguished it by argument and
irresistible logic—at first. But after a few weeks
he found that this labor was not necessary; that
he could leave the new project alone and it would
extinguish itself the same night. Orion thought
he would like to become a lawyer. Mr. Bates en-
couraged him, and he studied law nearly a week,
then of course laid it aside to try something new.
He wanted to become an orator. Mr. Bates gave
him lessons. Mr. Bates walked the floor reading
from an English book aloud and rapidly turning
the English into French, and he recommended this
exercise to Orion. But as Orion knew no French,
he took up that study and wrought at it with enthusiasm two or three days; then gave it up. During his apprenticeship in St. Louis he joined a number of churches, one after another, and taught in
the Sunday-schools—changing his Sunday-school every time he changed his religion. He was correspondingly erratic in his politics—Whig to-day,
Democrat next week, and anything fresh that he
could find in the political market the week after. I
may remark here that throughout his long life he was
always trading religions and enjoying the change of
scenery. I will also remark that his sincerity was
never doubted; his truthfulness was never doubted;
and in matters of business and money his honesty
was never questioned. Notwithstanding his for-
ever-recurring caprices and changes, his principles
were high, always high, and absolutely unshakable.

He was the strangest compound that ever got mixed in a human mold. Such a person as that is given to acting upon impulse and without reflection; that was Orion's way. Everything he did he did with conviction and enthusiasm and with a vainglorious pride in the thing he was doing—and no matter what that thing was, whether good, bad, or indifferent, he repented of it every time in sackcloth and ashes before twenty-four hours had sped. Pessimists are born, not made. Optimists are born, not made. But I think he was the only person I have ever known in whom pessimism and optimism were lodged in exactly equal proportions. Except in the matter of grounded principle, he was as unstable as water. You could dash his spirits with a single word; you could raise them into the sky again with another one. You could break his heart with a word of disapproval; you could make him as happy as an angel with a word of approval. And there was no occasion to put any sense or any vestige of mentality of any kind into these miracles; anything you might say would answer.

He had another conspicuous characteristic, and it was the father of those which I have just spoken of. This was an intense lust for approval. He was so eager to be approved, so girlishly anxious to be approved by anybody and everybody, without discrimination, that he was commonly ready to forsake his notions, opinions, and convictions at a moment's notice in order to get the approval of any person who disagreed with them. I wish to be understood as reserving his fundamental principles all the time. He never forsook those to please anybody. Born and reared among slaves and slave-holders, he was yet an abolitionist from his boyhood to his death. He was always truthful; he was always sincere; he was always honest and honorable. But in light matters—matters of small consequence, like religion and politics and such things—he never acquired a conviction that could survive a disapproving remark from a cat.

He was always dreaming; he was a dreamer from birth, and this characteristic got him into trouble now and then. Once when he was twenty-three or twenty-four years old, and was become a journeyman, he conceived the romantic idea of coming to Hannibal without giving us notice, in order that he might furnish to the family a pleasant surprise. If he had given notice, he would have been informed that we had changed our residence and that that gruff old bass-voiced sailorman, Doctor Meredith, our family physician, was living in the house which we had formerly occupied and that Orion's former room in that house was now occupied by Doctor Meredith's two ripe old-maid sisters. Orion arrived at Hannibal per steamboat in the middle of the night, and started with his customary eagerness on his excursion, his mind all on fire with his romantic project and building and enjoying his surprise in advance. He was always enjoying things in advance; it was the make of him. He never could wait for the event, but he must build it out of dream-stuff and enjoy it beforehand—consequently sometimes when the event happened he saw that it was not as good as the one he had invented in his imagination, and so he had lost profit by not keeping the imaginary one and letting the reality go.

When he arrived at the house he went around to the back door and slipped off his boots and crept upstairs and arrived at the room of those old maids without having wakened any sleepers. He undressed in the dark and got into bed and snuggled up against somebody. He was a little surprised, but not much, for he thought it was our brother Ben. It was winter, and the bed was comfortable, and the supposed Ben added to the comfort—and so he was dropping off to sleep very well satisified with his progress so far and full of happy dreams of what was going to happen in the morning. But something else was going to happen sooner than that, and it happened now. The old maid that was being crowded squirmed and struggled and presently came to a half waking condition and protested against the crowding. That voice paralyzed Orion. He couldn't move a limb; he couldn't get his breath; and the crowded one began to paw around, found Orion's new whiskers, and screamed, "Why, it's a man!" This removed the paralysis, and Orion was out of the bed and clawing around in the dark for his clothes in a fraction of a second. Both maids began to scream, so Orion did not wait to get his whole outfit. He started with such parts of it as he could grab. He flew to the head of the stairs and started down, and he was paralyzed again at that point, because he saw the faint yellow flame of a candle soaring up the stairs from below and he judged that Doctor Meredith was behind it, and he was. He had no clothes on to speak of, but no matter, he was well enough fixed for an occasion like this, because he had a butcher knife in his hand. Orion shouted to him, and this saved his life, for the doctor recognized his voice. Then, in those deep sea-going bass tones of his that I used to admire so much when I was a little boy, he explained to Orion the change that had been made, told him where to find the Clemens family, and closed with some quite unnecessary advice about posting himself before he undertook another adventure like that—advice which Orion probably never needed again as long as he lived.

When my father died, in 1847, the disaster happened—as is the customary way with such things—just at the very moment when our fortunes had changed and we were about to be comfortable once more, after several years of grinding poverty and privation which had been inflicted upon us by the dishonest act of one Ira Stout, to whom my father had lent several thousand dollars—a fortune in those days and in that region. My father had just been elected clerk of the Surrogate Court. This modest prosperity was not only quite sufficient for us and for our ambitions, but he was so esteemed—held in such high regard and honor throughout the county—that his occupancy of that dignified office would, in the opinion of everybody, be his possession as long as he might live. He went to Palmyra, the county-seat, to be sworn in, about the end of February. In returning home, horseback, twelve miles, a storm of sleet and rain assailed him and he arrived at the house in a half-frozen condition. Pleurisy followed and he died on the 24th of March.

Thus our splendid new fortune was snatched from us and we were in the depths of poverty again. It is the way such things are accustomed to happen.

The Clemens family was penniless again. Orion came to the rescue.

[*Thursday, March 29, 1906*

Mr. Clemens as apprentice to Mr. Ament.—Wilhelm II's dinner, and the potato incident.—The printing of Rev. Alexander Campbell's sermon.—Incident of dropping watermelon on Henry's head.—Orion buys Hannibal "Journal," which is a failure—then he goes to Muscatine, Iowa, and marries.—Mr. Clemens starts out alone to see the world—visits St. Louis, New York, Philadelphia, Washington, then goes to Muscatine and works in Orion's office—finds fifty-dollar bill—thinks of going to explore the Amazon and collect coca—gets Horace Bixby to train him as pilot—starts with Orion for Nevada when Orion is made Secretary to Territory of Nevada.

BUT I am in error. Orion did not come to Hannibal until two or three years after my father's death. He remained in St. Louis. He was a journeyman printer and earning wages. Out of his wage he supported my mother and my brother Henry, who was two years younger than I. My sister Pamela helped in this support by taking piano pupils. Thus we got along, but it was pretty hard sledding. I was not one of the burdens, because I was taken from school at once upon my father's death and placed in the office of the Hannibal *Courier,* as printer's apprentice, and Mr. Ament, the editor and proprietor of the paper, allowed me the usual emolument of the office of apprentice —that is to say, board and clothes, but no money. The clothes consisted of two suits a year, but one of the suits always failed to materialize and the other suit was not purchased so long as Mr. Ament's old clothes held out. I was only about half as big as Ament, consequently his shirts gave me the uncomfortable sense of living in a circus tent, and I had to turn up his pants to my ears to make them short enough.

There were two other apprentices. One was Wales McCormick, seventeen or eighteen years old, and a giant. When he was in Ament's clothes they fitted him as the candle mold fits the candle—thus he was generally in a suffocated condition, particularly in the summertime. He was a reckless, hilarious, admirable creature; he had no principles and was delightful company. At first we three apprentices had to feed in the kitchen with the old slave cook and her very handsome and bright and well-behaved young mulatto daughter. For his own amusement—for he was not generally laboring for other people's amusement—Wales was constantly and persistently and loudly and elaborately making love to that mulatto girl and distressing the life out of her and worrying the old mother to death. She would say, "Now, Marse Wales, Marse Wales, can't you behave yourself?" With encouragement like that, Wales would naturally renew his attentions and emphasize them. It was killingly funny to Ralph and me. And, to speak truly, the old mother's distress about it was merely a pretense. She quite well understood that by the customs of slaveholding communities it was Wales's right to make love to that girl if he wanted to. But the girl's distress was very real. She had a refined nature, and she took all Wales's extravagant love-making in earnest.

We got but little variety in the way of food at that kitchen table, and there wasn't enough of it, anyway. So we apprentices used to keep alive by arts of our own—that is to say, we crept into the cellar nearly every night, by a private entrance which we had discovered, and we robbed the cellar of potatoes and onions and such things, and carried them downtown to the printing-office, where we slept on pallets on the floor, and cooked them at the stove and had very good times. Wales had a secret of cooking a potato which was noble and wonderful and all his own. Since Wales's day I have seen a potato cooked in that way only once. It was when Wilhelm II, Emperor of Germany, commanded my presence at a private feed toward the end of the year 1891. And when that potato appeared on the table it surprised me out of my discretion and made me commit the unforgivable sin, before I could get a grip on my discretion again

—that is to say, I made a joyful exclamation of welcome over the potato, addressing my remark to the Emperor at my side without waiting for him to take the first innings. I think he honestly tried to pretend that he was not shocked and outraged, but he plainly was; and so were the other half-dozen grandees who were present. They were all petrified, and nobody could have said a word if he had tried. The ghastly silence endured for as much as half a minute, and would have lasted until now, of course, if the Emperor hadn't broken it himself, for no one else there would have ventured that. It was at half past six in the evening, and the frost did not get out of the atmosphere entirely until close upon midnight, when it did finally melt away—or wash away—under generous floods of beer.

As I have indicated, Mr. Ament's economies were of a pretty close and rigid kind. By and by, when we apprentices were promoted from the basement to the ground floor and allowed to sit at the family table, along with the one journeyman, Pet MacMurray, the economies continued. Mrs. Ament was a bride. She had attained to that distinction very recently, after waiting a good part of a lifetime for it, and she was the right woman in the right place, according to the Amentian idea, for she did not trust the sugar bowl to us, but sweetened our coffee herself. That is, she went through the motions. She didn't really sweeten it. She seemed to put one heaping teaspoonful of brown sugar into each cup, but, according to Wales, that was a deceit. He said she dipped the spoon in the coffee first to make the sugar stick, and then scooped the sugar out of the bowl with the spoon upside down, so that the effect to the eye was a heaped-up spoon, whereas the sugar on it was nothing but a layer. This all seems perfectly true to me, and yet that thing would be so difficult to perform that I suppose it really didn't happen, but was one of Wales's lies.

I have said that Wales was reckless, and he was. It was the recklessness of ever-bubbling and indestructible good spirits flowing from the joy of youth. I think there wasn't anything that that vast boy wouldn't do to procure five minutes' entertainment for himself. One never knew where he would break out next. Among his shining characteristics was the most limitless and adorable irreverence. There didn't seem to be anything serious in life for him; there didn't seem to be anything that he revered.

Once the celebrated founder of the at that time new and widespread sect called Campbellites arrived in our village from Kentucky, and it made a prodigious excitement. The farmers and their families drove or tramped into the village from miles around to get a sight of the illustrious Alexander Campbell and to have a chance to hear him preach. When he preached in a church many had to be disappointed, for there was no church that would begin to hold all the applicants; so in order to accommodate all, he preached in the open air in the public square, and that was the first time in my life that I had realized what a mighty population this planet contains when you get them all together.

He preached a sermon on one of these occasions which he had written especially for that occasion. All the Campbellites wanted it printed, so that they could save it and read it over and over again, and get it by heart. So they drummed up sixteen dollars, which was a large sum then, and for this great sum Mr. Ament contracted to print five hundred copies of that sermon and put them in yellow paper covers. It was a sixteen-page duodecimo pamphlet, and it was a great event in our office. As we regarded it, it was a book, and it promoted us to the dignity of book printers. Moreover, no such mass of actual money as sixteen dollars, in one bunch, had ever entered that office on any previous occasion. People didn't pay for their paper and for their advertising in money; they paid in dry-goods, sugar, coffee, hickory wood, oak wood, turnips, pumpkins, onions, watermelons—and it was very seldom indeed that a man paid in money, and when that happened we thought there was something the matter with him.

We set up the great book in pages—eight pages to a form—and by help of a printer's manual we managed to get the pages in their apparently crazy but really sane places on the imposing-stone. We printed that form on a Thursday. Then we set up the remaining eight pages, locked them into a form, and struck a proof. Wales read the proof, and presently was aghast, for he had struck a snag. And it was a bad time to strike a snag, because it was Saturday; it was approaching noon; Saturday afternoon was our holiday, and we wanted to get away and go fishing. At such a time as this Wales struck that snag and showed us what had happened. He had left out a couple of words in a thin-spaced page of solid matter and there wasn't another break-line for two or three pages ahead. What in the world was to be done? Overrun all those pages in order to get in the two missing words? Apparently there was no other way. It would take an hour to do it. Then a revise must be sent to the great minister; we must wait for him to read the revise; if he encountered any errors we must correct them. It looked as if we might lose half the afternoon before we could get away. Then Wales had one of his brilliant ideas. In the line in which the "out" had been made occurred the name Jesus Christ. Wales reduced it in the French way to J. C. It made room for the missing words, but it took 99 per cent of the solemnity out of a particularly solemn sentence. We sent off the revise and waited. We were not intending to wait long. In the circumstances we meant to get out and go fishing before that revise should get back, but we were not speedy enough. Presently that great Alexander Campbell appeared at the far end of that sixty-foot room, and his countenance cast a gloom over the whole place. He strode down to our end and what he said was brief, but it was very stern, and it was to the point. He read Wales a lecture. He said, "So long as you live, don't you ever diminish the Saviour's name again. Put it *all* in." He repeated this admonition a couple of times to emphasize it, then he went away.

In that day the common swearers of the region had a way of their own of *emphasizing* the Saviour's name when they were using it profanely, and this fact intruded itself into Wales's incorrigible mind. It offered him an opportunity for a momentary entertainment which seemed to him to be more precious and more valuable than even fishing and swimming could afford. So he imposed upon himself the long and weary and dreary task of over-running all those three pages in order to improve upon his former work and incidentally and thoughtfully improve upon the great preacher's admonition. He enlarged the offending J. C. into Jesus H. Christ. Wales knew that that would make prodigious trouble, and it did. But it was not in him to resist it. He had to succumb to the law of his make. I don't remember what his punishment was, but he was not the person to care for that. He had already collected his dividend.

It was during my first year's apprenticeship in the *Courier* office that I did a thing which I have been trying to regret for fifty-five years. It was a summer afternoon and just the kind of weather that a boy prizes for river excursions and other frolics, but I was a prisoner. The others were all gone holidaying. I was alone and sad. I had committed a crime of some sort and this was the punishment. I must lose my holiday, and spend the afternoon in solitude besides. I had the printing-office all to myself, there in the third story. I had one comfort, and it was a generous one while it lasted. It was the half of a long and broad watermelon, fresh and red and ripe. I gouged it out with a knife, and I found accommodation for the whole of it in my person—though it did crowd me until the juice ran out of my ears. There remained then the shell, the hollow shell. It was big enough to do duty as a cradle. I didn't want to waste it, and I couldn't think of anything to do with it which could afford entertainment. I was sitting at the open window which looked out upon the sidewalk of the main street three stories below, when it occurred to me to drop it on somebody's head. I doubted the judiciousness of this, and I had some compunctions about it, too, because so much of the resulting entertainment would fall to my share and so little to the other person. But I thought I would chance it. I watched out of the window for the right person to come along—the safe person— but he didn't come. Every time there was a candidate he or she turned out to be an unsafe one, and I had to restrain myself. But at last I saw the right one coming. It was my brother Henry. He was the best boy in the whole region. He never did harm to anybody, he never offended anybody. He was exasperatingly good. He had an overflowing abundance of goodness—but not enough to save him this time. I watched his approach with eager interest. He came strolling along, dreaming his pleasant summer dream and not doubting but that Providence had him in His care. If he had known where I was he would have had less confidence in that superstition. As he approached his form became more and more foreshortened. When he was almost under me he was so foreshortened that nothing of him was visible from my high place except the end of his nose and his alternately approaching feet. Then I poised the watermelon, calculated my distance, and let it go, hollow side down. The accuracy of that gunnery was beyond admiration. He had about six steps to make when I let that canoe go, and it was lovely to see those two bodies gradually closing in on each other. If he had had seven steps to make, or five steps to make, my gunnery would have been a failure. But he had exactly the right number to make, and that shell smashed down right on the top of his head and drove him into the earth up to the chin, the chunks of that broken melon flying in every direction like a spray. I wanted to go down there and condole with him, but it would not have been safe. He would have suspected me at once. I expected him to suspect me, anyway, but as he said nothing about this adventure for two or three days—I was watching him in the meantime in order to keep out of danger—I was deceived into believing that this time he didn't suspect me. It was a mistake. He was only waiting for a sure opportunity. Then he landed a cobblestone on the side of my head which raised a bump there so large that I had to wear two hats for a time. I carried this crime to my mother, for I was always anxious to get Henry into trouble with her and could never succeed. I thought that I had a sure case this time when she should come to see that murderous bump. I showed it to her, but she said it was no matter. She didn't need to inquire into the circumstances. She knew I had deserved it, and the best way would be for me to accept it as a valuable lesson, and thereby get profit out of it.

About 1849 or 1850 Orion severed his connection with the printing-house in St. Louis and came up to Hannibal and bought a weekly paper called the Hannibal *Journal,* together with its plant and its good-will, for the sum of five hundred dollars cash. He borrowed the cash, at ten per cent interest, from an old farmer named Johnson who lived five miles out of town. Then he reduced the subscription price of the paper from two dollars to one dollar. He reduced the rates for advertising in about the same proportion, and thus he created one absolute and unassailable certainty—to wit: that the business would never pay him a single cent of profit. He took me out of the *Courier* office and engaged my services in his own at three dollars and a half a week, which was an extravagant wage, but Orion was always generous, always liberal with everybody except himself. It cost him nothing in my case, for he never was able to pay me a single penny as long as I was with him. By the end of the first year he found he must make some economies. The office rent was cheap, but it was not cheap enough. He could not afford to pay rent of any kind, so he moved the whole plant into the house we lived in, and it cramped the dwelling-place cruelly. He kept that paper alive during four years, but I have at this time no idea how he accomplished it. Toward the end of each year he had to turn out and scrape and scratch for the fifty dollars of interest due Mr. Johnson, and that fifty dollars was about the only cash he ever received or paid out, I suppose, while he was proprietor of that newspaper, except for ink and printing-paper. The paper was a dead failure. It had to be that from the start. Finally he handed it over to Mr. Johnson, and went up to Muscatine, Iowa, and acquired a small interest in a weekly newspaper there. It was not a sort of property to marry on——but no matter. He came across a winning and pretty girl who lived in Quincy, Illinois, a few miles below Keokuk, and they became engaged. He was always falling in love with girls, but by some accident or other he had never gone so far as engagement before. And now he achieved nothing but misfortune by it, because he straightway fell in love with a Keokuk girl——at least he imagined that he was in love with her, whereas I think she did the imagining for him. The first thing he knew he was engaged to her; and he was in a great quandary. He didn't know whether to marry the Keokuk one or the Quincy one, or whether to try to marry both of them and suit every one concerned. But the Keokuk girl soon settled that for him. She was a master spirit and she ordered him to write the Quincy girl and break off that match, which he did. Then he married the Keokuk girl and they began a struggle for life which turned out to be a difficult enterprise, and very unpromising.

To gain a living in Muscatine was plainly impossible, so Orion and his new wife went to Keokuk to live, for she wanted to be near her relatives. He bought a little bit of a job-printing plant—on credit, of course—and at once put prices down to where not even the apprentices could get a living out of it, and this sort of thing went on.

I had not joined the Muscatine migration. Just before that happened (which I think was in 1853) I disappeared one night and fled to St. Louis. There I worked in the composing-room of the *Evening News* for a time, and then started on my travels to see the world. The world was New York City, and there was a little World's Fair there. It had just been opened where the great reservoir afterward was, and where the sumptuous public library is now being built—Fifth Avenue and 42d Street. I arrived in New York with two or three dollars in pocket change and a ten-dollar bank bill concealed in the lining of my coat. I got work at villainous wages in the establishment of John A. Gray & Green in Cliff Street, and I found board in a sufficiently villainous mechanics' boarding-house in Duane Street. The firm paid my wages in wildcat money at its face value, and my week's wage merely sufficed to pay board and lodging. By and by I went to Philadelphia and worked there some months as a "sub" on the *Inquirer* and the *Public Ledger*. Finally I made a flying trip to Washington to see the sights there, and in 1854 I went back to the Mississippi Valley, sitting upright in the smoking-car two or three days and nights. When I reached St. Louis I was exhausted. I went to bed on board a steamboat that was bound for Muscatine. I fell asleep at once, with my clothes on, and didn't wake again for thirty-six hours.

I worked in that little job office in Keokuk as much as two years, I should say, without ever collecting a cent of wages, for Orion was never able to pay anything—but Dick Higham and I had good times. I don't know what Dick got, but it was probably only uncashable promises.

One day in the midwinter of 1856 or 1857—I think it was 1856—I was coming along the main street of Keokuk in the middle of the forenoon. It was bitter weather—so bitter that that street was deserted, almost. A light dry snow was blowing here and there on the ground and on the pavement, swirling this way and that way and making all sorts of beautiful figures, but very chilly to look at. The wind blew a piece of paper past me and it lodged against a wall of a house. Something about the look of it attracted my attention and I gathered it in. It was a fifty-dollar bill, the only one I had ever seen, and the largest assemblage of money I had ever seen in one spot. I advertised it in the papers and suffered more than a thousand dollars' worth of solicitude and fear and distress during the next few days lest the owner should see the advertisement and come and take my fortune away. As many as four days went by without an applicant; then I could endure this kind of misery no longer.

I felt sure that another four could not go by in this safe and secure way. I felt that I must take that money out of danger. So I bought a ticket for Cincinnati and went to that city. I worked there several months in the printing-office of Wrightson & Company. I had been reading Lieutenant Herndon's account of his explorations of the Amazon and had been mightily attracted by what he said of coca. I made up my mind that I would go to the head-waters of the Amazon and collect coca and trade in it and make a fortune. I left for New Orleans in the steamer *Paul Jones* with this great idea filling my mind. One of the pilots of that boat was Horace Bixby. Little by little I got acquainted with him, and pretty soon I was doing a lot of steering for him in his daylight watches. When I got to New Orleans I inquired about ships leaving for Pará and discovered that there weren't any, and learned that there probably wouldn't be any during that century. It had not occurred to me to inquire about these particulars before leaving Cincinnati, so there I was. I couldn't get to the Amazon. I had no friends in New Orleans and no money to speak of. I went to Horace Bixby and asked him to make a pilot out of me. He said he would do it for five hundred dollars, one hundred dollars cash in advance. So I steered for him up to St. Louis, borrowed the money from my brother-in-law, and closed the bargain. I had acquired this brother-in-law several years before. This was Mr. William A. Moffett, a merchant, a Virginian—a fine man in every way. He had married my sister Pamela, and the Samuel E. Moffett of whom I have been speaking was their son. Within eighteen months I was become a competent pilot, and I served that office until the Mississippi River traffic was brought to a standstill by the breaking out of the Civil War.

Meantime Orion had been sweating along with his little job office in Keokuk, and he and his wife were living with his wife's family—ostensibly as boarders, but it is not likely that Orion was ever able to pay the board. On account of charging nothing for the work done in his job office, he had almost nothing to do there. He was never able to get it through his head that work done on a profit-less basis deteriorates and is presently not worth anything, and that customers are obliged to go where they can get better work, even if they must pay better prices for it. He had plenty of time, and he took up Blackstone again. He also put up a sign which offered his services to the public as a lawyer. He never got a case, in those days, nor even an applicant, although he was quite willing to transact law business for nothing and furnish the stationery himself. He was always liberal that way.

Presently he moved to a wee little hamlet called Alexandria, two or three miles down the river, and he put up that sign there. He got no bites. He was by this time very hard aground. But by this time I was beginning to earn a wage of two hundred and fifty dollars a month as pilot, and so I supported him thenceforth until 1861, when his ancient friend, Edward Bates, then a member of Mr. Lincoln's first Cabinet, got him the place of Secretary of the new Territory of Nevada, and Orion and I cleared for that country in the overland stagecoach, I paying the fares, which were pretty heavy, and carrying with me what money I had been able to save—this was eight hundred dollars, I should say—and it was all in silver coin and a good deal of a nuisance because of its weight. And we had another nuisance, which was an Unabridged Dictionary. It weighed about a thousand pounds, and was a ruinous expense, because the stagecoach company charged for extra baggage by the ounce. We could have kept a family for a time on what that dictionary cost in the way of extra freight—and it wasn't a good dictionary, anyway—didn't have any modern words in it—only had obsolete ones that they used to use when Noah Webster was a child.

[*Friday, March 30, 1906*

Mr. Clemens's interview with Tchaykoffsky.—Presides at a meeting of the association formed in interest of the adult blind.—His first meeting with Helen Keller.—Helen Keller's letter, which Mr. Clemens read at this meeting.

I WILL drop Orion for the present and return and pick him up by and by. For the moment I am more interested in the matters of to-day than I am in Orion's adventures and mine of forty-five years ago.

Three days ago a neighbor brought the celebrated Russian revolutionist, Tchaykoffsky, to call upon me. He is grizzled, and shows age—as to exteriors—but he has a Vesuvius, inside, which is a strong and active volcano yet. He is so full of belief in the ultimate and almost immediate triumph of the revolution and the destruction of the fiendish autocracy, that he almost made me believe and hope with him. He has come over here expecting to arouse a conflagration of noble sympathy in our vast nation of eighty millions of happy and enthusiastic freemen. But honesty obliged me to pour some cold water down his crater. I told him what I believed to be true: that our Christianity which we have always been so proud of—not to say so vain of—is now nothing but a shell, a sham, a hypocrisy; that we have lost our ancient sympathy with oppressed peoples struggling for life and liberty; that when we are not coldly indifferent to such things we sneer at them, and that the sneer is about the only expression the newspapers and the nation deal in with regard to such things; that his mass meetings would not be attended by people entitled to call themselves representative Americans, even if they may call themselves Americans at all; that his audiences will be composed of foreigners who have suffered so recently that they have not yet had time to become Americanized and their hearts turned to stone in their breasts; that these audiences will be drawn from the ranks of the poor, not those of the rich; that they will give and give freely, but they will give from their poverty and the money result will not be large. I said that when our windy and flamboyant President conceived the idea, a year ago, of advertising himself to the world as the new Angel of Peace, and set himself the task of bringing about the peace between Russia and Japan and had the misfortune to accomplish his misbegotten purpose, no one in all this nation except Doctor Seaman and myself uttered a public protest against this folly of follies. That at that time I believed that that fatal peace had postponed the Russian nation's imminent liberation from its age-long chains indefinitely—probably for centuries; that I believed at that time that Roosevelt had given the Russian revolution its death-blow, and that I am of that opinion yet.

I will mention here, in parenthesis, that I came across Doctor Seaman last night for the first time in my life, and found that his opinion also remains to-day as he expressed it at the time that that infamous peace was consummated.

Tchaykoffsky said that my talk depressed him profoundly, and that he hoped I was wrong.

I said I hoped the same.

He said, "Why, from this very nation of yours came a mighty contribution only two or three months ago, and it made us all glad in Russia. You raised two millions of dollars in a breath—in a moment, as it were—and sent that contribution, that most noble and generous contribution, to suffering Russia. Does not that modify your opinion?"

"No," I said, "it doesn't. That money came not from Americans, it came from Jews; much of it from rich Jews, but the most of it from Russian and Polish Jews on the East Side—that is to say, it came from the very poor. The Jew has always been benevolent. Suffering can always move a Jew's heart and tax his pocket to the limit. He will be at your mass meetings. But if you find any Americans there put them in a glass case and exhibit them. It will be worthy fifty cents a head to go and look at that show and try to believe in it."

He asked me to come to last night's meeting and speak, but I had another engagement and could not do it. Then he asked me to write a line or two which could be read at the meeting, and I did that cheerfully.

(From The New York Times.)

ARMS TO FREE RUSSIA, TCHAYKOFFSKY'S APPEAL

REVOLUTIONIST SPEAKS TO CHEERING AUDIENCE OF 3,000

SAYS THE BATTLE IS NEAR

Mark Twain Writes That He Hopes Czars and Grand Dukes Will Soon Become Scarce

"Tovarishzy!"

When Nicholas Tchaykoffsky, hailed by his countrymen here as the father of the revolutionary movement in Russia, spoke this word last night in Grand Central Palace 3,000 men and women rose to their feet, waved their hats, and cheered madly for three minutes. The word means "Comrades!" It is the watchword of the revolutionists.

The spirit of revolution possessed the mass meeting called to greet the Russian patriot now visiting New York.

Fight is what he wants, and arms to fight with. He told the audience so last night and, by their cheers, they promised to do their part in supplying the sinews of war.

Mark Twain could not attend because he had already accepted an invitation to another meeting, but he sent this letter:

DEAR MR. TCHAYKOFFSKY:

I thank you for the honor of the invitation, but I am not able to accept it because Thursday evening I shall be presiding at a meeting whose object is to find remunerative work for certain classes of our blind who would gladly support themselves if they had the opportunity.

My sympathies are with the Russian revolution, of course. It goes without saying. I hope it will succeed, and now that I have talked with you I take heart to believe it will. Government by falsified promises, by lies, by treachery, and by the butcher knife, for the aggrandizement of a single family of drones and its idle and vicious kin has been borne quite long enough in Russia, I should think. And it is to be hoped that the roused nation, now rising in its strength, will presently put an end to it and set up the republic in its place. Some of us, even the white-headed, may live to see the blessed day when czars and grand dukes will be as scarce there as I trust they are in heaven.

Most sincerely yours,
MARK TWAIN.

Mr. Tchaykoffsky made an impassioned appeal for help to inaugurate a real revolution and overturn the Czar and all his allies.

The engagement which I spoke of to Tchaykoffsky was to act as chairman at the first meeting of the association which was formed five months ago in the interest of the adult blind. Joseph H. Choate and I had a very good time there, and I came away with the conviction that that excellent enterprise is going to flourish, and will bear abundant fruit. The State of New York contains six thousand listed blind persons and also a thousand or so who have not been searched out and listed. There are between three and four hundred blind children. The state confines its benevolence to these. It confers upon them a book education. It teaches them to read and write. It feeds them and shelters them. And of course it pauperizes them, because it furnishes them no way of earning a living for themselves. The state's conduct toward the adult blind—and this conduct is imitated by the legislatures of most of the other states—is purely infamous. Outside of the blind asylums the adult blind person has a hard time. He lives merely by the charity of the compassionate, when he has no relatives able to support him—and now and then, as a benevolence, the state stretches out its charitable hand and lifts him over to Blackwell's Island and submerges him among that multitudinous population of thieves and prostitutes.

But in Massachusetts, in Pennsylvania, and in two or three other states, associations like this new one we have formed have been at work for some years, supported entirely by private subscriptions, and the benefits conferred and the work accomplished are so fine and great that their official reports read like a fairy-tale. It seems almost proven that there are not so very many things accomplishable by persons gifted with sight which a blind person cannot learn to do and do as well as that other person.

Helen Keller was to have been present last night, but she is ill in bed and has been ill in bed during several weeks, through overwork in the interest of the blind, the deaf, and the dumb. I need not go into any particulars about Helen Keller. She is fellow to Cæsar, Alexander, Napoleon, Homer, Shakespeare, and the rest of the immortals. She will be as famous a thousand years from now as she is to-day.

I remember the first time I ever had the privilege of seeing her. She was fourteen years old then. She was to be at Laurence Hutton's house on a Sunday afternoon, and twelve or fifteen men and women had been invited to come and see her. Henry Rogers and I went together. The company had all assembled and had been waiting awhile. The wonderful child arrived now, with her about equally wonderful teacher, Miss Sullivan. The girl began to deliver happy ejaculations, in her broken speech. Without touching anything, and without seeing anything, of course, and without hearing anything, she seemed to quite well recognize the character of her surroundings. She said, "Oh the books, the books, so many, many books. How lovely!"

The guests were brought one after another and introduced to her. As she shook hands with each she took her hand away and laid her fingers lightly against Miss Sullivan's lips, who spoke against them the person's name. When a name was difficult, Miss Sullivan not only spoke it against Helen's fingers, but spelled it upon Helen's hand with her own fingers—stenographically, apparently, for the swiftness of the operation was suggestive of that.

Mr. Howells seated himself by Helen on the sofa and she put her fingers against his lips and he told her a story of considerable length, and you could see each detail of it pass into her mind and strike fire there and throw the flash of it into her face. Then I told her a long story, which she interrupted all along and in the right places, with cackles, chuckles, and care-free bursts of laughter. Then Miss Sullivan put one of Helen's hands against her lips and spoke against it the question, "What is Mr. Clemens distinguished for?" Helen answered, in her crippled speech, "For his humor." I spoke up modestly and said, "And for his wisdom." Helen said the same words instantly— "And for his wisdom." I suppose it was a case of mental telegraphy, since there was no way for her to know what it was I had said.

After a couple of hours spent very pleasantly, some one asked if Helen would remember the feel of the hands of the company after this considerable interval of time, and be able to discriminate the hands and name the possessors of them. Miss Sullivan said, "Oh, she will have no difficulty about that." So the company filed past, shook hands in turn, and with each handshake Helen greeted the owner of the hand pleasantly and spoke the name that belonged to it without hesitation, until she encountered Mr. Rogers, toward the end of the procession. She shook hands with him, then paused, and a reflecting expression came into her face. Then she said: "I am glad to meet you now. I have not met you before." Miss Sullivan told her she was mistaken; this gentleman was introduced to her when she first arrived in the room. But Helen was not affected by that. She said no, she never had met this gentleman before. Then Mr. Rogers said that perhaps the confusion might be explained —by the fact that he had his glove on when he was introduced to Helen. Of course that explained the matter.

This was not in the afternoon, as I have misstated. It was in the forenoon, and by and by the assemblage proceeded to the dining-room and sat down to luncheon. I had to go away before it was over, and as I passed by Helen I patted her lightly on the head and passed on. Miss Sullivan called to me and said: "Stop, Mr. Clemens. Helen is distressed because she did not recognize your hand. Won't you come back and do that again?" I went back and patted her lightly on the head, and she said at once, "Oh, it's Mr. Clemens."

Perhaps some one can explain this miracle, but I have never been able to do it. Could she feel the wrinkles in my hand through her hair? Some one else must answer this. I am not competent.

As I have said, Helen was not able to leave her sick-bed, but she wrote a letter, two or three days ago, to be read at the meeting, and Miss Holt, the secretary, sent it to me by a messenger at midafternoon yesterday. It was lucky for me that she didn't reserve it and send it to me on the platform last night, for in that case I could not have gotten through with it. I read it to the house without a break in my voice, and also without even a tremor in it that could be noticed, I think. But it was because I had read it aloud to Miss Lyon at mid-afternoon, and I knew the dangerous places and how to be prepared for them. I told the house in the beginning that I had this letter and that I would read it at the end of the evening's activities. By and by when the end had arrived and Mr. Choate had spoken, I introduced the letter with a few words. I said that if I knew anything about literature, here was a fine and great and noble sample of it; that this letter was simple, direct, unadorned, unaffected, unpretentious, and was moving and beautiful and eloquent; that no fellow to it had ever issued from any girl's lips since Joan of Arc, that immortal child of seventeen, stood alone and friendless in her chains, five centuries ago, and confronted her judges—the concentrated learning and intellect of France—and fenced with them week by week and day by day, answering them out of her great heart and her untaught but marvelous mind, and always defeating them, always camping on the field and master of it as each day's sun went down. I said I believed that this letter, written by a young woman who has been stone deaf, dumb, and blind ever since she was eighteen months old, and who is one of the most widely and thoroughly educated women in the world, would pass into our literature as a classic and remain so. I will insert the letter here.

MY DEAR MR. CLEMENS:

It is a great disappointment to me not to be with you and the other friends who have joined their strength to uplift the blind. The meeting in New York will be the greatest occasion in the movement which has so long engaged my heart: and I regret keenly not to be present and feel the inspiration of living contact with such an assembly of wit, wisdom and philanthropy. I should be happy if I could have spelled into my hand the words as they fall from your lips, and receive, even as it is uttered, the eloquence of our newest Ambassador to the blind. We have not had such advocates before. My disappointment is softened by the thought that never at any meeting was the right word so sure to be spoken. But, superfluous as all other appeal must seem after you and Mr. Choate have spoken, nevertheless, as I am a woman, I cannot be silent, and I ask you to read this letter, knowing that it will be lifted to eloquence by your kindly voice.

To know what the blind man needs, you who can see must imagine what it would be not to see, and you can imagine it more vividly if you remember that before your journey's end you may have to go the dark way yourself. Try to realize what blindness means to those whose joyous activity is stricken to inaction.

It is to live long, long days, and life is made up of days. It is to live immured, baffled, impotent, all God's world shut out. It is to sit helpless, defrauded, while your spirit strains and tugs at its fetters, and your shoulders ache for the burden they are denied, the rightful burden of labor.

The seeing man goes about his business confident and self-dependent. He does his share of the work of the world in mine, in quarry, in factory, in counting-room, asking of others no boon, save the opportunity to do a man's part and to receive the laborer's guerdon. In an instant accident blinds him. The day is blotted out. Night envelops all the visible world. The feet which once bore him to his task with firm and confident stride stumble and halt and fear the forward step. He is forced to a new habit of idleness, which like a canker consumes the mind and destroys its beautiful faculties. Memory confronts him with his lighted past. Amid the tangible ruins of his life as it promised to be he gropes his pitiful way. You have met him on your busy thoroughfares with faltering feet and outstretched hands, patiently "dredging" the universal dark, holding out for sale his petty wares, or his cap for your pennies; and this was a Man with ambitions and capabilities.

It is because we know that these ambitions and capabilities can be fulfilled, that we are working to improve the condition of the adult blind. You cannot bring back the light to the vacant eyes; but you can give a helping hand to the sightless along their dark pilgrimage. You can teach them new skill. For work they once did with the aid of their eyes you can substitute work that they can do with their hands. They ask only opportunity, and opportunity is a torch in darkness. They crave no charity, no pension, but the satisfaction that comes from lucrative toil, and this satisfaction is the right of every human being.

At your meeting New York will speak its word for the blind, and when New York speaks, the world listens. The true message of New York is not the commercial ticking of busy telegraphs, but the mightier utterances of such gatherings as yours. Of late our periodicals have been filled with depressing revelations of great social evils. Querulous critics have pointed to every flaw in our civic structure. We have listened long enough to the pessimists. You once told me you were a pessimist, Mr. Clemens, but great men are usually mistaken about themselves. You are an optimist. If you were not, you would not preside at the meeting. For it is an answer to pessimism. It proclaims that the heart and the wisdom of a great city are devoted to the good of mankind, that in this busiest city in the world no cry of distress goes up but receives a compassionate and generous answer. Rejoice that the cause of the blind has been heard in New York; for the day after, it shall be heard round the world.

Yours sincerely,

HELEN KELLER.

[*Monday, April 2, 1906*

Government of new Territory of Nevada.—Governor Nye and the practical jokers.—Mr. Clemens begins journalistic life on Virginia City "Enterprise"—reports legislative sessions.—He and Orion prosper.—Orion builds $12,000 house.—Governor Nye turns Territory of Nevada into a state.

PROMOTION FOR BARNES, WHOM TILLMAN BERATED

HAD WOMAN ⌐JECTED FROM WHITE HOUSE; TO BE POSTMASTER.

MERRITT GETS NEW PLACE

Present Postmaster at Washington to be Made Collector at Niagara—Platt Not Consulted.

(Special to The New York Times.)

WASHINGTON, March 31.—President Roosevelt surprised the capital this afternoon by announcing that he would appoint Benjamin F. Barnes as Postmaster of Washington, to succeed John A. Merritt of New York. Mr. Merritt, who for several years has been Postmaster here, has been chosen for Collector of the Port of Niagara, succeeding the late Major James Low.

Mr. Barnes is at present assistant secretary to the President. Only a short time ago he figured extensively in the newspapers for having ordered the forcible ejection from the White House of Mrs. Minor Morris, a Washington woman who had called to see the President. What attracted attention to the case was not the ejection itself, but the violence with which it was performed.

Mrs. Morris, who had been talking to Barnes in an ordinary conversational tone, and with no indications of excitement, so far as the spectators observed, was seized by two policemen and dragged by the arms out of the building and across the asphalt walk in front of the White House, a distance corresponding to that of two ordinary city blocks. During a part of the journey a negro carried her by the feet. Her dress was torn and trampled.

She was locked up on a charge of disorderly conduct, and when it was learned that she would be released on that charge a policeman, a relative of Barnes's, was sent to the House of Detention to prefer a charge of insanity against her so that she would have to be held. She was held accordingly until two physicians had examined her and pronounced her sane. He was denounced by Mrs. Morris, by various newspapers, and by Mr. Tillman in the Senate.

The appointment of Barnes to be Postmaster so soon after this incident has created endless talk here. It is taken to be the President's way of expressing confidence in Barnes and repaying him for the pain he suffered as a result of the newspaper criticisms of his course.

· · · · · ·

Orion Clemens again. To continue.

The government of the new Territory of Nevada was an interesting menagerie. Governor Nye was an old and seasoned politician from New York— politician, not statesman. He had white hair. He was in fine physical condition. He had a winningly friendly face and deep lustrous brown eyes that could talk as a native language the tongue of every feeling, every passion, every emotion. His eyes could outtalk his tongue, and this is saying a good deal, for he was a very remarkable talker, both in private and on the stump. He was a shrewd man. He generally saw through surfaces and perceived what might be going on inside without being suspected of having an eye on the matter.

When grown-up persons indulge in practical jokes, the fact gauges them. They have lived narrow, obscure, and ignorant lives, and at full manhood they still retain and cherish a job lot of left-over standards and ideals that would have been discarded with their boyhood if they had then moved out into the world and a broader life. There were many practical jokers in the new Territory. I do not take pleasure in exposing this fact, for I liked those people; but what I am saying is true. I wish I could say a kindlier thing about them instead. If I could say they were burglars, or hatrack thieves, or something like that, that wouldn't be utterly uncomplimentary. I would prefer it, but I can't say those things. They would not be true. These people were practical jokers, and I will not try to disguise it. In other respects they were plenty good enough people; honest people; reputable and likable. They played practical jokes upon each other with success, and got the admiration and applause and also the envy of the rest of the community. Naturally they were eager to try their arts on big game, and that was what the Governor was. But they were not able to score. They made several efforts, but the Governor defeated these efforts without any trouble and went on smiling his pleasant smile as if nothing had happened. Finally the joker chiefs of Carson City and Virginia City conspired together to see if their combined talent couldn't win a victory, for the jokers were getting into a very uncomfortable place. The people were laughing at them, instead of at their proposed victim. They banded themselves together to the number of ten and invited the Governor to what was a most extraordinary attention in those days—pickled-oyster stew and champagne—luxuries very seldom seen in that region, and existing rather as fabrics of the imagination than as facts.

The Governor took me with him. He said, disparagingly: "It's a poor invention. It doesn't deceive. Their idea is to get me drunk and leave me under the table, and from their standpoint this will be very funny. But they don't know me. I am familiar with champagne and have no prejudices against it."

The fate of the joke was not decided until two o'clock in the morning. At that hour the Governor was serene, genial, comfortable, contented, happy, and sober, although he was so full that he couldn't laugh without shedding champagne tears. Also, at that hour the last joker joined his comrades under the table, drunk to the last perfection. The Governor remarked: "This is a dry place, Sam. Let's go and get something to drink and go to bed."

The Governor's official menagerie had been drawn from the humblest ranks of his constituents at home —harmless good fellows who had helped in his campaigns, and now they had their reward in petty salaries payable in greenbacks that were worth next to nothing. Those boys had a hard time to make both ends meet. Orion's salary was eighteen hundred dollars a year, and he couldn't even support his dictionary on it. But the Irishwoman who had come out on the Governor's staff charged the menagerie only ten dollars a week apiece for board and lodging. Orion and I were of her boarders and lodgers; and so, on these cheap terms the silver I had brought from home held out very well.

At first I roamed about the country seeking silver, but at the end of '62 or the beginning of '63 when I came up from Aurora to begin a journalistic life on the Virginia City *Enterprise,* I was presently sent down to Carson City to report the legislative session. Orion was soon very popular with the members of the legislature, because they found that whereas they couldn't usually trust each other, nor anybody else, they could trust him. He easily held the belt for honesty in that country, but it didn't do him any good in a pecuniary way, because he had no talent for either persuading or scaring legislators. But I was differently situated. I was there

every day in the legislature to distribute compliment
and censure with evenly balanced justice and spread
the same over half a page of the *Enterprise* every
morning; consequently I was an influence. I got the
legislature to pass a law requiring every corporation doing business in the territory to record its
charter in full, without skipping a word, in a record
to be kept by the Secretary of the Territory—my
brother. All the charters were framed in exactly the
same words. For this record service he was authorized to charge forty cents a folio of one hundred
words for making the record; five dollars for furnishing a certificate of each record, and so on.
Everybody had a toll-road franchise, but no toll
road. But the franchise had to be recorded and
paid for. Everybody was a mining corporation, and
had to have himself recorded and pay for it. Very
well, we prospered. The record service paid an
average of one thousand dollars a month, in gold.

Governor Nye was often absent from the Territory. He liked to run down to San Francisco every
little while and enjoy a rest from Territorial civ-
ilization. Nobody complained, for he was prodi-
giously popular. He had been a stage-driver in his
early days in New York or New England, and had
acquired the habit of remembering names and faces,
and of making himself agreeable to his passengers.
As a politician this had been valuable to him, and
he kept his arts in good condition by practice. By
the time he had been Governor a year he had shaken
hands with every human being in the Territory of
Nevada, and after that he always knew these people

instantly at sight and could call them by name. The whole population, of 20,000 persons, were his personal friends, and he could do anything he chose to do and count upon their being contented with it. Whenever he was absent from the Territory—which was generally—Orion served his office in his place, as Acting Governor, a title which was soon and easily shortened to "Governor." Mrs. Governor Clemens enjoyed being a Governor's wife. No one on this planet ever enjoyed a distinction more than she enjoyed that one. Her delight in being the head of society was so frank that it disarmed criticism, and even envy. Being the Governor's wife and head of society, she looked for a proper kind of house to live in—a house commensurate with these dignities—and she easily persuaded Orion to build that house. Orion could be persuaded to do anything. He built and furnished the house at a cost of twelve thousand dollars, and there was no other house in that capital that could approach this property for style and cost.

When Governor Nye's four-year term was drawing to a close, the mystery of why he had ever consented to leave the great State of New York and help inhabit that sage-brush desert was solved. He had gone out there in order to become a United States Senator. All that was now necessary was to turn the Territory into a State. He did it without any difficulty. That patch of sand and that sparse population were not well fitted for the heavy burden of a State government, but no matter, the people were willing to have the change, and so the Governor's game was made.

Orion's game was made, too, apparently, for he was as popular because of his honesty as the Governor was for more substantial reasons. But at the critical moment the inborn capriciousness of his character rose up without warning, and disaster followed.

[Wednesday, April 4, 1906

The Morris case again.—Scope of this autobiography, a mirror.—More about Nast sale; laurels for Mr. Clemens.— Clippings in regard to Woman's University Club reception; Mr. Clemens comments on them.—Vassar benefit at Hudson Theater; Mr. Clemens meets many old friends.

MRS. MORRIS CASE IN SENATE.

NOMINATION OF BARNES OPENS WAY FOR AN INQUIRY.

(Special to The New York Times.)

WASHINGTON, April 3.—Criticism of the appointment of Mr. Roosevelt's Assistant Secretary, B. F. Barnes, to be Postmaster of Washington continues. It now seems likely that the appointment may have a hard time in passing the Senate. Barnes's action in having Mrs. Minor Morris put out of the White House is the chief ground of opposition. The Senate Committee on Post Offices and Post Roads has determined to investigate Barnes's action in the Morris case, and eye witnesses of the affair have been summoned to appear before the committee to-morrow and tell what they saw. This is the same investigation which Mr. Tillman requested and which the Senate refused to grant. It now comes as the result of the President's action in appointing

Barnes Postmaster. The witnesses who are to appear before the committee were not asked to testify in the investigation which the President made when he decided that Barnes's course was justified.

There was much speculation to-day as to who Mr. Barnes's successor as Assistant Secretary would be. The *Evening Star* to-night devotes a column and a half to suggestions on the subject, saying that the leading candidates are John L. McGrew, a clerk in the White House offices; Warren Young, Chief Executive Clerk; M. C. Latta, the President's personal stenographer; James J. Corbett of New York, Robert Fitzsimmons, Augustus Ruhlin, and James J. Jeffries.

The article is illustrated with two pictures of Corbett and Fitzsimmons.

That is neat, and causes me much gentle delight. The point of that whole matter lies in the last four names that are mentioned in it. These four men are prize-fighters—the most celebrated ones now living.

Is the incident now closed? Again we cannot tell. The smell of it may linger in American history a thousand years yet.

This autobiography of mine differs from other autobiographies—differs from *all* other autobiographies, except Benvenuto's, perhaps. The conventional biography of all the ages is an open window. The autobiographer sits there and examines and discusses the people that go by—not all of them, but the notorious ones, the famous ones; those that wear fine uniforms, and crowns when it is not raining; and very great poets and great statesmen—

illustrious people with whom he has had the high privilege of coming in contact. He likes to toss a wave of recognition to these with his hand as they go by, and he likes to notice that the others are seeing him do this, and admiring. He likes to let on that in discussing these occasional people that wear the good clothes he is only interested in interesting his reader. and is in a measure unconscious of himself.

But this autobiography of mine is not that kind of an autobiography. This autobiography of mine is a mirror, and I am looking at myself in it all the time. Incidentally I notice the people that pass along at my back—I get glimpses of them in the mirror—and whenever they say or do anything that can help advertise me and flatter me and raise me in my own estimation, I set these things down in my autobiography. I rejoice when a king or a duke comes my way and makes himself useful to this autobiography, but they are rare customers, with wide intervals between. I can use them with good effect as lighthouses and monuments along my way, but for real business I depend upon the common herd.

Here is some more about the Nast sale:

30 CENTS FOR McCURDY POEM.

OTHER LITERARY CURIOSITIES FROM THE NAST COLLECTION AT AUCTION.

The sale of autograph letters, wash drawings, pencil and pen and ink sketches, the property of the late Thomas Nast, the cartoonist, was continued yesterday by the Merwin-Clayton Company.

Five letters from Theodore Roosevelt as Police Commissioner, colonel of the Rough Riders, Governor, and President, to Mr. Nast, thanking him for sketches and expressing warm friendship for the cartoonist, brought prices ranging from $1.50 to $2.25.

Richard A. McCurdy's autograph letter and original autograph poem addressed to Nast, with a typewritten copy of the poem, brought 30 cents the lot.

The following letter written by Gen. Philip H. Sheridan to Nast was bid in at $12.25 by J. H. Manning, a son of the late Daniel Manning:

May 12, 1875.

"DEAR NAST:

"It is true. I will be married on the 30th of June coming unless there is a slip between the cup and the lip, which is scarcely possible. I will not have any wedding for many reasons, among them the recent death of my father.

"I am very happy, but wish the d—d thing was over.

"Yours truly,

SHERIDAN.

"P. S. and M. I.—I send the inclosed for your oldest. Please send me yours to be kept for mine.

"P. H. S."

A letter written by Lincoln, and which was laid over a piece of white silk bearing a faded red stain, sold for $38. The attached certificate stated that the silk was from the dress of Laura Keene, worn on the night of Lincoln's assassination, and that the stain was made by his blood.

Gen. W. T. Sherman's letter to Nast, dated March 9, 1879, indorsing a testimonial of the cartoonist's services to the army and navy, sold for $6.

A scrapbook containing sketches of Lincoln, Sumner,

Greeley, Walt Whitman, and many water-color sketches, brought $75.

A sketch of William M. Tweed and his companion, Hunt, under arrest, brought $21. Two companion Christmas sketches by Nast, representing a child telephoning to Santa Claus, brought $43 each. A sketch of Gen. Grant was bid in for $36. A sketch of the "G. O. P." elephant brought $28. A sketch representing the Saviour, full face, with nimbus, brought $65.

An autograph photograph of Theodore Roosevelt, dated 1884, was bid in at $5.

It is a great satisfaction to me to notice that I am still ahead—ahead of Roosevelt, ahead of Sherman, ahead of Sheridan, even ahead of Lincoln. These are fine laurels, but they will not last. A time is coming when some of them will wither. A day will come when a mere scratch of Mr. Lincoln's pen will outsell a whole basketful of my letters. A time will come when a scratch of the pens of those immortal soldiers, Sherman and Sheridan, will outsell a thousand scratches of mine, and so I shall enjoy my supremacy now, while I may. I shall read that clipping over forty or fifty times, now, while it is new and true, and let the desolating future take care of itself.

Day before yesterday all Vassar, ancient and modern, packed itself into the Hudson Theater, and I was there. The occasion was a benefit arranged by Vassar and its friends to raise money to aid poor students of that college in getting through the college course. I was not aware that I was to be a feature of the show, and was distressed and most uncomfortably inflamed with blushes when I found it out. Really the distress and the blushes were manufactured, for at bottom I was glad. I held a reception on that stage for an hour or two, and all Vassar, ancient and modern, shook hands with me. Some of the moderns were too beautiful for words, and I was very friendly with those. I was so hoping somebody would want to kiss me for my mother, but I didn't dare to suggest it myself. Presently, however, when it happened, I did what I could to make it contagious, and succeeded. This required art, but I had it in stock. I *seemed* to take the old and the new as they came, without discrimination, but I averaged the percentage to my advantage, and without anybody's suspecting, I think.

Among that host I met again as many as half a dozen pretty old girls whom I had met in their bloom at Vassar that time that Susy and I visited the college so long ago. Yesterday at the University Club, almost all the five hundred were of the young and lovely, untouched by care, unfaded by age. There were girls there from Smith, Wellesley, Radcliffe, Vassar, and Barnard, together with a sprinkling of college girls from the South, from the Middle West and the Pacific coast.

I delivered a moral sermon to the Barnard girls at Columbia University a few weeks ago, and now it was like being among old friends. There were dozens of Barnard girls there, scores of them, and I had already shaken hands with them at Barnard. As I have said, the reporter heard many things there yesterday, but there were several which he didn't hear. One sweet creature wanted to whisper in my ear, and I was nothing loath. She raised her dainty form on tiptoe, lifting herself with a grip of her velvet hands on my shoulders, and put her lips to my ear and said, "How do you like being the belle of New York?" It was so true, and so gratifying, that it crimsoned me with blushes, and I could make no reply. The reporter lost that.

Two girls, one from Maine, the other from Ohio, were grandchildren of fellow-passengers who sailed with me in the *Quaker City* in the *Innocents Abroad* excursion thirty-nine years ago.

[*Thursday, April 5, 1906*

Ellen Terry's farewell banquet, on fiftieth anniversary.— Mr. Clemens's cablegram.—Mr. Clemens has fine new idea for a play; Mr. Hammond Trumbull squelches it.—Orion Clemens is defeated as Secretary of State.—At Mr. Camp's suggestion Mr. Clemens speculates unfortunately.—Mr. Camp offers to buy Tennessee land for $200,000.—Orion refuses.—Mr. Clemens just discovers that he still owns one thousand acres of the Tennessee land.—Orion comes East, gets position on Hartford "Evening Post."—After various business ventures he returns to Keokuk and tries raising chickens.

THE other day I furnished a sentiment in response to a man's request—to wit:

"The noblest work of God?" Man.

"Who found it out?" Man.

I thought it was very good, and smart, but the other person didn't. . . .

Ellen Terry has been a queen of the English stage for fifty years, and will retire from it on the 28th of this month, which will be the fiftieth anniversary. She will retire in due form at a great banquet in London, and cablegrams meet for the occasion will flow in upon the banqueters from old friends of hers in America and other formerly distant regions of the earth—there are no distant regions now. The American cablegrams are being collected by a committee in New York, and by request I have furnished mine. To do these things by cable, at twenty-five cents a word, is the modern way and the only way. They could go by post at no expense, but it wouldn't be good form. [Privately I will remark that they *do* go by mail—dated to suit the requirements.]

Cablegram to Ellen Terry, London.

Age has not withered, nor custom staled, the admiration and affection I have felt for you so many many years. I lay them at your honored feet with the strength and freshness of their youth upon them undiminished.

MARK TWAIN.

She is a lovely character, as was also Sir Henry Irving, who lately departed this life. I first knew them thirty-four years ago in London, and thenceforth held them in high esteem and affection.

ORION CLEMENS RESUMED

There were several candidates for all the offices in the gift of the new State of Nevada save two—

United States Senator (Governor Nye) and Secretary of State (Orion Clemens). Nye was certain to get a Senatorship, and Orion was so sure to get the Secretaryship that no one but him was named for that office. But he was hit with one of his spasms of virtue on the very day that the Republican party was to make its nominations in the convention. Orion refused to go near the convention. He was urged, but all persuasions failed. He said his presence there would be an unfair and improper influence, and that if he was to be nominated the compliment must come to him as a free and unspotted gift. This attitude would have settled his case for him without further effort, but he had another spasm of virtue on the same day, and that made it absolutely sure. It had been his habit for a great many years to change his religion with his shirt, and his ideas about temperance at the same time. He would be a teetotaler for a while and the champion of the cause; then he would change to the other side for a time. On nomination day he suddenly changed from a friendly attitude toward whisky—which was the popular attitude—to uncompromising teetotalism, and went absolutely dry. His friends besought and implored, but all in vain. He could not be persuaded to cross the threshold of a saloon. The paper next morning contained the list of chosen nominees. His name was not in it. He had not received a vote.

His rich income ceased when the State government came into power. He was without an occupation. Something had to be done. He put up his sign as attorney at law, but he got no clients. It was strange. It was difficult to account for. I cannot account for it—but if I were going to guess at a solution I should guess that by the make of him he would examine both sides of a case so diligently and so conscientiously that when he got through with his argument neither he nor a jury would know which side he was on. I think that his client would find out his make in laying his case before him, and would take warning and withdraw it in time to save himself from probable disaster.

I had taken up my residence in San Francisco about a year before the time I have just been speaking of. One day I got a tip from Mr. Camp, a bold man who was always making big fortunes in ingenious speculations and losing them again in the course of six months by other speculative ingenuities. Camp told me to buy some shares in the Hale and Norcross. I bought fifty shares at three hundred dollars a share. I bought on a margin, and put up 20 per cent. It exhausted my funds. I wrote Orion and offered him half, and asked him to send his share of the money. I waited and waited. He wrote and said he was going to attend to it. The stock went along up pretty briskly. It went higher and higher. It reached a thousand dollars a share. It climbed to two thousand, then to three thousand; then to twice that figure. The money did not come, but I was not disturbed. By and by that stock took a turn and began to gallop down. Then I wrote urgently. Orion answered that he had sent the money long ago—said he had sent it to the Occidental Hotel. I inquired for it. They said it was not there. To cut a long story short, that stock went on down until it fell below the price I had paid for it. Then it began to eat up the margin, and when at last I got out I was very badly crippled.

When it was too late, I found out what had become of Orion's money. Any other human being would have sent a check, but he sent gold. The hotel clerk put it in the safe and never thought of it again, and there it reposed all this time, enjoying its fatal work, no doubt. Another man might have thought to tell me that the money was not in a letter, but was in an express package, but it never occurred to Orion to do that.

Later, Mr. Camp gave me another chance. He agreed to buy our Tennessee land for two hundred thousand dollars, pay a part of the amount in cash and give long notes for the rest. His scheme was to import foreigners from grape-growing and wine-making districts in Europe, settle them on the land, and turn it into a wine-growing country. He knew what Mr. Longworth thought of those Tennessee grapes, and was satisfied. I sent the contracts and things to Orion for his signature, he being one of the three heirs. But they arrived at a bad time— in a doubly bad time, in fact The temperance virtue was temporarily upon him in strong force, and he wrote and said that he would not be a party to debauching the country with wine. Also he said how could he know whether Mr. Camp was going to deal fairly and honestly with those poor people

from Europe or not?—and so, without waiting to
find out, he quashed the whole trade, and there it
fell, never to be brought to life again. The land,
from being suddenly worth two hundred thousand
dollars, became as suddenly worth what it was before—nothing, and taxes to pay. I had paid the
taxes and the other expenses for some years, but
I dropped the Tennessee land there, and have never
taken any interest in it since, pecuniarily or otherwise, until yesterday.

I had supposed, until yesterday, that Orion had
frittered away the last acre, and indeed that was
his impression. But a gentleman arrived yesterday
from Tennessee and brought a map showing that
by a correction of the ancient surveys we still own
a thousand acres, in a coal district, out of the hundred thousand acres which my father left us when
he died in 1847. The gentleman brought a proposition; also he brought a reputable and well-to-do
citizen of New York. The proposition was that the
Tennesseean gentleman should sell that land; that
the New York gentleman should pay all the expenses
and fight all the lawsuits, in case any should turn
up, and that of such profit as might eventuate the
Tennesseean gentleman should take a third, the New
Yorker a third, and Sam Moffett and his sister
(Mrs. Charles L. Webster), and I—who are the
surviving heirs—the remaining third.

This time I hope we shall get rid of the Tennessee land for good and all and never hear of it
again. It was created under a misapprehension; my
father loaded himself up with it under a misappre-

hension; he unloaded it on to us under a misapprehension, and I should like to get rid of the accumulated misapprehensions and what is left of the land as soon as possible.

I came East in January, 1867. Orion remained in Carson City perhaps a year longer. Then he sold his twelve-thousand-dollar house and its furniture for thirty-five hundred in greenbacks at about 30 per cent discount. He and his wife took first-class passage in the steamer for New York. In New York they stopped at an expensive hotel; explored the city in an expensive way; then fled to Keokuk, and arrived there about as nearly penniless as they were when they had migrated thence in July, '61. About 1871 or '72 they came to New York. They were obliged to go somewhere. Orion had been trying to make a living in the law ever since he had arrived from the Pacific coast, but he had secured only two cases. Those he was to try free of charge—but the possible result will never be known, because the parties settled the case out of court without his help.

I had bought my mother a house in Keokuk. I was giving her a stated sum monthly, and Orion another stated sum. They all lived together in the house.

But, as I say, they came East and Orion got a job as proofreader on the New York *Evening Post* at ten dollars a week. They took a single small room, and in it they cooked, and lived on that money. By and by Orion came to Hartford and wanted me to get him a place as reporter on a Hartford paper. Here was a chance to try my scheme again, and I did it. I made him go to the Hartford *Evening Post,* without any letter of introduction, and propose to scrub and sweep and do all sorts of things for nothing, on the plea that he didn't need money, but only needed work, and that was what he was pining for. Within six weeks he was on the editorial staff of that paper at twenty dollars a week, and he was worth the money. He was presently called for by some other paper at better wages, but I made him go to the *Post* people and tell them about it. They stood the raise and kept him. It was the pleasantest berth he had ever had in his life. It was an easy berth. He was in every way comfortable. But ill luck came. It was bound to come.

A new Republican daily was to be started in Rutland, Vermont, by a stock company of well-to-do politicians, and they offered Orion the chief editorship at three thousand a year. He was eager to accept. His wife was equally eager—no, twice as eager, three times as eager. My beseechings and reasonings went for nothing. I said:

"You are as weak as water. Those people will find it out right away. They will easily see that you have no backbone; that they can deal with you as they would deal with a slave. You may last six months, but not longer. Then they will not dismiss you as they would dismiss a gentleman: they will fling you out as they would fling out an intruding tramp."

It happened just so. Then Orion and his wife migrated to that persecuted and unoffending Keokuk

once more. Orion wrote from there that he was
not resuming the law; that he thought that what
his health needed was the open air, in some sort
of outdoor occupation; that his old father-in-law
had a strip of ground on the river border a mile
above Keokuk with some sort of a house on it, and
his idea was to buy that place and start a chicken
farm and provide Keokuk with chickens and eggs,
and perhaps butter—but I don't know whether you
can raise butter on a chicken farm or not. He said
the place could be had for three thousand dollars
cash, and I sent the money. Orion began to raise
chickens, and he made a detailed monthly report to
me, whereby it appeared that he was able to work
off his chickens on the Keokuk people at a dollar and
a quarter a pair. But it also appeared that it cost
a dollar and sixty cents to raise the pair. This did
not seem to discourage Orion, and so I let it go.
Meantime he was borrowing a hundred dollars per
month of me regularly, month by month. Now to
show Orion's stern and rigid business ways—and he
really prided himself on his large business capacities—the moment he received the advance of a hundred dollars at the beginning of each month, he
sent me his note for the amount, and with it he
sent, out of that money, *three months' interest* on
the hundred dollars at 6 per cent per annum, these
notes being always for three months. I did not
keep them, of course. They were of no value to
anybody.

As I say, he always sent a detailed statement of
the month's profit and loss on the chickens—at least

the month's loss on the chickens—and this detailed statement included the various items of expense—corn for the chickens, a bonnet for the wife, boots for himself, and so on; even car fares, and the weekly contribution of ten cents to help out the missionaries who were trying to damn the Chinese after a plan not satisfactory to those people. But at last when among those details I found twenty-five dollars for pew rent I struck. I told him to change his religion and sell the pew.

[*Friday, April 6, 1906*

Mr. Clemens's present house unsatisfactory because of no sunshine.—Mr. Clemens meets Etta in Washington Square. Recalls ballroom in Virginia City forty-four years ago.—Orion resumed; he invents wood-sawing machine; invents steam canal boat.—Orion's autobiography.—His death.

THIS house is No. 21 Fifth Avenue, and stands on the corner of Ninth Street within a couple of hundred yards of Washington Square. It was built fifty or sixty years ago by Renwick, the architect of the Roman Catholic Cathedral. It is large, and every story has good and spacious rooms, but not enough sunshine.

Yesterday I went down to Washington Square, turned out to the left to look at a house that stands on the corner of the Square and University Place. Presently I stepped over to the corner of the Square to take a general look at the frontage of the house.

While crossing the street I met a woman, and was conscious that she recognized me, and it seemed to me that there was something in her face that was familiar to me. I had the instinct that she would turn and follow me and speak to me, and the instinct was right. She was a fat little woman, with a gentle and kindly but aged and homely face, and she had white hair, and was neatly but poorly dressed. She said:

"Aren't you Mr. Clemens?"

"Yes," I said, "I am."

She said, "Where is your brother Orion?"

"Dead," I said.

"Where is his wife?"

"Dead," I said; and added, "I seem to know you, but I cannot place you."

She said, "Do you remember Etta Booth?"

I had known only one Etta Booth in my lifetime, and that Etta rose before me in an instant, and vividly. It was almost as if she stood alongside of this fat little antiquated dame in the bloom and diffidence and sweetness of her thirteen years, her hair in plaited tails down her back and her fiery-red frock stopping short at her knees. Indeed I remembered Etta very well. And immediately another vision rose before me, with that child in the center of it and accenting its sober tint like a torch with her red frock. But it was not a quiet vision; not a reposeful one. The scene was a great ball-room in some ramshackle building in Gold Hill or Virginia City, Nevada. There were two or three hundred stalwart men present and dancing with cordial energy. And in the midst of the turmoil Etta's crimson frock was swirling and flashing; and she was the only dancer of her sex on the floor. Her mother, large, fleshy, pleasant, and smiling, sat on a bench against the wall in lonely and honored state and watched the festivities in placid contentment. She and Etta were the only persons of their sex in the ballroom. Half of the men represented ladies, and they had a handkerchief tied around the left arm so that they could be told from the men. I did not dance with Etta, for I was a lady myself. I wore a revolver in my belt, and so did all the other ladies—likewise the gentlemen. It was a dismal old barn of a place, and was lighted from end to end by tallow-candle chandeliers made of barrel hoops suspended from the ceiling, and the grease dripped all over us. That was in the beginning of the winter of 1862. It has taken forty-four years for Etta to cross my orbit again.

I asked after her father.

"Dead," she said.

I asked after her mother.

"Dead," she said.

Another question brought out the fact that she had long been married, but had no children. We shook hands and parted. She walked three or four steps, then turned and came back, and her eyes filled, and she said:

"I am a stranger here, and far from my friends—in fact I have hardly any friends left. Nearly all of them are dead. I must tell my news to you. I *must* tell it to somebody. I can't bear it by myself, while it is so new. The doctor has just told me that my husband can live only a very little while, and I was not dreaming it was so bad as this."

ORION RESUMED

I think the poultry experiment lasted only a year, possibly two years. It had then cost me six thousand dollars. It is my impression that Orion was not able to give the farm away, and that his father-in-law took it back as a kindly act of self-sacrifice.

Orion returned to the law business, and I suppose he remained in that harness off and on for the succeeding quarter of a century, but so far as my knowledge goes he was only a lawyer in name, and had no clients.

My mother died in her eighty-eighth year, in the summer of 1890. She had saved some money, and she left it to me, because it had come from me. I gave it to Orion and he said, with thanks, that I had supported him long enough and now he was going to relieve me of that burden and would also hope to pay back some of that expense, and maybe the whole of it. Accordingly, he proceeded to use up that money in building a considerable addition to the house, with the idea of taking boarders and getting rich. We need not dwell upon this venture. It was another of his failures. His wife tried hard to make the scheme succeed, and if anybody could have made it succeed she would have done it. She was a good woman and was greatly liked. Her vanity was pretty large and inconvenient, but she had a practical side, too, and she would have made that boarding-house lucrative if circumstances had not been against her.

Orion had other projects for recouping me, but as they always required capital I stayed out of them, but they did not materialize. Once he wanted to start a newspaper. It was a ghastly idea, and I squelched it with a promptness that was almost rude. Then he invented a wood-sawing machine and patched it together himself, and he really sawed wood with it. It was ingenious; it was capable; and it would have made a comfortable little fortune for him; but just at the wrong time Providence interfered again. Orion applied for a patent and found that the same machine had already been patented and had gone into business and was thriving.

Presently the State of New York offered a fifty-thousand-dollar prize for a practical method of navigating the Erie Canal with steam canal boats. Orion worked at that thing two or three years, invented and completed a method, and was once more ready to reach out and seize upon imminent wealth, when somebody pointed out a defect. His steam canal boat could not be used in the winter-time; and in the summertime the commotion its wheels would make in the water would wash away the State of New York on both sides.

Innumerable were Orion's projects for acquiring the means to pay off his debt to me. These projects extended straight through the succeeding thirty years, but in every case they failed. During all those thirty years Orion's well-established honesty kept him in offices of trust where other people's money had to be taken care of, but where no salary was paid. He was treasurer of all the benevolent institutions; he took care of the money and other property of widows and orphans; he never lost a cent for anybody, and never made one for himself. Every time he changed his religion the church of his new faith was glad to get him; made him treasurer at once, and at once he stopped the graft and the leaks in that church. He exhibited a facility in changing his political complexion that was a marvel to the whole community. Once this curious thing happened, and he wrote me all about it himself.

One morning he was a Republican, and upon invitation he agreed to make a campaign speech at the Republican mass meeting that night. He prepared the speech. After luncheon he became a Democrat and agreed to write a score of exciting mottoes to be painted upon the transparencies which the Democrats would carry in their torchlight procession that night. He wrote these shouting Democratic mottoes during the afternoon, and they occupied so much of his time that it was night before he had a chance to change his politics again; so he actually made a rousing Republican campaign speech in the open air while his Democratic transparencies passed by in front of him, to the joy of every witness present.

He was a most strange creature—but in spite of his eccentricities he was beloved, all his life, in whatsoever community he lived. And he was also held in high esteem, for at bottom he was a sterling man.

About twenty-five years ago—along there somewhere—I wrote and suggested to Orion that he write an autobiography. I asked him to try to tell the straight truth in it; to refrain from exhibiting himself in creditable attitudes exclusively, and to honorably set down all the incidents of his life which he had found interesting to him, including those which were burned into his memory because he was ashamed of them. I said that this had never been done, and that if he could do it his autobiography would be a most valuable piece of literature. I said I was offering him a job which I could not duplicate in my own case, but I would cherish the hope that he might succeed with it. I recognize now that I was trying to saddle upon him an impossibility. I have been dictating this autobiography of mine daily for three months; I have thought of fifteen hundred or two thousand incidents in my life which I am ashamed of, but I have not gotten one of them to consent to go on paper yet. I think that that stock will still be complete and unimpaired when I finish this autobiography, if I ever finish it. I believe that if I should put in all those incidents I would be sure to strike them out when I came to revise this book.

While we were living in Vienna in 1898 a cablegram came from Keokuk announcing Orion's death. He was seventy-two years old. He had gone down to the kitchen in the early hours of a bitter December morning; he had built the fire, and then sat down at a table to write something, and there he died, with the pencil in his hand and resting against the paper in the middle of an unfinished word—an indication that his release from the captivity of a long and troubled and pathetic and unprofitable life was swift and painless.

[*Monday, April 9, 1906*

Letter from French girl inclosing cable about "Huck Finn."—The Juggernaut Club.—Letter from librarian of Brooklyn Public Library in regard to "Huckleberry Finn" and "Tom Sawyer."—Mr. Clemens's reply.—The deluge of reporters trying to discover contents of that letter.

THIS morning's mail brings me from France a letter from a French friend of mine, inclosing this New York cablegram:

MARK TWAIN INTERDIT

NEW YORK, 27 mars. (*Par dépêche de notre correspondant particulier.*)—Les directeurs de la bibliothèque de Brooklyn ont mis les deux derniers livres de Mark Twain à l'index pour les enfants au-dessous de quinze ans, les considérant comme malsains.

Le célèbre humoriste a écrit a des fonctionnaires une lettre pleine d'esprit et de sarcasme. Ces messieurs se refusent à la publier, sous le prétexte qu'ils n'ont pas l'autorisation de l'auteur de le faire.

The letter is from a French girl who lives at St. Dié, in Joan of Arc's region. I have never seen this French girl, but she wrote me about five years

ago and since then we have exchanged friendly letters three or four times a year. She closes her letter
with this paragraph:

Something in a newspaper that I read this morning has
surprised me very much. I have cut it out because, often,
these informations are forged and, if this is the case, the
slip of paper will be my excuse. Please, allow me to smile,
my dear unseen Friend! I cannot imagine for a minute that
you have been very sorry about it.—In France, such a
measure would have for immediate result to make every one
in the country buy these books, and I—for one,—am going
to get them as soon as I go through Paris, perfectly sure
that I'll find them as wholesome as all you have written.
I know your pen well. I know it has never been dipped
in anything but clean, clear ink.

I must go back now to that French cablegram.
Its information is not exactly correct, but it is near
enough. *Huck Finn* and *Tom Sawyer* are not recent
books. *Tom* is more than thirty years old. The
other book has been in existence twenty-one years.
When Huck appeared, twenty-one years ago, the
public library of Concord, Massachusetts, flung him
out indignantly, partly because he was a liar and
partly because after deep meditation and careful
deliberation he made up his mind on a difficult point,
and said that if he'd got to betray Jim or go to
hell, he would go to hell—which was profanity, and
those Concord purists couldn't stand it.

After this disaster, Huck was left in peace for
sixteen or seventeen years. Then the public library
of Denver flung him out. He had no similar trouble

until four or five months ago—that is to say, last November. At that time I received the following letter:

SHEEPSHEAD BAY BRANCH
BROOKLYN PUBLIC LIBRARY
1657 SHORE ROAD
BROOKLYN-NEW YORK, *Nov. 19th, '05*

DEAR SIR:

I happened to be present the other day at a meeting of the children's librarians of the Brooklyn Public Library. In the course of the meeting it was stated that copies of "Tom Sawyer" and "Huckleberry Finn" were to be found in some of the children's rooms of the system. The Sup't of the Children's Dep't—a conscientious and enthusiastic young woman—was greatly shocked to hear this, and at once ordered that they be transferred to the adults' department. Upon this I shamefacedly confessed to having read "Huckleberry Finn" aloud to my defenseless blind people, without regard to their age, color, or previous condition of servitude. I also reminded them of Brander Matthews's opinion of the book, and stated the fact that I knew it almost at heart, having got more pleasure from it than from any book I have ever read, and reading is the greatest pleasure I have in life. My warm defense elicited some further discussion and criticism, from which I gathered that the prevailing opinion of Huck was that he was a deceitful boy who said "sweat" when he should have said "perspiration." The upshot of the matter was that there is to be further consideration of these books at a meeting early in January which I am especially invited to attend. Seeing you the other night at the performance of "Peter Pan" the thought came to me that you (who know Huck as well as I—you *can't* know him better or love him more—) might be willing to give me a word or two to say in witness of his good character though he "warn't no more quality than a mud cat."

I would ask as a favor that you regard this communication as confidential, whether you find time to reply to it or not; for I am loath for obvious reasons to bring the institution from which I draw my salary into ridicule, contempt or reproach.

Yours very respectfully,
Asa Don Dickinson.

(In charge Department for the Blind and Sheepshead Bay Branch, Brooklyn Public Library.)

That was a very private letter. I didn't know the author of it, but I thought I perceived that he was a safe man and that I could venture to write a pretty private letter in return and trust that he would not allow its dreadful contents to leak out and get into the newspapers. I wrote him on the 21st:

21 Fifth Avenue,
November 21, 1905

Dear Sir:

I am greatly troubled by what you say. I wrote Tom Sawyer and Huck Finn for adults exclusively, and it always distresses me when I find that boys and girls have been allowed access to them. The mind that becomes soiled in youth can never again be washed clean; I know this by my own experience, and to this day I cherish an unappeasable bitterness against the unfaithful guardians of my young life, who not only permitted but compelled me to read an unexpurgated Bible through before I was 15 years old. None can do that and ever draw a clean sweet breath again this side of the grave. Ask that young lady—she will tell you so.

Most honestly do I wish I could say a softening word or two in defence of Huck's character, since you wish it, but really in my opinion it is no better than those of Solomon, David, Satan, and the rest of the sacred brotherhood.

If there is an unexpurgated in the Children's Department, won't you please help that young woman remove Huck and Tom from that questionable companionship?

Sincerely yours,

(Signed) S. L. CLEMENS.

I shall not show your letter to anyone—it is safe with me.

A couple of days later I received this handsome rejoinder in return:

SHEEPSHEAD BAY BRANCH
BROOKLYN PUBLIC LIBRARY
1657 SHORE ROAD
BROOKLYN-NEW YORK, *Nov. 23rd, '05*

DEAR SIR:

Your letter rec'd. I am surprised to hear that you think Huck and Tom would have an unwholesome effect on boys and girls. But relieved to hear that you would not place them in the same category with many of the scriptural reprobates. I know of one boy who made the acquaintance of Huck in 1884, at the age of eight, and who has known him intimately ever since, and I can assure you he is not an atom the worse for the 20 years' companionship. On the contrary he will always feel grateful to Huck's father— I don't mean Pop—for the many hours spent with him and Jim, when sickness and sorrow were forgotten.

Huckleberry Finn was the first book I selected to read

to my blind (for selfish reasons I am afraid), and the amount of innocent enjoyment it gave them, has never been equalled by anything I have since read.

Thanking you for the almost unhoped for courtesy of your reply, I am

Yours very respectfully,

Asa Don Dickinson.

Four months drifted tranquilly by. Then there was music! There came a freshet of newspaper reporters and they besieged my secretary all day. Of course I was in bed. I am always in bed. She barred the stairs against them. They were bound to see me, if only for a moment, but none of them got by her guard. They said a report had sprung up that I had written a letter some months before to the Brooklyn Public Library; that according to that report the letter was pungent and valuable, and they wanted a copy of it. They said the head officials of the Brooklyn Library declared that they had never seen the letter and that they had never heard of it until the reporters came and asked for it. I judged by this that my man—who was not in the head library, but in a branch of it—was keeping his secret all right, and I believed he could be trusted to continue to keep that secret, for his own sake as well as mine. That letter would be a bombshell for me if it got out—but it would hoist him, too. So I feel pretty confident that for his own sake, if for no other, he would protect me.

My secretary had a hard day of it, but I had a most enjoyable one. She never allowed any reporter to get an idea of the nature of the letter; she smoothed all those young fellows down and sent them away empty.

They renewed the assault next day, but I told her to never mind—human nature would win the victory for us. There would be an earthquake somewhere, or a municipal upheaval *here*, or a threat of war in Europe—something would be sure to happen in the way of a big excitement that would call the boys away from No. 21 Fifth Avenue for twenty-four hours, and that would answer every purpose; they wouldn't think of that letter again, and we should have peace.

I knew the reporters would get on the right track very soon, so I wrote Mr. Dickinson and warned him to keep his mouth hermetically sealed. I told him to be wise and wary. His answer bears date March 28th.

BAY RIDGE BRANCH
BROOKLYN PUBLIC LIBRARY
73D STREET AND SECOND AVENUE
BROOKLYN-NEW YORK, *Mar. 28, '06*

DEAR MR. CLEMENS:

Your letter of the 26th inst. rec'd this moment. As I have now been transferred to the above address, it has been a long time reaching me.

I have tried to be wary and wise and am very grateful to you for your reticence. The poor old B. P. L. has achieved some very undesirable notoriety. I thought my head was coming off when I heard from my chief on the telephone night before last. But yesterday he began to be amused, I think, at the teapot tempest.

Last night I reached home at 11.30 and found a Herald man sitting on the steps, leaning his head against the door post. He had been there since 7.30 and said he would cheerfully sit there till morning if I would give him the least hint of the letter's contents. But I was wise and wary.

At the January meeting it was decided not to place Huck and Tom in the *Children's* rooms along with "Little Nellie's Silver Mine" and "Dotty Dimple at Home." But the books have not been "restricted" in any sense whatever. They are placed on open shelves among the adult fiction, and any child is free to read adult fiction if he chooses.

I am looking forward with great eagerness to seeing and hearing you to-morrow night at the Waldorf. As I have a wild scheme for a national library for the blind, they have been generous enough to place a couple of boxes at my disposal. The "young lady" whom you mentioned in your letter—the Sup't of the Children's Dep't—and several other B. P. L.'s, I hope will be present.

I am very sorry to have caused you so much annoyance through reporters, but be sure that I have said nothing nor will say anything to them about the contents of that letter. And please don't you tell on me!

Yours very respectfully,

ASA DON DICKINSON.

I saw him at the Waldorf the next night, where Choate and I made our public appeal in behalf of the blind, and found him to be a very pleasant and safe and satisfactory man.

Now that I have heard from France, I think the incident is closed—for it had its brief run in England, two or three weeks ago, and in Germany also. When people let Huck Finn alone he goes peacefully along, damaging a few children here and there and yonder, but there will be plenty of children in heaven without those, so it is no great matter. It is only when well-meaning people expose him that he gets his real chance to do harm. Temporarily, then, he spreads havoc all around in the nurseries and no doubt does prodigious harm while he has his chance. By and by, let us hope, people that really have the best interests of the rising generation at heart will become wise and not stir Huck up.

[Tuesday, April 10, 1906

Child's letter about "Huckleberry Finn" being flung out of Concord Library.—Ambassador White's autobiography.— Mr. Clemens's version of the Fiske-Cornell episode.—Another example of his great scheme for finding employment for the unemployed.—This client wins the Fiske lawsuit.

WHEN *Huck Finn* was flung out of the Concord Public Library twenty-one years ago, a number of letters of sympathy and indignation reached me— mainly from children, I am obliged to admit—and I kept some of them so that I might reread them now and then and apply them as a salve to my soreness. I have overhauled those ancient letters this morning and among them I find one from a little girl who resents that library's treatment of Huck and then goes innocently along and gives me something more of a dig than even the library had done. She says:

I am eleven years old, and I live on a farm near Rockville, Maryland. Once this winter we had a boy to work for us named John. We lent him "Huck Finn" to read, and one night he let his clothes out of the window and left in the night. The last we heard from him he was out in Ohio; and father says if we had lent him "Tom Sawyer" to read he would not have stopped on this side of the ocean.

Bless her gentle heart, she was trying to cheer me up, and her effort is entitled to the praise which the country journalist conferred upon the Essex band after he had praised the whole Fourth of July celebration in detail, and had exhausted his stock of compliments. But he was obliged to lay something in the nature of a complimentary egg, and with a final heroic effort he brought forth this, "The Essex band done the best they could."

I have been reading another chapter or two in Ambassador White's autobiography, and I find the book charming, particularly where he talks about me. I find any book charming that talks about me. I am expecting this one of mine to do something in that line, and it is my purpose that it shall not lose sight of that subject long at a time. Mr. White was the first president of Cornell University, and he gives the university's side of the Willard Fiske trouble. I stopped at that point. I didn't read his version, for I want to give another version first, and as this version may conflict with his, I wish to set it down now before its complexion shall have a chance to undergo a change by coming in contact with his version.

This brings me back to another example of my great scheme for finding work for the unemployed. The famous Fiske-Cornell episode of a quarter of

a century ago grew up in this way. About fifty
years ago, when Willard Fiske was a poor and
untaught and friendless boy of thirteen, he and
Bayard Taylor took steerage passage in a sailing
ship and crossed the ocean. They found their way
to Iceland, and Willard Fiske remained there a
year or two. He acquired the Norse languages and
perfected himself in them. He also became an expert scholar in the literature of those languages.
By and by he returned to America, and while still
a very young man and hardly of age, he got a place
as instructor in that kind of learning in the infant
Cornell University. This seat of learning was at
Ithaca, New York, and Mr. McGraw was a citizen
of that little town. He had made a fortune in the
electric telegraph, and it was his purpose to leave
a large part of it to the university. He had a lovely
young daughter, and she and young Fiske fell in
love with each other. They were aware of this; the
girl's parents were aware of it; the university was
aware of it; Ithaca was aware of it. All these
parties expected Fiske to propose, but he didn't do
it. There was no way to account for it, and so
all the parties, including the girl, went on from
month to month and year to year in a condition of
suppressed surprise, waiting for the mystery to solve
itself. Which it still didn't do. At last Mr.
McGraw died, and the fact developed that he had
left no will. Therefore the daughter was sole heir.
However, she knew what her father's intention had
been, so she turned over to the university a good

part of the fortune and thus made the intention good.

The years drifted along and the relations between Fiske and Miss McGraw remained the same. But there was no proposal. Fiske had a quite definite reason for not proposing. It was that he was very poor and the girl very rich, and he was not willing to seem to marry her for her money. This was good morals, good principle, good sentiment—but it was not business. Things remained just in this way for years and years, and the devotion of the couple to each other went along unimpaired by time. At last, when they were well stricken in years, and when Miss McGraw had developed pulmonary consumption, she invited Fiske and Charles Dudley Warner and his wife to make a trip up the Nile with her in the old-fashioned dahabiyeh, a trip which occupied a matter of three months. Miss McGraw had already been on the other side of the ocean several months, and she had been buying all sorts of beautiful things—pictures, sculpture, costly rugs, and so on—wherewith to adorn a little palace which she was building in Ithaca.

At last there on board the dahabiyeh a sorrowful time came—for Miss McGraw's malady was making great progress and it was manifest that she could not live long. Then she came out frankly and said she wanted to marry Fiske so that she could leave her fortune to him. Fiske wanted to marry her, but his ideas remained unimpaired in his heart and head and he was not willing to accept the fortune. The Warners wrought with him.

They used their best persuasions. He was as anxious for the marriage as was Miss McGraw, but he wouldn't accept the fortune. At last he was persuaded to a modification of the terms. He was willing to accept the little palace and its furnishings and three hundred thousand dollars; he would accept nothing more. The marriage took place. Mrs. Fiske made a will, and in the will she left the palace and its furnishings and three hundred thousand dollars to her husband, Willard Fisk. She left the residue of the fortune to Cornell University.

By and by Fiske arrived at an understanding of the fact that he had not acted wisely. The income of three hundred thousand dollars was wholly inadequate. He could not live in the Ithaca house on any such income as that. He did not try to live in it. There it stood, with all those beautiful things in it which Miss McGraw had gathered in her travels in Europe, and Fiske lived elsewhere—lived most comfortably elsewhere—lived where three hundred thousand dollars was really a fortune, and he was entirely satisfied. He lived in Italy. He was as dear and sweet a soul as I have ever known. His was a character which won friends for him, and whoso became his friend remained so, ever afterward.

Now followed this curious circumstance. Cornell had received by Mrs. Fiske's will a noble addition to its endowment—two million dollars, if I remember rightly. No doubt Cornell University was satisfied. But the university's lawyers, picking and searching around through Mrs. Fiske's will, found a defect in it which neither Mrs. Fiske nor Charley Warner, who drew the will, suspected was there. It was something about "residue." It was the opinion of those lawyers that the university might claim the little palace and its rich equipment, and make the claim good in a court of law.

The claim was put forward. Fiske and Warner were outraged by this insolence, this greed. Both knew that it was the desire of the dying wife that her husband should live in that house and have the sacred companionship of those things which had been selected by her own hands for its adornment. Both knew that but for Fiske's stubborn resistance he would have had not only the house, but a great sum of money besides, and now that the university proposed to take the house away from Fiske—well, it was time for the worm to turn. The worm turned. Fiske was the worm. Fiske resisted the university's claim and the university brought suit.

Now then, I must go back to a point antedating the bringing of this suit three or four years. One day in Hartford a young fellow called and wanted to see me. I think he said he was from Canada. He said he had a strong desire, an irresistible desire, to become a lawyer, and he thought that if he could get some work to do that would support him, he could meantime use his off hours, if he had any, in studying Blackstone. He thought he could be a journalist. He thought he could at least become a good reporter, and his idea was to get me to use my influence with the Hartford newspaper people to the end that he might get the sort of chance he was after.

I said: "Certainly, I will get you a berth in any newspaper in the town. Choose your own paper."

He was very grateful. These clients of mine always are, until they learn the conditions. I furnished him the conditions in the same old way. He considered a moment and then said:

"How simple that is; how sure it is; how certain it is; how actually infallible it is, human nature being constructed as it is—how is it that that has not been thought of before?" Then he added, as he went out of the door, "I choose the *Courant*, and I will have the job before night."

About three months afterward he came out to report progress. He had moved along so briskly, from sweeper-out, up through the several grades, that he was now on the editorial staff, and was very happy, particularly as staff work allowed him a good deal of off time for the study of the law, and the law was where his high ambition lay.

I come back now to that Fiske lawsuit. We had gone to Elmira one summer to spend the summer, as usual, at Quarry Farm, and we were visiting Mrs. Clemens's family down in the town for a while. A young man called and said he would like to see me. I went to the library and saw him there. It was the young man of whom I have been talking, but as I had not seen him for three or four years I did not at first recall him. He said that while he was on the *Courant* he saved all the money he could, and studied the law diligently in his off hours—that now, recently, he had given up journalism and was going to make a break into the law; that he had canvassed the field and had decided that he would become office assistant to David B. Hill of Elmira, New York—that is to say, he had decided to do this, evidently without requiring Mr. Hill to state whether he wanted it so or not. Hill was a very distinguished lawyer and a big politician, a man of vast importance and influence—and he is still that to-day, in his old age. The application was made and Hill said promptly that he didn't need anybody's assistance. But young Bacon said he didn't want any pay, he only wanted a chance to work; he could support himself. He would do anything that could be of any assistance to Mr. Hill, even to sweeping out the office; that he wanted to work, and he wanted to be near a man like Hill because he was determined to become a lawyer. Well, as he was not expensive and showed a determination that pleased Hill, Hill gave him office room. Very well, the usual thing happened, the thing that always happens. Little by little Bacon got to beguiling out of Hill things to do, and presently Hill was furnishing him the things to do without any beguilement.

"Now then," Bacon said, "Mr. Clemens, I've got a chance—I've got a chance." Professor Willard Fiske brought his case to Mr. Hill. Mr. Hill examined it carefully and declined to take it. He said Fiske had no case, and therefore he did not wish to take it merely to lose it. Fiske insisted, and presently Hill said: "Well, here's this young fellow here in my office. If he wants to take your case, all right; I will advise him and help him to the best of my ability without charge"; and he asked if Fiske was willing to put the case into Bacon's hands. Fiske did it.

Then young Bacon had this happy idea. There being nothing for Fiske in the apparent conditions, he went to the university charter to see what he might find there. He found a very pleasant thing there; to use a phrase of the day, he struck oil in that charter. He brought the charter to Mr. Hill and showed him this large fact: that Cornell University was not privileged to accept or to acquire any property if, at the time, it already possessed property worth three millions of dollars. Cornell University possessed property worth more than that at the time that Mrs. Fiske made her will, and it still possessed that amount.

Hill said, "Well, Bacon, the case is yours—that is to say, well, Bacon, the case is Fiske's. It is the university, now, that has no show."

Bacon won the case. It was his first case. He charged Fiske a hundred thousand dollars for his services. Fiske handed him the check, and his thanks therewith.

I didn't see Bacon again for some years—I don't know how many—and then he told me that that first lawsuit of his was also his last one; that that first fee of his was the only one he had ever received; that he had hardly pocketed his check until he ran across a most charming young widow possessed of a great fortune and he took them both in.

I think I will say nothing more about my great scheme for providing jobs for the unemployed. I think I have proven that it is a good and effective scheme.

[*Wednesday, April 11, 1906*

Mr. Frank Fuller and his enthusiastic launching of Mr. Clemens's first New York lecture.—Results not in fortune, but in fame.—Leads to a lecture tour under direction of Redpath.—Clipping in regard to Frank Fuller, and Mr. Clemens's comments.

I AM not glancing through my books to find out what I have said in them. I refrain from glancing through those books for two reasons: first—and this reason always comes first in every matter connected with my life—laziness. I am too lazy to examine the books. The other reason is—well, let it go. I had another reason, but it had slipped out of my mind while I was arranging the first one. I think it likely that in the book called *Roughing It* I have mentioned Frank Fuller. But I don't know, and it isn't any matter.

When Orion and I crossed the continent in the overland stagecoach in the summer of 1861, we stopped two or three days in Great Salt Lake City. I do not remember who the Governor of Utah Territory was at that time, but I remember that he was absent—which is a common habit of territorial Governors, who are nothing but politicians who go out to the outskirts of countries and suffer the pri-

vations there in order to build up States and come
back as United States Senators.   But the man who
was acting in the Governor's place was the Secretary
of the Territory, Frank Fuller—called Governor,
of course, just as Orion was in the great days when
he got that accident-title through Governor Nye's
absences.   Titles of honor and dignity once acquired
in a democracy, even by accident and properly usable
for only forty-eight hours, are as permanent here as
eternity is in heaven.   You can never take away those
titles.   Once a justice of the peace for a week, always "judge" afterward.   Once a major of militia for a campaign on the Fourth of July, always
a major.   To be called colonel, purely by mistake
and without intention, confers that dignity on a
man for the rest of his life.   We adore titles and
heredities in our hearts, and ridicule them with our
mouths.   This is our democratic privilege.

Well, Fuller was acting Governor, and he gave
us a very good time during those two or three days
that we rested in Great Salt Lake City.   He was an
alert and energetic man; a pushing man; a man who
was able to take an interest in anything that was
going—and not only that, but take five times as
much interest in it as it was worth, and ten times
as much as anybody else could take in it—a very
live man.

I was on the Pacific coast thereafter five or six
years, and returned to the States by the way of the
Isthmus in January, '67.   In the previous year I
had spent several months in the Sandwich Islands
for the Sacramento *Union,* and had returned to San

Francisco empty as to cash, but full of information —information proper for delivery from the lecture platform. My letters from the Islands had given me a large notoriety—local notoriety. It did not extend eastward more than a hundred miles or so, but it was a good notoriety to lecture on, and I made use of it on the platform in California and Nevada and amassed twelve or fifteen hundred dollars in the few nights that I labored for the instruction and amusement of my public. Fifteen hundred dollars was about half—the doorkeeper got the rest. He was an old circus man and knew how to keep door.

When I arrived in New York I found Fuller there in some kind of business. He was very hearty, very glad to see me, and wanted to show me his wife. I had not heard of a wife before; had not been aware that he had one. Well, he showed me his wife, a sweet and gentle woman with most hospitable and kindly and winning ways. Then he astonished me by showing me his daughters. Upon my word, they were large and matronly of aspect, and married—he didn't say how long. Oh, Fuller was full of surprises. If he had shown me some little children, that would have been well enough, and reasonable. But he was too young-looking a man to have grown children. Well, I couldn't fathom the mystery and I let it go. Apparently it was a case where a man was well along in life, but had a handsome gift of not showing his age on the outside.

Governor Fuller—it is what all his New York

friends called him now, of course—was in the full
storm of one of his enthusiasms. He had one enthusiasm per day, and it was always a storm. He
said I must take the biggest hall in New York and
deliver that lecture of mine on the Sandwich Islands
—said that people would be wild to hear me. There
was something catching about that man's prodigious
energy. For a moment he almost convinced me that
New York was wild to hear me. I knew better.
I was well aware that New York had never heard
of me, was not expecting to hear of me, and didn't
want to hear of me—yet that man almost persuaded
me. I protested, as soon as the fire which he had
kindled in me had cooled a little, and went on pro-
testing. It did no good. Fuller was sure that I
should make fame and fortune right away without
any trouble. He said leave it to him—just leave
everything to him—go to the hotel and sit down
and be comfortable—he would lay fame and fortune
at my feet in ten days.

I was helpless. I was persuadable, but I didn't
lose *all* of my mind, and I begged him to take a
very small hall, and reduce the rates to side-show
prices. No, he would not hear of that—said he
would have the biggest hall in New York City. He
would have the basement hall in Cooper Institute,
which seated three thousand people and there was
room for half as many more to stand up; and he said
he would fill that place so full, at a dollar a head,
that those people would smother and he could charge
two dollars apiece to let them out. Oh, he was all
on fire with his project. He went ahead with it.

He said it shouldn't cost me anything. I said there would be no profit. He said: "Leave that alone. If there is no profit that is my affair. If there is profit it is yours. If it is loss, I stand the loss myself, and you will never hear of it."

He hired Cooper Institute, and he began to advertise this lecture in the usual way—a small paragraph in the advertising columns of the newspapers. When this had continued about three days I had not yet heard anybody or any newspaper say anything about that lecture, and I got nervous. "Oh," he said, "it's working around underneath. You don't see it on the surface." He said, "Let it alone; now, let it work."

Very well, I allowed it to work—until about the sixth or seventh day. The lecture would be due in three or four days more—still I was not able to get down underneath, where it was working, and so I was filled with doubt and distress. I went to Fuller and said he must advertise more energetically.

He said he would. So he got a barrel of little things printed that you hang on a string—fifty in a bunch. They were for the omnibuses. You could see them swinging and dangling around in every omnibus. My anxiety forced me to haunt those omnibuses. I did nothing for one or two days but sit in buses and travel from one end of New York to the other and watch those things dangle, and wait to catch somebody pulling one loose to read it. It never happened—at least it happened only once. A man reached up and pulled one of those things loose, said to his friend, "Lecture on the Sandwich Islands by Mark Twain. Who can that be, I wonder"—and he threw it away and changed the subject.

I couldn't travel in the omnibuses any more. I was sick. I went to Fuller and said: "Fuller, there is not going to be anybody in Cooper Institute that night, but you and me. It will be a dead loss, for we shall both have free tickets. Something must be done. I am on the verge of suicide. I would commit suicide if I had the pluck and the outfit." I said, "You must paper the house, Fuller. You must issue thousands of complimentary tickets. You *must* do this. I shall die if I have to go before an empty house that is not acquainted with me and that has never heard of me, and that has never traveled in the bus and seen those things dangle."

"Well," he said, with his customary enthusiasm, "I'll attend to it. It shall be done. I will paper that house, and when you step on the platform you shall find yourself in the presence of the choicest audience, the most intelligent audience, that ever a man stood before in this world."

And he was as good as his word. He sent whole basketsful of complimentary tickets to every public-school teacher within a radius of thirty miles of New York—he deluged those people with complimentary tickets—and on the appointed night they all came. There wasn't room in Cooper Institute for a third of them. The lecture was to begin at half past seven. I was so anxious that I had to go to that place at seven. I couldn't keep away.

I wanted to see that vast vacant Mammoth Cave and die. But when I got near the building I found that all the streets for a quarter of a mile around were blocked with people, and traffic was stopped. I couldn't believe that those people were trying to get into Cooper Institute, and yet that was just what was happening. I found my way around to the back of the building and got in there by the stage door. And sure enough, the seats, the aisles, the great stage itself, was packed with bright-looking human beings raked in from the centers of intelligence—the schools. I had a deal of difficulty to shoulder my way through the mass of people on the stage, and when I had managed it and stood before the audience, that stage was full. There wasn't room enough left for a child.

I was happy, and I was excited beyond expression. I poured the Sandwich Islands out on to those people with a free hand, and they laughed and shouted to my entire content. For an hour and fifteen minutes I was in Paradise. From every pore I exuded a divine delight—and when we came to count up we had thirty-five dollars in the house.

Fuller was just as jubilant over it as if it had furnished the fame and the fortune of his prophecy. He was perfectly delighted, perfectly enchanted. He couldn't keep his mouth shut for several days. "Oh," he said, "the fortune didn't come in—that didn't come in—that's all right. That's coming in later. The fame is already here, Mark. Why, in a week you'll be the best-known man in the United

States. This is no failure. This is a prodigious success."

That episode must have cost him four or five hundred dollars, but he never said a word about that. He was as happy, as satisfied, as proud, as delighted, as if he had laid the fabled golden egg and hatched it.

He was right about the fame. I certainly did get a working quantity of fame out of that lecture. The New York newspapers praised it. The country newspapers copied those praises. The lyceums of the country—it was right in the heyday of the old lyceum lecture system—began to call for me. I put myself in Redpath's hands, and I caught the tail end of the lecture season. I went West and lectured every night, for six or eight weeks, at a hundred dollars a night—and I now considered that the whole of the prophecy was fulfilled. I had acquired fame, and also fortune. I don't believe these details are right, but I don't care a rap. They will do just as well as the facts. What I mean to say is, that I don't know whether I made that lecturing excursion in that year or whether it was the following year. But the main thing is that I made it, and that the opportunity to make it was created by that wild Frank Fuller and his insane and immortal project.

All this was thirty-eight or thirty-nine years ago. Two or three times since then, at intervals of years, I have run across Frank Fuller for a moment—only a moment, and no more. But he was always young. Never a gray hair; never a suggestion of age about him; always enthusiastic; always happy and glad to be alive. Last fall his wife's brother was murdered in a horrible way. Apparently a robber had concealed himself in Mr. Thompson's room, and in the night had beaten him to death with a club. A couple of months ago I ran across Fuller on the street, and he was looking so very, very old, so withered, so moldy, that I could hardly recognize him. He said his wife was dying of the shock caused by the murder of her brother; that nervous prostration was carrying her off, and she could not live more than a few days—so I went with him to see her.

She was sitting upright on a sofa and was supported all about with pillows. Now and then she leaned her head for a little while on a support. Breathing was difficult for her. It touched me, for I had seen that picture so many, many times. During two or three months Mrs. Clemens sat up like that, night and day, struggling for breath. When she was made drowsy by opiates and exhaustion she rested her head a little while on a support, just as Mrs. Fuller was doing, and got naps of two minutes' or three minutes' duration.

I did not see Mrs. Fuller alive again. She passed to her rest about three days later.

INDEX

THE END

BOOKS BY MARK TWAIN

Special Editions in Color

THE ADVENTURES OF TOM SAWYER

THE PRINCE AND THE PAUPER

THE ADVENTURES OF HUCKLEBERRY FINN

THE MYSTERIOUS STRANGER

Uniform Cloth Edition
(Crown 8vo.)

THE AMERICAN CLAIMANT

CHRISTIAN SCIENCE

A CONNECTICUT YANKEE IN KING ARTHUR'S COURT

EUROPE AND ELSEWHERE

FOLLOWING THE EQUATOR

THE GILDED AGE

THE ADVENTURES OF HUCKLEBERRY FINN

IN DEFENSE OF HARRIET SHELLEY

INNOCENTS ABROAD

JOAN OF ARC

THE PRINCE AND THE PAUPER

LIFE ON THE MISSISSIPPI

THE MAN THAT CORRUPTED HADLEYBURG

MARK TWAIN'S SPEECHES

THE MYSTERIOUS STRANGER AND OTHER STORIES

PUDD'NHEAD WILSON

ROUGHING IT

SKETCHES NEW AND OLD

THE $30,000 BEQUEST

TOM SAWYER ABROAD

THE ADVENTURES OF TOM SAWYER

A TRAMP ABROAD

WHAT IS MAN?

Thin-Paper Limp-Leather Edition
(12mo.)

THE AMERICAN CLAIMANT

THE ADVENTURES OF TOM SAWYER

THE ADVENTURES OF HUCKLEBERRY FINN

CHRISTIAN SCIENCE

A CONNECTICUT YANKEE IN KING ARTHUR'S COURT

FOLLOWING THE EQUATOR (2 Vols.)

IN DEFENSE OF HARRIET SHELLEY

THE GILDED AGE (2 Vols.)

WHAT IS MAN?

INNOCENTS ABROAD (2 Vols.)

JOAN OF ARC (2 Vols.)

Ingram Content Group UK Ltd.
Milton Keynes UK
UKHW052033050423
419731UK00006B/85

9 780766 161313